OTHER BOOKS BY ORIANA JOSSEAU KALANT:

The Amphetamines - Toxicity and Addiction
1st edition   1966
2nd edition, revised   1973

Drugs, Society and Personal Choice   1971
French translation: Drogues,
Société et Option Personnelle   1973
Norwegian translation: Stoffbruk,
Samfunn, Personlig Valg   1974

Amphetamines and Related Drugs:
Clinical Toxicity and Dependence   1974

Alcohol and Drug Problems in Women   1980

Cannabis: Health Risks - A Comprehensive
Annotated Bibliography (1844-1982)   1983

Maier's "Cocaine Addiction"
(Der Kokainismus - English Translation)   1987

The author at the peak of her scientific career in Canada

ORIANA

Memoirs of a Patagonian

Oriana Josseau

iUniverse, Inc.
Bloomington

Oriana
Memoirs of a Patagonian

iUniverse books may be ordered through booksellers or by contacting:

iUniverse
1663 Liberty Drive
Bloomington, IN 47403
www.iuniverse.com
1-800-Authors (1-800-288-4677)

ISBN: 978-1-4759-0707-0 (sc)
ISBN: 978-1-4759-0709-4 (hc)
ISBN: 978-1-4759-0708-7 (e)

Printed in the United States of America

iUniverse rev. date: 5/3/2012

Dedicated to Mary V. Seeman, dear friend and literary muse,
who inspired and encouraged the writing of this book.

Contents

From Patagonia with Hesitation

I am seventy-five years old as I write this, but I have not always been that old. In fact, I was just a baby when, at 2:30 in the afternoon of November 6, 1920, I was born. This event, important as it turned out to be for me, went largely unnoticed everywhere except at 544 Calle Valdivia in Punta Arenas, Chile. This was the home of my parents, Pablo and Maria Josseau, who shared it with my father's nine younger brothers and sisters. They were a lively bunch of young people ranging in age from fifteen to twenty-nine or so, my four Josseau uncles and five aunts. At thirty, my father was the oldest and the surrogate father of the family. My mother, at twenty-three, ranked fourth in a family of eight, presided over by my grandparents, Mateo and Gerónima Eterovic, who lived across the street from my parents' home. At the time, however, only four or five of the eight still lived at home, the others having gone to Argentina or to Santiago to pursue their careers. There were no Josseau grandparents because they had died some fifteen years earlier. This left me in the very privileged situation of having two grandparents, two parents and sixteen young aunts and uncles, most of them within reach of my undoubtedly robust screams, and no competition.

Although I already had six Eterovic cousins at the time of my birth, they did not live in Punta Arenas. And since I was unquestionably the firstborn in the Josseau family, I had, for a couple of years or so, the more or less undivided attention of some sixteen grown-ups. From the family tales I've been told, I soaked up all this attention like a sponge and thrived on it but,

1

understandably, the situation created problems for my parents, especially my mother. In a nutshell, there wasn't enough of me to go around and so there were fights for the right to hold me and to play with me.

One of the first problems that arose was my very name. My mother, inspired by the graceful beauty of the *S.S. Oriana*, a ship of the P. & O. Lines that had docked at Punta Arenas on its way to the Pacific coast of Chile, decided to name me after it. But my aunts objected strenuously and proposed alternative names. After some apparently quite heated arguments, my mother won the day, but not before agreeing to add two more names in order to appease my demanding and possessive aunts. Thus I came to be known officially as Oriana Yolanda Liliana. But I wasn't through being named yet, because the priest that later baptised me claimed that all three names were pagan, and so he added the Christian "Maria" to the list, to give the Catholic stamp of approval - if not to me, at least to my name.

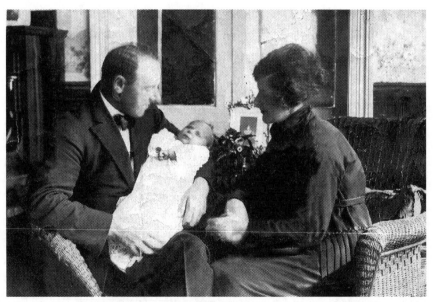

The proud parents admiring Oriana not long after her birth

Neither I nor my parents had any choice on the matter of being born in Punta Arenas. My mother wasn't actually born there but brought by her mother at the age of three from Croatia. But my grandparents, all of whom were Europeans, literally chose to settle and raise their families in this forbidding last corner of the world. Let me explain this description of my birthplace. Punta Arenas is a port on the northern shore of the Strait of Magellan, which connects the Atlantic to the Pacific at latitude 53 degrees south. The strait slices off the archipelago of Tierra del Fuego from the mainland at the southernmost tip of South America. From the time that Magellan discovered it in 1520, during the first trip around the world, to the opening of the Panama Canal in 1914, the strait was the only relatively sheltered passage between the Atlantic and the Pacific. It permitted ships to bypass the tempestuous and treacherous waters around Cape Horn, where the tail end of the Andes submerges into the confluence of the South Atlantic and the South Pacific.

The Josseau family home in Punta Arenas, Chile. This photo was taken recently, after it had been converted to a club for merchant seamen.

One would think that because of this advantageous geographical location, implying equally advantageous trading and commercial opportunities, a port or two on the shores of the strait would have thrived from the beginning, in the sixteenth century. But that was not the case. In fact, nothing much happened for another three centuries, until 1849 when Punta Arenas was founded as a penal settlement of the Chilean government. It took another three decades, until the 1880s, for significant European and Chilean immigration to begin the development of the city into the thriving port of approximately one hundred and fifty thousand people that it is today.

The reasons for this slow development are first and foremost the abominable climate of the whole region, and secondly the distance and inaccessibility from big centers of population to the north, in both Chile on the west and

Argentina on the east. Chile, that strange long stringbean of a country, stretches nearly 4,000 kilometers from Punta Arenas in the south to Arica on the border with Peru in the north, practically the same distance as from Montreal to Vancouver, or form New York to Seattle, but it is only a little over 160 kilometers across at its widest point. For the most part, the climate of Punta Arenas is determined by the geographical location of the region. Cape Horn, the southernmost tip of Tierra del Fuego, is at a latitude of 56 degrees south. This means that it is hundreds of kilometers closer to the South Pole than its main rival, the southern coast of Tasmania in Australia. The land, barren and of relatively low altitude, is surrounded by the ice-cold waters and is open and exposed to horrendous winds, especially from the west.

The area, described by some as one of the most inhospitable regions of the earth, has one of the world's most unpleasant climates. The temperature ranges narrowly between 0°C in the winter and 11°C in the summer, so it is never very cold or very warm, but always cloudy, windy or rainy, with virtually no significant seasonal variations. However, it sometimes snows in the winter - as it did in 1995, when a snowfall of a meter and a half killed close to three hundred thousand sheep - and there are impressive dust storms in the summer. No wonder that it took nearly three and a half centuries for anybody to consider seriously settling in the region! And if I had had any voice in the matter at all, I would have suggested that my mother and father meet much, much farther north, say in Santiago, or in the south of France. But they met in Punta Arenas and I'm stuck with my inhospitable heritage.

In this setting the vegetation is as sparse and skimpy as the population. It consists mainly of grasslands, where at least the sheep thrive and grow thick and profuse woollen coats. There is some forest, but the trees - evergreens and eucalyptus - are sometimes denuded on the west side, their manes combed towards the east by the fierce west winds. No future for vain trees down there! But the strawberries are superbly fragrant and the *calafate* (currant) bush produces smooth black berries of great renown, at least locally!

It was not until the 1880s that significant numbers of Europeans and Chileans from the north - mainly hired labor - came and settled in the region, of which Punta Arenas is the main urban center. Before that, the interest of Europeans in the area had been pretty well confined to exploration and mapping. Probably the most notable and thorough of these expeditions was the voyage of the Beagle between 1826 and 1836, under the command of King and Fitzroy of the British admiralty, who played host to one Charles Darwin. The profusion of British place names - such as Beagle Channel, Dawson Island, Brunswick Peninsula, Londonderry Island - is mainly due to this expedition. These non-committal names are in amusing contrast to the plaintively descriptive Spanish labels such as Isla Desolación (Desolation

Island), Bahía Inútil (Useless Bay), Ultima Esperanza (Last Hope), and Golfo de Penas (Gulf of Sorrows).

All of this is of course part of Patagonia, a land shared between Chile and Argentina and, probably because of its emptiness and desolation and of its distance from everything else, a magnetic source of attraction for writers as disparate as Melville, Chatwin and Theroux. To Melville the term Patagonia meant "the outlandish, the monstrous and fatally attractive" (quoted by Chatwin, in *Nowhere is a Place),* while Jorge Luis Borges is claimed to have said: "You will find nothing there. There is nothing in Patagonia." Nothing, unless you are seduced by "the enormity of the desert or the sight of a tiny flower" as Theroux has put it, or in Chatwin's words "as a metaphor for The Ultimate, the point beyond which one could not go". For better or for worse, and not by design but by sheer chance, I am therefore entitled to proudly declare myself, for the first time in my life, to be a Patagonian.

Despite these awesome conceptualizations, however, there were mundane lures towards the end of the nineteenth century, powerful enough to attract Europeans and others to the region. The main lures were gold and sheep ranching. Thousands of people came from everywhere in search of gold, but the most numerous single group among them were people, mainly peasants, from the Dalmatian coast of Croatia, part of the Austro-Hungarian Empire at the time. My grandparents Eterovic and their first five children were part of this group.

To the best of my knowledge, however, Jean-Marie Josseau, my paternal grandfather, landed on the shores near the Atlantic end of the Strait of Magellan without any preconceived plans of making his fortune from either gold or sheep, but through a sheer nautical accident which took place some fifteen years before the arrival of the Eterovics. Yet the accident in question determined, in a way, not only his destiny as a successful sheep rancher but that of his family and the Eterovics, and the subsequent connection between them, from which I eventually emerged.

Neither my father nor any of my Josseau aunts and uncles ever talked to us about their parents. The story that follows, therefore, is based on what my mother told us on numerous occasions, on a few old newspaper clippings and other documents that I have preserved, and on the present recollections of my aunt Catalina Eterovic, now ninety-six years old and the only survivor of her generation of Eterovics. I now wish I had asked more questions and kept more notes, but alas I didn't.

In the summer of 1884 the *Arctique,* a ship of the French merchant marine, sailed from Saint-Malo on the north shore of Brittany with a cargo of merchandise for Chile, but primarily with the purpose of loading with nitrates in the north of the country. On board was Jean-Marie Josseau, a young cadet about eighteen years of age, who came from the nearby port of Lorient on the south or Atlantic side of Brittany. The intended trip, by itself, would have been quite an adventure for such a young man, but much more was in store, not only for young Jean-Marie, but for the whole crew under the command of captain Joseph Hulot.

After a long voyage south through the Atlantic, the Arctique had entered the Strait of Magellan when, on September 23 of the same year, it was shipwrecked in the midst of one of the characteristically horrendous storms of the region. The whole crew, including Jean-Marie, were rescued by the Chilean Navy and taken to Punta Arenas, where they waited for another French ship to take them back home. I don't know exactly what happened, especially in Jean-Marie's head, but the fact is that while all his shipmates eventually returned home to France, he did not.

Some time after the shipwreck of the Arctique the Chilean authorities sent a crew of fifty men to Cape Vírgenes, the actual place of the incident, to salvage the ship's merchandise. As the men began digging in the sand in order to set up camp and to build a makeshift wharf to unload the ship, they found gold in such quantities that, breaking their contract, they ignored and abandoned the Arctique's cargo altogether. This chance finding caused a stampede of prospectors exploring for gold, not only on the shores of the strait but in Tierra del Fuego as well. This, in its turn, led to the large migrations of people from all over the world that I have already mentioned.

Whether Jean-Marie Josseau decided to stay in Punta Arenas because of the prospect of making a quick fortune in gold, or because prosperous sheep ranching appeared to him as a tempting proposition, is a moot question. According to *tía* Catalina, he stayed because of "economic reasons". However, staying in Chile instead of sailing back to France with the rest of the crew turned him into a *de facto* deserter, afoul of the law in his own country. This fact strongly suggests to me that he may have had other personal and private reasons of which I know nothing. His subsequent behavior and ultimate fate bear witness to a very complex and tormented young man. My curiosity about these fascinating aspects of my grandfather's early life, and the accompanying frustration at not having more facts at hand, are making me fantasize quite seriously about going down there to my birthplace in order to flesh out my story more substantially and more soundly. But for the time being I shall have to make do with only my meager resources and recollections and their respective huge gaps.

One of these gaps relates to the six years that elapsed between Jean-Marie's arrival at Punta Arenas in 1884 and the date of birth of his first-born in 1890. I presume he must have married my grandmother a year or so before, when he was just twenty-three. My grandmother, Marie Blanc, was of French-Swiss extraction, but I do not know why she, and presumably her family, happened to be in the south of Chile at the time. The first child of Jean-Marie and Marie was Pablo, my father, who was followed in quick succession by his fourteen brothers and sisters, of whom the nine already mentioned survived into adulthood.

The surviving children thrived in Palomares ("Dove Cotes"), the *estancia* (ranch) that Jean-Marie had acquired along the way, just on the outskirts of Punta Arenas. There, according to family legend, they spoke only French until they first went to school. And the sheep also thrived, producing vast quantities of wool for the export market, especially Britain. The wool business turned my grandfather into a very wealthy man before he was forty. Wealthy enough to have owned, in addition to Palomares, extensive and valuable real estate holdings at the core of the city of Punta Arenas.

But despite his family, his sheep and his affluence, Jean-Marie had turned into a very troubled and unhappy man, who frequently drank to excess and who violently abused his wife when he did. His drinking was so bad that on one occasion he traded a solid block of buildings facing the main square of Punta Arenas for a case of whisky. Apparently he was also pathologically jealous, especially of an old friend who used to visit the family frequently because he felt extremely sorry for my grandmother. But life went on at the estancia until one day, in 1905, when Jean-Marie shot his wife dead and then turned the gun on himself. My father was then fifteen, and his youngest sibling, Magdalena, was fifteen months old.

In addition to his heavy drinking, the only other salient and strange fact that I know with certainty about Jean-Marie Josseau is that, after settling permanently in Punta Arenas, he never again contacted his family back in Lorient, France. Because of my father's extreme reluctance to tell us anything about his parents, I do not know what, if anything, he knew about his relatives in Europe. And so my brothers and I grew up harboring the mystery of the very real possibility of a distant French side of the family. So much so that when I began to travel abroad in my twenties, I invariably made it a point to look up the name Josseau in the telephone directories of every city I visited. But no luck. Not even in Paris, where my husband and I spent the Christmas holidays of 1955. We had intended to go to Brittany the following summer to search in the very place that Jean-Marie had come from, but other events intervened and that expedition never took place.

The story would have ended right there but for a remarkable incident that occurred in Mexico City in 1961, where Fernando, my youngest brother, was writing scripts for the Mexican film industry. It was there that he met Manolo Fabregas, the renowned Mexican actor, who promptly informed him that he knew a French woman by the name of Marie Josseau, well known in local theatrical circles because she was a prominent *modiste* who provided wardrobes for the most important theater companies of Mexico City. Since they agreed that Fernando and Marie might be related, a visit to her home was arranged.

It was instant recognition on the part of Marie who, setting eyes for the first time on Fernando's facial features and general appearance, exclaimed "Pure Josseau!". An understandably emotional meeting ensued, during which they compared family notes. Although they couldn't draw definitive conclusions for lack of some specific details, they both became convinced that they belonged to the same family. Marie Josseau explained that she was the youngest daughter of a Josseau family from Lorient in Brittany. One of her uncles, whose name she couldn't recall, but presumably my grandfather, had sailed on a trip to South America toward the end of the nineteenth century, never to return or be heard from again. Her father had worried about the fate of his lost brother for the rest of his life.

The families were contacted immediately with this utterly surprising news and with requests for further details. Fernando wrote to my mother in Santiago, who in turn wrote to my father in Tierra del Fuego and to me in Toronto, while Elisabeth, Marie's daughter, wrote to her aunts in Paris. A long international correspondence, mainly between Santiago and Paris, ensued, leaving no doubt about the family connections. It became clear, however, that except for Marie's daughter in Mexico City, there were no other descendants of my own generation in the New World.

I know nothing about my father's feelings or overall response to the tragic end of his parents when he was just fifteen years old. Amazingly, however, and according to my own recollections and to what *tía* Catalina has told me recently, he took charge of the family - his nine brothers and sisters - and of the family business, the sheep ranch at Palomares. He apparently hired an administrator and other help to run the estancia, and servants to look after his family in the country house at Palomares and in their city house in Punta Arenas. Besides his being very strict in all matters concerning the upbringing of his siblings, I know virtually nothing about this period of my father's life.

I do know that he later grew into a very difficult man, extremely ill-tempered and uncommunicative, and that these traits were often explained at home, especially by my mother, on the basis of his enormously traumatic early family experience. "It is no wonder! ", those who knew the story would say. Not so his siblings, however, because despite these traits of my father's, they all grew up to be quite normal, outgoing and well-adjusted people who later married and went on to have their own families. And at the time my father married my mother, in 1918, when he was twenty-eight years old, he was still a personable and attractive man, still the head of the family and of their business enterprises. And they, the ten of them, were the healthy, happy and prosperous young people that I introduced at the beginning of my story.

I wish I could say that my father was a handsome young man at the time. But I can't, not quite, because he had a rather prominent nose about which he would always be extremely sensitive. He was tall by Chilean standards, fair and blue-eyed and, perhaps most importantly, impeccably dressed. I remember my mother telling us that he then had twenty pairs of shoes - an exorbitant number, it seemed to me, by Chilean or any other standards. He was a horseman and a hunter, and for these activities he wore British clothes: fine leather and tweeds, riding breeches and peak-caps. In the city he sometimes wore a cape and carried a silver-headed cane, and in his circles he was known as the Prince.

Pablo Josseau, a.k.a. "The Prince", with Oriana aged 2. They are sitting on a park bench in the main square of Punta Arenas, near the huge statue of Magellan that dominates the park.

The young Josseaus lived in the big house in Calle Valdivia with the help of two servants, and that is where my mother moved after her marriage. She always talked about this place as very well furnished and comfortable, and was particularly impressed by the library, a luxury unknown to her before. The Josseaus, who then owned three cars, including a Rolls-Royce, and lived like millionaires, were apparently a very sociable bunch, forever organizing picnics in the country and dinner and other parties in the city. But my father was the one who presided over all these activities, as well as over the sheep ranching and the family finances, with great ease and success.

The story of the Eterovics, my mother's family, is neither as romantic nor as tragic as that of the Josseaus. Mateo and Gerónima Eterovic had met and married in Pučisča, a small village on the island of Brač (Brazza) which is located in the Adriatic sea, facing the port of Split (Spoletto) on the Dalmatian coast of Croatia. Although their point of origin qualified them as Croatian and technically as Austrian subjects of the then Austro-Hungarian Empire, and although Yugoslavia didn't come into existence until well after their departure from Europe, I never heard any of the Eterovics call themselves anything but Yugoslavs. As I have already noted, they were part of a very large group of Yugoslavs who emigrated to the south of Chile in search of a better life. By the time my grandparents' fifth child — my mother — was born in Pučisča, my grandfather had already left for Punta Arenas.

I presume that the big attraction was the apparently transitory turn-of-the-century gold boom and the accompanying prosperity because, as far as I know, my grandfather was never involved in the sheep business. Only one of his sons, *tío* Pedro, would much later become a very successful sheep rancher in the Argentinian part of Patagonia. For over three years my grandfather worked very hard as a clerk in a grocery store in order to save enough money to bring his family over to join him in Chile. Therefore, when my grandmother and her first five children arrived in Punta Arenas by ship in 1899, my mother was already three-and-a-half years old.

Subsequently, three more children were born to the Eterovic family which prospered sufficiently for my grandfather to become the owner of his own grocery store. By the time of my mother's marriage, her father's store was in the Calle Valdivia, right across the street from the Josseaus. He remained a grocer until his retirement in Santiago, many years later, and the closest he ever came to gold was a stash of British sovereigns that he was rumored to keep hidden in the mattress. Considering that both he and my grandmother were illiterate peasants, and that consequently they never learned to speak Spanish properly, I've often wondered how they managed to run a store successfully. But they did, at least well enough to raise their family modestly but most respectably.

The Eterovic siblings, four boys and four girls, all spoke Croatian at home and Spanish in school and elsewhere, but I have it on good authority that their "Yugoslavian", except in the case of one of the boys who later became the Yugoslavian consul in Santiago, left a great deal to be desired. All I know first-hand is that by the time I was old enough to judge, my mother always talked to my grandmother in some sort of Croatian, and that when the latter switched to Spanish to address me, the difference was not all that great. She spoke a unique blend of both languages, the proportion of each varying according to the primary language of whoever she was speaking to. More Spanish for me, more Croatian for my mother. I always found this quirk of my grandmother's both amusing and charming, but I'm not so sure about the charm, now that something very similar is happening to me with Spanish and English. One gradually forgets, or loses command of, the original language without ever having acquired complete mastery of the second one, especially if the latter was learned in adulthood, as happened to my grandmother and me.

Just as with the Josseaus, the Eterovic boys got a better education than the girls, or at least more years of schooling. I have objective evidence of this in the respective quality of their handwriting, which for their generation was a sort of index or badge of the level of education attained. My father's and my uncles' writing is regular, even, sophisticated and I would say mature, while my mother's and my aunts' is small, uneven, straight up-and-down and girlish. Tempted as I am to refer to and draw conclusions about my level of education as reflected in my own rather pathetic handwriting, I will refrain because such standards no longer seem to apply. Outside of school, however, the girls' education included the acquisition of all those skills such as baking, sewing, embroidering, playing the piano and singing that would combine to turn them into fine young "ladies".

María Eterovic, at age 18, in Croatian folk
costume for a festival in Punta Arenas.

My mother was also quite beautiful, probably the best looking of all the Eterovics and Josseaus combined. And because of her sewing skills she also dressed very well, copying dress patterns from store windows and Paris catalogues. I don't know much about my mother's temperament and personality as a young woman because my father, unlike my mother, never talked much about their youth. But I do know that she was hard working to a fault, clean, tidy, well organized and extremely well groomed. She was also loving and even-tempered, fitting into the Josseau family even better than some of its own members. I had the very clear impression, as I grew up, that during the six or so years that they had all lived together, she had become a sort of mother figure to them all, or at least their very wise and kind older sister. For the rest of their lives, well after they had all dispersed both geographically and socially, she seemed to me to have remained as the center of the family, the magnet that drew them all together. And she achieved all this without fanfare or ambitious plans of any sort. She never, on her own initiative, organized family reunions or parties to preserve the Josseau family bonds. She was simply there, and sooner or later they all came, just as her own brothers and sisters did.

These were, in broad outline, the setting and the set into which I was born and lived for the first four years of my life. Nothing worth noting happened during the first two years, except, of course, that I learned to walk and talk. I've been told by many that I was quite precocious and that by the time I was two I was so talkative that my aunts would sit me at the dinner table and let me entertain — and probably dismay and distract — their guests. I had simply become, by a sheer accident of birth, the toy, the pet, the center of attention for all the young people that surrounded me. One of them, *tío* Julio, called me "Chiporrito" (Little Lamb) at the time — the only nickname I've ever had.

Then, shortly after I had turned two in November of 1922, my cozy little universe collapsed quite abruptly after the, at least for me, unexpected intrusion of my twin brothers, Raúl and Orlando. Knowing how reticent my parents always were about anything at all dealing with reproduction, I'm quite certain that I may have been told, at best, that a new baby was coming —from Paris, of course, as everybody knew all babies did. However, nobody knew, least of all me, that it would be not just one healthy baby, but two very sickly baby boys. When the attending doctor told my mother that their chances of survival were nil and that she would be lucky if they survived the month, she determined with all her will to prove him wrong. And so she did. She donned a nurse's uniform and for the following year, especially for the critical first few weeks, she cared for them with all the skills and resolve at her command. While another two sets of twins born at the same time in the city perished, my brothers not only survived but before they were a year old they had turned into two lovely healthy babies, her pride and joy.

Oriana at age 2, dressed in Croatian folk costume
for another festival in Punta Arenas.

However, there was a casualty to this otherwise very happy affair, and that casualty was me. I reacted so intensely and violently —"hysterically" was the term my mother always used when retelling this story — to being suddenly abandoned by my mother for two alien intruders that before long I was sent packing across the street to be looked after by my young aunt, *tía* Catalina. And this she did, very lovingly, for a few weeks, while my mother looked after my brothers. She made me pretty little dresses, curled my notoriously straight hair, and took me with her everywhere she went to amuse and distract me. On one of these occasions, I'm pleased to report, I was elected queen of a children's party to which she had taken me. But on another, she says that I cried so violently when confronted with a lady who had a moustache, that she had no recourse but to take me back home. I couldn't stand ugly people, she concluded, or perhaps I told her. Although the outward demonstrations of raw anger about my mother's abandonment of me subsided, the resentment stayed, for good. This is clearly evident in a photo-portrait of mine taken by a professional photographer at the time. Although I'm very nicely groomed, and my hair nicely curled, the expression on my face says it all: I did not want my picture taken, but I was forced to pose. In fact, I remember that in one of the takes my right leg is dangling down from the settee I was sitting on, in preparation for my escape, but to no avail.

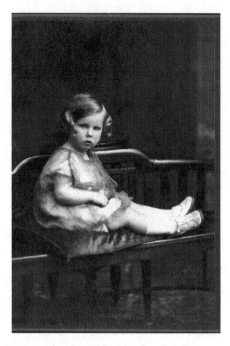

An angry Oriana, displaced by the birth of her twin brothers.

Although I had been dethroned, disgraced and even exiled, I did survive this episode more or less intact, but there were long-lasting repercussions. I don't, of course, remember any of this first-hand but, judging by my later feelings for my mother, this was the event that changed them from a sense of closeness and warmth to a polite distant mixture of duty and mistrust. We would never be close again. As for my father, I know even less. I've been told that he adored me up to the age of two, that I was the apple of his eye. But not afterwards, at least not demonstrably. By the time my own memories begin, roughly at age six, he seemed to me to care a lot more about my brothers than about me. I have the theory that my obnoxious reaction and behavior at the birth of my twin brothers put him off, pretty well for good. I base this, partly at least, on the fact that he always claimed that children were adorable, but only up to the age of two when, in his judgment, they seemed to turn into little monsters. His claim is consistent with the fact that the only visitors to the house he ever paid any attention to were little children, even up to the age of five, whom he entertained very happily indeed.

Things at Calle Valdivia pretty well returned to normal until two years later, when Fernando, my youngest brother, was born. As far as I know, I didn't make any fuss about his arrival into the family. On the contrary, I suspect that in a way I welcomed him as my new ally, a status he would keep for the rest of my life. I have no idea what the twins felt about me, but when Fernando appeared on the scene they thought he was a dog and barked at him accordingly. Some dog! He was a sweet and beautiful baby who turned into a very good-natured and goodlooking boy, the best looking of the lot.

At that time, or shortly afterwards, the Josseaus, all of them adults by then, held a family council and decided to sell Palomares and the family house and its contents. Quite understandably, all of them, especially the men, wanted their independence, financially and otherwise, in order to start their own businesses and get married. So the big pie got cut into ten equal small pieces that made them all at least temporarily comfortable, but not as affluent as they had been before. As a result, my father's portion amounted to one hundred thousand pesos, a sum that at the time would have bought ten three-bedroom brick town houses in mid-town Santiago. In addition, there were my mother's jewels, worth twenty thousand pesos, as I recall.

My parents' first move was to buy a smaller nearby house in Punta Arenas, where we lived for the next two years. What effect, if any, this important change from the big extended family to the relatively small nuclear family of six had on me, I do not remember. I am rather surprised to realize in retrospect that I don't seem to have become especially attached or close to any of my Josseau aunts and uncles in particular. I was fond of them all and as I grew up I came to know and be closer to some of them, more because of geographical proximity than because of any special preference. My youngest aunt, *tía* Magdalena, however, seemed always to be especially fond of me and her feelings were amply reciprocated. She was also my father's favorite sibling, a pretty young woman, who was crowned Beauty Queen of Punta Arenas at around that time, before my parents made the big move to Santiago.

My first real memories of Punta Arenas belong to this period, between 1924 and 1926. I remember my mother opening big wooden crates which had just arrived from France. There she was, pulling china, silver, fabrics and, of course, most importantly for me, those terrific toys — dolls, a teddy bear, a wagon — all those wonderful things that she had ordered from Parisian catalogues, just as I imagined she had ordered my three little brothers some time back. And then there was the wind. I remember walking downhill the two or three blocks to my grandparents' store and hanging on for dear life to door knobs, lamp posts or anything else at hand, so as to not be blown away altogether and be lost forever. And the wind, that made the window panes whistle ferociously and let the dust come in through the cracks in such quantities that my brothers and I could make mountains and rivers and valleys on the floor below to play with, and that, for the same reason, forced my mother to dust the house several times a day.

Perhaps it was the same relentless wind that finally persuaded my mother to agree with my father to leave Punta Arenas for good and move to the benign climate of Santiago. Be that as it may, we all left, some time during 1926, leaving behind most of my father's and my mother's families. As I understand it, however, my father's primary motive to leave was not the climate, but business opportunities. Why he didn't stay in the sheep and wool business, the one thing he was an expert at, I'll never know. Perhaps his capital was not enough to buy a viable ranch, or perhaps he simply thought there were easier ways of investing and making lots of money. Whatever the reason, we all left for Santiago, the promised land.

Educationally and culturally this change was radical. I am positively sure that had my family stayed in Punta Arenas, which would have been the normal thing to do but for my father's restless and adventurous spirit, I would have never gone to university, the nearest one being at least one thousand kilometers away. And now, instead of writing this story in Canada, I would very likely be minding sheep at the other end of the world, in Patagonia.

One only has to look at a map of the southern third or so of Chile to understand immediately that no roads or railroads were then possible. The land between the Andes and the Pacific is all broken up into countless islands of all sizes, channels, fjords and glaciers. It is, as the Chilean writer Benjamin Subercaseaux has said: " ... a submerged chunk of Chile, in which the Central Valley continues beneath the channels and the mountains emerge as islands". Since commercial aviation had not yet been developed, and the Austral Highway, far from finished even today, was decades away from conception, the only option to travel from Punta Arenas to Santiago was by boat, at least to Puerto Montt, where the islands and the channels end and the Central Valley and its main north-south railroad began.

And so it was that one day the six of us sailed from Punta Arenas on a long and arduous trip through endless channels, islands and gulfs, because the maritime route stays away from the open Pacific Ocean altogether in order to avoid its fierce storms. We had been warned that the worst and most perilous part of the trip was the crossing of the Golfo de Penas (Gulf of Sorrows) which, true to its name, nearly wrecked the ship. Family legend has it that everybody on board was sick for days, except for the captain and my father, who consequently looked after the rest of the wretched human cargo single-handedly. I think it was then that I began to see my father as a most courageous figure, a veritable hero, and my mother as a victim of misfortune, forever in charge of four small children who threatened to get sick at the slightest opportunity. At any rate, we all made it through the Golfo de Penas and reached Puerto Montt safely, to take the train on the long trip to Santiago.

Map of Chile, showing Patagonia y Punta Arenas in the far south,
over 2,000 km from Santiago and the main part of the country.

Santiago, A Cool Welcome

Once there — I wish I could remember our triumphant but anxious arrival, but I don't — we settled for a while in a "*pensión*" or boarding house, while my parents looked for an appropriate house. I remember the place, in downtown Santiago, as horrendously dingy but, worse still, full of gigantic rats that surfaced at night, when the lights were turned off. Here again my father was the hero, spending a good deal of his nights chasing rats like a mad huntsman. But we survived the dinginess and the rats and eventually settled in a lower duplex with a back yard in a not particularly attractive middle class — very middle, with a tendency towards low rather than high — district of Santiago. Our only relatives there at that time were *tio* Antonio Eterovic, his wife and their three daughters, and *tia* Luisa, the oldest of my Josseau aunts, who was then single and ran a very respectable boarding house in downtown Santiago. It was in that duplex, some time later, that we were all initiated into the vagaries of earthquakes for which Chile, but especially the central part, is duly notorious.

I was awakened one night by a tremendous noise and by everything around me, including my bed, trembling madly. The first thought that crossed my mind was that a ferocious gang of bandits, holed up in the vacant duplex above, was coming down the stairs to attack us. In an instant, my mother had crossed the hallway between my parents' bedroom and ours and, sitting at the foot of one of our beds, had gathered us all around her to protect us, like a weeping madonna. But by then the worst part of the upheaval was over, since most earthquakes do not last more than a minute. Nothing had fallen over our heads, or anywhere else for that matter, except for huge amounts of dust through the cracks all over the ceilings and the walls. Everything went back to normal very quickly, but the memory of the ominous and inexplicable noise, coupled with the unsettling tremor, and the memory of my mother trying to protect us with nothing but her body, would stay with me for life.

Just as in California, mild tremors, each a potential sign of worse things to come, are routine experiences in the central zone of Chile. But every once in a while there is a devastating earthquake, and for this reason one grows up there, as I did, with a sort of extra sense tuned in to the possibility of the earth revolting and quitting from under one's feet. Except for modern and expensive aseismic buildings, there is not much that can be done against these acts of nature. All I remember being taught after that experience at age six, was to keep my coat at the foot of the bed, always, and to either crawl under a table or stand under a door frame to stave off the possibility of falling bricks or lumber. The idea of always keeping a coat handy is wiser than it sounds. It may not protect one from falling bricks, but it will from the embarrassment endured by a very proper and polished young friend of mine who, during one earthquake, landed at the front door of his house wearing only his pajama tops and his hat!

My memories of life in this house are still scattered, disconnected samples, instead of the more or less continuous whole that begins only a year later. Two of them stand out and they perhaps illustrate the beginnings of my unusual personality —"you are different", everybody says, without ever specifying "different" from what and in what way. Our back yard was simply a moderate-sized square of packed dirt that was sprinkled and swept daily, a lonely tree at the back, and a fenced-in corner for the chickens from which we got eggs and eventually the chickens themselves to eat. This yard was separated from the neighbors' by a picket fence through which it was easy to interact with the people next door.

Among them there was a boy, slightly older than me, with whom I apparently had established some sort of relationship. I can't remember his face, or even his name, but I do remember very well that when Christmas came and I was given a lovely miniature sewing machine as a gift, I entered into negotiations with this boy which led me to exchange with him my toy sewing machine for, of all things, a bag of maize, presumably for the chickens! It goes without saying that when my parents found out about this dismal business transaction of mine, the goods involved were returned to their original owners, I was severely punished and admonished never to have anything to do with the boy next door, or any other boy, for that matter.

Since I was clearly the loser in this, my first business deal, and since I know that I wasn't so dumb as to have failed to realize that, I've tried very hard to find a cogent explanation ever since, but I invariably come up empty-handed. As I was writing this anecdote, however, the memory of this incident has connected with the fact that my mother often told us, with a big grin on her face, that her main wish or dream when she was a child was to be a chicken. Could it be that I saw her as a chicken with my mind's eye, a chicken that I could look after and feed with my very own maize? The real chickens in the yard were being fed by my parents after all, but I already knew that something was amiss with my father's ability to provide for the family, the most important member of which, from the point of view of my day-to-day survival, was clearly my mother.

The other memory connected with this first house in Santiago relates to my perception of my father's relationship to his sons on the one hand and to me on the other. He would come home at noon every day and after lunch we would go to the backyard to play with him. But I invariably felt left out. I thought that he either preferred to play with the boys or that perhaps he didn't think the games they played were appropriate for a little girl. But since I felt quite able and eager to play, it occurred to me one day that if I tucked my pretty little skirts into my panties, the difference between me and my brothers wouldn't be so obvious and everybody would be happy— my own early version of "if you can't lick them, join them". But my stratagem backfired because instead of solving the problem I infuriated my father, who not only punished me severely, but made it absolutely clear that pants were not for me then or ever, the wearing of pants thereby becoming in my mind a veritable sin, I guess the first sin I ever knew.

As a result, I never wore pants of any description in his presence for the rest of his life, but I defied him by doing so for sports in other settings and much, much later, when pants became fashionable for women, by wearing them as a matter of course. His rigid attitudes concerning boys and girls, men and women, are further illustrated by the fact that when, in that year of 1926, my cousin Viola, who was then sixteen, bobbed her hair very short, without a moment's hesitation he condemned her soul to burn in hell forever. Whatever other consequences conflicts of these types with my father had on my further development, my defiance never made up for the fact that I never got to play with him as my brothers did.

Earthquakes aside, other earth-shattering events of quite another sort were happening to me and my family at the same time. My father had not come to Santiago with the idea of looking for a job of any sort, but clearly to invest in commercial transactions with the capital he had obtained from the liquidation of the Josseau estate. He apparently had put most if not all of his money into one single deal that came to be known to us as "*el negocio de las tripas*", or the gut business. I haven't the slightest idea what this was all about. The only commercial applications of gut — sheep gut, more specifically — that I know of are catgut used for surgical sutures, and condoms. So, for all I know, my father's mysterious business amounted to buying sheep gut in Punta Arenas — a sort of by-product of sheep ranching — and selling it to manufacturers of sutures and condoms in Santiago.

What I do know for sure, however, is that my father had a partner or partners in this business, crooks as it turned out, who promptly swindled him out of all his money. Presumably, a huge load of gut had been bought by these men in Punta Arenas and loaded on a ship destined for Valparaíso. However, when my father tried to take possession of the load, there was no such cargo on board. It was nowhere to be found. It had either been stolen in transit, or never been loaded in the first place. Inexplicably, my father was never able to obtain satisfaction from his so-called partners. He was ruined. It was as simple as that. All that was left at the end of that first year in Santiago were my mother's jewels. Characteristically, in search of at least a modicum of security for her brood, she pleaded with my father to buy a house with the profits from their sale. But he did not agree, and lost that money as well in some further "business" deals.

This was a very unsettling period for all of us. Virtually overnight, the financial and social status of my family had changed from upper middle class respectability and affluence in Punta Arenas, to humiliating destitution in Santiago, albeit in an incomparably superior climate. My father spent the rest of his life dreaming up schemes to restore his former fortune, but never made it.

We then moved from the earthquake-shaken duplex to a more modest rented house nearby, while the question of my going to school arose. A law had been passed in Chile in 1920 making primary education mandatory for all children over six years of age. The government was in dead earnest about this, and inspectors were sent periodically to all neighborhoods in search of delinquent parents. One day they appeared at the front door of our house and my mother had quite a bit of explaining to do in order to justify the fact that her oldest child, already seven years old and very tall for her age, was not in school. I presume the explanation, which appeared to satisfy the inspectors, was that we were in transit between Punta Arenas and La Estrella, our next destination.

La Estrella, My Very Own Paradise Lost

In the wake of my father's economic ruin he had met an acquaintance from Punta Arenas by the name of Floro Menendez. The name and the point of origin immediately suggest to anyone at all familiar with the social history of the extreme south of Chile that Floro Menendez was a member of the Menendez clan, the biggest and richest landowners and business entrepreneurs in the region. And indeed he was, but a member in bad standing, the black sheep of the white-sheep-raising family. As rumor had it, he had been bought out, given enough money, that is, to leave Punta Arenas and go as far north as he could, to mind his own business and leave the rest of the family alone. He had bought a comparatively small farm in La Estrella, south-west of Santiago, which consisted basically of only three prosperous vineyards, but which had a house disproportionately large and well appointed, as well as a beautiful orchard and a vegetable garden big enough to serve all the needs of its inhabitants and their servants.

Every time that I've remembered La Estrella throughout my life, I've thought of it as an almost exotic and remote place, which of course it is from Toronto but not, I've just discovered to my amazement, from Santiago. What I always thought of as a very distant village, reached only after a long and arduous trip, happens to be only one hundred and twenty kilometers south-west of Santiago as the crow flies, or one hundred and seventy kilometers by railway and road. It is, in effect, twenty kilometers nearer to Santiago than our present cottage on Georgian Bay is to Toronto, a routine two and a half hour trip by car. This comparison, although strictly speaking correct, is actually misleading, if not somewhat fraudulent, because of the enormous changes in transportation between the 1920s and the 1990s, and the differences between Chile and Canada. And also because the perceptions of a small child introduce a factor of scale that tends to make everything experienced then seem more grand, or at least larger than the perceptions of an adult.

At any rate, Floro Menendez and my father soon entered into some sort of partnership to run the vineyards jointly. I presume the idea was that Menendez would provide the land with the developed vineyards, while my father would contribute the know-how as, a former ranch owner and, as it turned out, most of the work. How the profits would be distributed between them, I have no idea.

The fact is that some time during 1927 my parents packed their four children and all their belongings into a train destined for San Fernando, where a second-hand model A Ford roadster that my father had bought for the occasion was waiting for us. It was a red two-seater with a rumble seat at the back in which most of the luggage and the four of us were precariously accommodated. My parents of course sat in the front seat, but it seemed to me that my father spent as much time getting out of the stalled car to crank up the engine manually as he did sitting behind the wheel. The road, some seventy-five kilometers long, was a one-lane dirt affair. If it had been designed at all, it had not been intended for motorized vehicles but for ox-carts and horse-drawn carriages which had inevitably carved deep ruts throughout its length, and an endless profusion of pot-holes exposing stones of all sizes. It probably took most of the day to reach our destination, by which time we were all tired, cranky, hungry and covered in dust. We must have been a sight to behold, the genuine Latin predecessors, by several decades but in reverse, of the Beverly Hillbillies!

And at last there was La Estrella, this tiny little village — probably two hundred inhabitants or so — built around its inevitable plaza of which the most impressive building was, of course, the church. Right across the river, a trickle in summer but swelling to dangerous proportions during the rainy winters, there was the house, looking mighty and impressive atop the raised land on the far side of the river.

I don't, alas, remember our actual arrival, or what if any reception we got from the Menendez family. But I do remember the feeling that the house was huge and important. In fact, it was the slightly run down, but gracious in its old age, former summer villa of some wealthy local landowners. It had the characteristic architectural structure of Spanish colonial houses, in which an inner open square is surrounded on all four sides by rooms with doors and windows to the inner courtyard but seldom windows to the outside. Between the rooms and the courtyard on all four sides was a tiled porch covered by a roof supported by pillars at regular intervals. In this particular case, three or four steps at the front of the house led to a large double wooden front door with wide verandas to either side, which ran the full width of the front of the house. Since it faced the road leading to and from the village across the river, in due time the verandas became my favorite watch tower, the place from which I could see the parade go by. In line with the front door, but on the opposite end of the house, there was an equally large double wooden door which opened onto the back yard. The main features of the yard were a gigantic walnut tree to the left, and at the center a wrought iron arbor, covered with grapevines on top and rose bushes below, which was, I'm sure, at least one hundred yards long.

At the other end of the arbor there was an adobe wall with yet another gate, beyond which lay one of the three vineyards. To the left of the arbor, beyond the walnut tree, was a very large vegetable garden that in season yielded a rich and varied profusion of produce, and beyond it an orchard of the more common fruit trees such as peaches, apricots, cherries, pears and apples. And the area to the right of the arbor exhibited the more unusual or exotic fruit trees including figs, pomegranates, chestnuts, persimmons and avocados, as well as almond and olive trees. I should add with some degree of amused embarrassment that at the far side of all this luxuriant growth, next to the adobe wall already mentioned, there sat the outhouse, a sobering reminder of the full reality of the human condition.

The inner courtyard of the house, on the other hand, was a flower garden which, unfortunately, I cannot describe with the same degree of detail. Clearly my interest in food at age seven was considerably greater than my interest in flowers, a deficiency which has since been corrected. Only the lemon and the orange trees, with their almost painfully fragrant blossoms in the spring, and the rose and jasmine bushes remain in my memory, together with the overall feeling that it was all quite beautiful, but to a considerable degree underappreciated by my as yet immature senses.

By previous agreement, each family would occupy one half of the house, mirror images of each other. The Menendezes were already living in the right side, so the left was ours to invade and settle. There was a front sitting room, a large dining room and spacious bedrooms, but I cannot recall the details of the kitchen, bathroom or servants' rooms, or for that matter how the place got to be furnished. I do remember, though, that my father made some furniture for the dining room out of local poplar. My mother made mattresses out of the sheep wool processed on the farm itself, and cotton curtains and bedding out of sugar bags. It was all very modest, and a far cry from the relative luxury of ordering things from Paris by catalogue, but my overall recollection is that it turned out to be quite comfortable, airy and clean to a fault. Needless to say, there was no electricity or running water, nor a telephone for miles around. But we managed quite nicely with kerosene lamps and candles for lighting, a wood stove with which my mother cooked and baked — especially bread — as well as she had with a gas stove before, and pure fresh water from a well in the back yard. This was all rather primitive compared to our comforts in Punta Arenas, but more than compensated for by the sun and the warmth for at least three quarters of the year — we could play outside year round — and by the freshness and abundance of just about everything that the earth can produce. A land of plenty!

Like my father, Don Floro was a man in his late thirties who seemed incomplete unless he held in one hand a glass of wine, of which there was more than plenty around, and a cigarette in the other. I realize in retrospect that his florid cheeks and his blood-shot eyes were already signs of the alcoholism that would eventually kill him prematurely. Neither he nor my father wore the *huaso* (Chilean cowboy) attire characteristic of farmers in the region, with their Spanish style flat-topped and wide-brimmed felt hats, colorful ponchos and outsized showy silver spurs. They wore instead the heavily British-influenced country attire they had worn in Punta Arenas, which included tweed sport jackets, breeches, knee-high leather boots and small spurs designed more for their intended purpose than for show or decoration. Even their polished-leather saddles stood in sharp contrast to the bulky huaso saddles made of multi-layered sheep skins. All of this contributed to their being easily identified as wealthy landlords, which of course they weren't, and more importantly, as outsiders, foreigners, colonizers. I very strongly suspect that I came to share this perception myself and to think and act accordingly.

Don Floro's wife, Señora (Sra.) Inés, as seen through my seven-year-old eyes, was a dark, tall, impressive woman, much more stern than my mother, who consequently evoked respect from us children, if not some degree of fear. I heard it said many times that Don Floro had met her in a brothel in Punta Arenas and that their two children, Mirella and Florito (little Floro) had been born out of wedlock. This, together with Don Floro's drinking and his consequent irresponsibility as a landlord, gave me the very clear impression that although he was the owner of the farm and thus financially superior to us, we had the upper hand in terms of propriety and respectability. Although I'm quite sure that I was then too young to articulate the issue in these terms, I can vouch for the fact that I had sensed my parents' ambivalence towards this family, as well as their own sense of righteousness. Nevertheless, Sra. Inés eventually became a highly respectable matriarch, presiding over both the farm and Florito's large family with considerable dignity and success.

The relationship between the two families was rather formal, each respecting the other's territory. Whatever interactions there were among the grown-ups were primarily centered around the workings of the farm between the two men and around common domestic chores between the two women. These, of course, were many more, and more varied, than in the city, including, in addition to the obvious, baking bread, making butter and cheese, grinding wheat between two stones to make flour, drying corn to feed the chickens throughout the year, preserving fruits for the winter and other similar tasks. Although the local women helped with this work, they were supervised by Sra. Inés and my mother, who also did her own cooking and house cleaning.

I suppose we must have played with the Menendez children, but I have no memories in this regard. Florito was probably about three at the time, so he very likely played more with my brothers than with me. The girl, Mirella, who might have been my obvious playmate because we were about the same age, was a very delicate sickly child who was kept indoors most of the time, often in bed. She was no match for my strong, healthy, energetic and rambunctious proclivities. We learned a few years later that she had died of tubercular meningitis. Since I wasn't in school and there were no other suitable children, according to my parents' standards, for miles around, I became the girl leader of this small pack of little boys. I suspect that this experience, nearly a whole year of nobody but small boys to play with, had some bearing on my subsequent tendency to be very assertive and occasionally bossy. I was quite aware then and later that my brothers resented this trait of mine, thereby introducing conflict and a strong element of ambivalence into my developing self-image as a potential leader. It was inevitable and even necessary in the circumstances, but also "sinful".

In addition to our games which, because of the comparative lack of toys and other products of technology, were quite physical, such as running, jumping, tree-climbing and ball-playing, I spent a good deal of time exploring my immediate surroundings and learning from the men and women who worked around the farm about their tasks and skills. Occasionally my field research got me into trouble, as when my investigations in the kitchen got me and my brothers thoroughly drunk.

The main produce of the farm was, of course, wine. After the grapes were harvested they were poured into large wooden vats and crushed to a pulp by the workers, all men, with their bare feet in the traditional way. This operation took place in a special building just across the road from the house, so that it was not a problem for me to watch. I presume that to-day this operation is done by machines, even in a "Third World" country such as Chile, but I am now talking of the mid 1920s. The mashed grapes were then allowed to ferment, an immensely complex process through which eventually the sugar in the grapes is turned into alcohol and, voilà, there is wine! I have no idea how long the mash must be allowed to ferment before it reaches its optimal alcohol concentration, and know nothing about how a good wine is made. But I do know that it is customary in Chile to decant some of the grape juice after the mash has fermented for twenty-four hours, and to drink it as a refreshment. Judging by its appearance, taste and effect this drink, called "chicha", must have an alcohol concentration of about three to four per cent, something like a light beer. It is, however, very deceptive because there is still enough sugar in it to make it sweet and it is fresh enough to preserve the color, the flavor and the aroma of fresh grapes.

And so it happened that one day my mother filled a large kitchen cauldron with chicha and left it on the kitchen floor. I am not exactly sure whether I remember the event itself or my mother's account of it. At any rate, the fact is that when my mother wasn't looking we found the cauldron filled to the top with this beautiful red juice and drank from it with the greatest of glee. What a find it must have been! I'm sure it was I who found both the blue enamelled cauldron and the ladle we used to drink the delicious chicha, for the very simple reason, as I have already said, that at that point in our lives I was the tallest and the most daring of the four of us. Fortunately for me, the experience did not lead any of my brothers to a life of alcoholic dissipation. As for me, it is a moot point whether my conduct then had any bearing on the development of my eventual drinking patterns. When my mother found us "in flagrante delictu" we were, as she repeatedly told us later, roaring drunk, so that she had to nurse us back to sobriety for several hours afterwards. The experience, however, did not lead to the banishment of wine from the dinner table or to any other drastic measures that I can recall.

My field explorations, however, were mostly positive, because every time I conjure up the memory of La Estrella, a whole fresco of country features and learning experiences appears in my mind. It was there that I saw, for the first time, an amazing variety of fruits ripen to exquisite sweetness on the trees; that I saw many of them being sun-dried on tin roofs for use in the winter; that I saw cows and goats being milked; that I saw the women making butter and cheese; that I saw the huasos thresh the wheat on horse-back; that I saw wine being made; that I saw the men, especially my father, fell huge eucalyptus trees and shear sheep; that I saw the women carding the greasy wool and then making pillows and mattresses; that I saw and smelled the roses, the jasmine and the orange blossoms; that I saw the animals mate and bring forth their offspring.

But it was also there that I saw what real poverty and destitution were like: the solemn taciturn men clad in rags, working the fields from dawn to dusk, and their toothless women forever holding babies in their arms and surrounded by swarms of barefoot, dirty, snotty-nosed children. It was there, I suppose, that I learned we were not poor, just broke. The deprivation of the peasants was destiny, ours only relative and, my family thought, transitory.

Finally, and perhaps most importantly, it was during that year that I learned to read and write. However, the only school available in the village, just across the small river from the house, was of course a public school whose student population consisted almost exclusively of the children of the local peons. My parents decided that was inappropriate company for their little girl and so, once again, I was not sent to school, in defiance of the law. During that year it was my mother, who had herself been pulled out of school at age twelve, who taught me to read and write. I don't think there was much printed material in the house, or for miles around, for that matter. The Menendez girl, who was my age, didn't go to school either.

My mother, therefore, arranged for tío Antonio in Santiago to send my cousins' discarded school books to La Estrella. I was in complete awe of their wealth and sophistication, reflected in their being in a position to send a parcel of discarded books to their poor cousin in the country. The three of them, but especialy Milena, the youngest and two years older than myself, were to have this effect on me for the rest of my school years. But I was even more awed and mystified by these mysterious objects called books, that once you had learned to read them could tell you an unheard-of variety of stories, many more than your mother had or could ever tell you. I was never to be the same again.

Unfortunately, I don't remember what the actual process of learning to read and write was really like for me. I simply assume, in retrospect, that it was easy because I was so keen about it, as I was about everything else. But it clearly had not been the only salient experience of the year we spent in the country.

The whole adventure and experience of La Estrella, however, which to this day I evoke as my very own Paradise Lost, was cut short. Before the year was over my father had come to grief with his alcoholic partner and had decided to move back to Santiago. This was tremendously exciting news to me because I strongly suspect that the nearly lyrical description of La Estrella written above is largely retrospective rather than what I actually appreciated at the time. It is by comparison with all the other places and years of my life that La Estrella has come to assume such an exalted status, my own expression or version of the Romantic eighteenth century ideal of the noble savage. The fact, however, was that moving back to Santiago, the capital, the great metropolis, meant that I would have my cousins, all girls, to play with and, above all, that I would be going to school with a whole bunch of girls like me, instead of the peasant children of La Estrella. My parents' daughter was already a snob, but she came by it honestly and there is nothing I can do about that now. The excitement, however, was contaminated with a fair amount of anxiety because I kept on wondering whether I would be accepted by my new playmates and classmates as one of their own, or whether I would be seen by them as the barefoot peasant I feared I had become.

I am sure it was for this reason that when we left, about half-way through 1928, I got dressed in my very best city clothes, including — and I remember this vividly — a brown beret and a little red purse. Because my father had by now sold the courageous red two-seater Ford, the trip to the San Fernando railway station, over the long and dusty dirt road, was made in a small horse-drawn cart with room enough for only the six of us and our belongings. This was clearly not very city-like, but no matter. We would arrive in Santiago by the far more civilized train and I was, no question about it, all dressed-up for the occasion. But then something happened that looms so large in my memory that it has erased all other memories of that very important trip.

My mother was sitting on the wooden bench right across from me, and probably just as dressed-up as I was, as the carriage made its way over the pot-holes and the stones. She kept on looking at me until, laughing quite openly, she said something like: "Look at her, she thinks she is a 'señorita', all dressed up like a grown-up!" This hurt more than all her spankings and other reprimands — being made to feel ridiculous for acting, or aspiring to act, as a little woman, as a girl. This wouldn't be the last time that she made fun of me in similar circumstances, but this particular memory stands out as a prototype. I am quite certain that the irony of it all did not escape my already well developed capacity to observe: I couldn't win. I was punished by my father when in his view I acted as a tomboy, and at the same time laughed at by my mother when I behaved as the girl that I was. Tough, especially since I had no allies, no sisters or peers to count on.

Once in Santiago we moved into a small but decent three-bedroom house in the Calle Manuel Infante just a couple of blocks from Avenida Providencia, the main artery that leads to the Barrio Alto, the well-to-do residential district extending towards the foot-hills of the Andes. It had a small fenced-in front garden and a larger dirt backyard, where my father, of course, promptly installed enough chickens to keep us well provided with eggs. It seems to me that we had chickens the way other people have cats and dogs, but there the similarity ends because eventually we always ate our pets. This time around, however, and beside the chickens, there were lots of children to play with in the street, especially those of the German consul, our next door neighbor. Our demographic circumstances therefore had improved substantially when compared with those of La Estrella, a fact further reinforced by the arrival from Punta Arenas of my Eterovic grandparents and their two youngest children, tia Catalina and tio Juan. They had bought a corner grocery store just a couple of blocks away from us, so that there was a lot of traffic back and forth, to say nothing of the candies and dried fruits, figs especially, that I always got when I visited.

Embassy Row

We arrived in Santiago in the middle of the school year, that in Chile begins at the end of the summer, in March, and ends in December, so I was not enrolled in school until the beginning of March of 1929. I was eight and a half years old by then, or a good two and half years behind everybody else. This, combined with the fact that I was considerably taller than average, was to cause me a lot of grief for the first couple of years of school life.

So the day came when my mother walked me to school, a good ten blocks away from home, to be left there all alone, at the mercy of the academic establishment for the first time. On our way, we crossed the "mighty" Mapocho, a small, short, precipitous river which, like the majority of rivers in Chile, has no time or distance to grow into anything very impressive, the distance between the Andes and the Pacific coast being so short. It cuts across Santiago, and during long hot summers becomes merely a trickle. But in a rainy long winter, or when the snow of the Andes melts in the spring, it has been known to overflow its embankments and flood the adjacent parts of the city. Non-natives like my husband laugh at my respect for the Mapocho, but to me it is what the Seine is to Parisians or the Thames to Londoners.

The first day of school is clearly a landmark in everybody's life but, regrettably, I remember nothing except for the walk with my mother. I know, however, that I was put in kindergarten with the five-and six-year-olds, where they kept me for a week, after which I was transferred to grade one. I am not sure whether it was my size, my age or my knowledge that impressed my teacher, but she transferred me to grade two at the end of the month, where I stayed for the rest of the year. I had no problems with the school work, but my social adjustment, especially the way I related to my classmates, was a different story. Because of my age, my blue eyes and blonde hair, my height, and my French name and noticeable accent, I was obviously "different", a term applied to me to this day although for different reasons, and about which I feel very ambivalent. It is flattering and embarrassing at the same time, and seldom explained satisfactorily. But a fortuitous happening during that year, I suspect, not only added to my sense of differentness but left a permanent mark in my mind.

One day my mother discovered that all four of us had become infested with lice, presumably by the peasant maid we had at the time. My mother was of course horrified, and promptly washed our hair in a vinegar solution, the customary procedure there at the time. I still remember dozens of small black things floating in the water with which our hair had been washed. Not only was the sight gruesome, but the mere idea of being lousy was a social disgrace of major proportions, it seemed to me, and clearly to my mother who, not content with the vinegar washing, had our heads shaved to the bare scalp.

Naturally this drastic procedure was of no consequence to my three younger brothers, who weren't even going to school yet, but the conspicuous mutilation was a severe trauma for me. When I next went to school I became the laughingstock of my class for weeks on end, until my hair grew back. Adding insult to injury, the girls called me "*Pedrito*" (little Pedro, or Peter in Spanish) from then on. I may have been no longer lousy, but I was certainly miserable in my self-conscious awkwardness, hair being such an important component of the appearance and identity not only of females generally but of little girls in particular. I don't think I ever got fully rid of that sense of awkwardness although for most of my adult life it was neatly stacked in the back of my mind. Old age is another matter.

I think this is as opportune a time as any to explain that schools in Chile, both primary and secondary, public and private, were segregated by gender. This applied not only to the students but also to the teachers and principals. Only the universities were co-educational. Therefore, except at home, I lived and grew up in an environment populated exclusively by females, from my first day of school until I graduated from high school, when I had just turned eighteen.

Among these females there was also Ivonne, my piano teacher at this time. Ivonne Laserre, who lived with her French family two houses away from ours, was a pupil of Señorita María Luisa Sepúlveda, the most renowned piano teacher in Santiago, and was simultaneously majoring in French at the

Instituto Pedagógico of the University of Chile. She was probably twenty years old at the time, and to me glamour personified, because in addition to her artistic and scholastic achievements, she was tall, slim and pretty. She became my mother's friend very quickly and took such a liking to me that she offered, or rather insisted, that I should take free piano lessons from her. My mother, who had herself taken piano lessons as a girl, was of course delighted, but I have no idea what I felt about all this myself.

What I do know is that from then on I had to go to Ivonne's house to take lessons and practice every day after school, because we didn't have a piano. Since Ivonne's piano was in the front sitting room, I could see and hear my brothers playing with our friends on the other side of the lace-curtained window, and would rush through my exercises (poor Diabelli!) like a prize sprinter. There is no question in my mind that playing physical games in the street was far more fun than practicing seemingly endless scales. But Ivonne not only persisted, she categorically insisted that I had talent — if only I would apply myself more seriously. She would show off by making me play for her friends when they came visiting and eventually, after a year and a half or so of lessons, she proudly announced to my mother and me that I was to play at a concert.

Once a year Ivonne's own piano teacher would present a recital by her best students in a downtown theater, the Club de Señoras, a recital that was an artistic and social event of some note. This time, however, she made an exception and either invited or allowed Ivonne to present two of her own students, as well as playing herself. Something like the grandchildren, as well as the children, being allowed to the feast. Ivonne selected me and another girl, a year younger than me, for the occasion, as well as the pieces we were going to play. For me she chose a piece called The Waltz of the Beaux and the companion piece, The Waltz of the Belles, for the other girl. And then, I practiced and practiced and practiced the benighted piece until I got to loathe it thoroughly, while my mother fretted over the dress I was to wear. She disinterred a pure silk peach-colored floor-length dress that she had made for me for the wedding of one of my aunts when I was a little girl in Punta Arenas, and which she had kept, together with other treasures, such as my soiled baptismal garments, in a trunk full of history. She dismantled the old dress, washed and ironed the fabric and then proceeded to make me a new but, for obvious reasons, very short dress suitable for the occasion.

When the fateful day came, Ivonne and her older sister decided, with prophetic forethought as things turned out, to have a dress-rehearsal some hours before the concert. As I was pulling the dress over my head we all heard the ominous sound of fabric tearing apart, and when we looked there was a vertical gash right in the middle of the yoke. I am sure that despite the momentary panic that this development caused among the grown-ups I must have given a big sigh of relief: no dress, no concert, no ordeal!

But Ivonne's resourceful older sister saved the day in a flash by promptly embroidering a large bouquet of rococo roses over the gash, thus transforming a pale and plain little dress into a high fashion piece but, by the same token, depriving me of the only way out of the dreaded event. However, even I thought the dress looked very pretty but could not suppress the fear that it might come apart again at any time. What if it happened when my turn came to play at the concert when no rescue was conceivably possible! What if! Oh Lord, the anguish of it all!

But my trials and tribulations were further compounded by another two items of my fancy apparel. My mother had bought me a pair of white shoes to go with my silk dress, and a wide white ribbon for my hair. The shoes were a bonus, a fantastic treat, because we rarely, if ever, had more than one pair of shoes at a time since, as my mother herself has written, shoes were about the only thing she could not make for us. But on that particular day, precisely because the shoes were brand new, they were tight as could be and my feet hurt to the point of making me limp. Then there was the bow on the top of my head. Because my hair was very fine, straight and silkier than usual since it had just been washed, the bow refused to stay in place until it was tied — to my brain, I thought! — with such vigor that I felt every hair on my head was being pulled out by its root. In summary then, my feet were hurting, my dress was threatening to come apart at any moment, anywhere, and my head was being scalped. It was in that state that they took me to the theater where everybody agreed, with amazing sensitivity, that I looked very pretty!

When my turn came, I walked across the stage to the piano and back as fast as my miserable feet allowed, and in between, I played The Waltz of the Beaux at great speed and with remarkable disregard for any musical merit it might have had. There was only one thought in my mind: get it over with. When the concert was over they all agreed I had played very well but, my mother asked, "Why were you in such a hurry, and why did you look so angry?" And therein lies a very important question of my own: Why have I always looked angry when I was simply — or maybe not so simply — in pain?

I continued to take lessons with Ivonne until her family moved to a new house too far away from ours to walk back and forth every day. A short time later we moved ourselves, twice as far again, and that marked the definitive end of my musical career and of my relationship with Ivonne. There is objective proof that such a concert really occurred because my mother kept the relevant newspaper clipping, and many years later sent it to me in Toronto.

The passage from second to third grade was uneventful except for the fact that we had moved yet again. My father's inability to provide for his family had begun to show because it was during the year or so that we lived in Calle Manuel Infante that my mother began to sew professionally, making dresses for relatively well-to-do women. She soon got an assistant named Aida whose main trait, as far as I was concerned, was to nervously cover her mouth with one hand every time she laughed because one of her front teeth was missing. But that didn't seem to deter my father from paying undue attention to her, right there in front of all of us. My mother seemed to take this otherwise humdrum episode with her characteristic dignity and superficial calm, while it got registered in my mind as the first nonsensical instance — my mother being so much more beautiful and attractive than this woman — of men's propensity for infidelity that I had witnessed first hand. I already knew about such things indirectly because it was well known in La Estrella that Don Floro had contributed significantly to the growth of the local population through his numerous illegitimate children.

Despite my mother's contribution to the family income, however, the rent in this ordinary two-storey brick house in Manuel Infante — the closest I would ever get to living in the Barrio Alto — was too high for us, and so we moved to an anything but ordinary small one-storey house in a more central part of the city. Vicuña Mackenna Avenue was not only embassy row — the British, French, Cuban and Argentinian embassies being within two blocks of the house — but also millionaire's row. Our (to say the least) modest and odd dwelling stuck out like a sore thumb between two mansions with large, carefully manicured gardens all around, inhabited by two elderly couples with no children.

It consisted simply of a row of six rooms, each connected to the next by a door and each opening onto a long narrow garden through a paned glass door. A tiled open corridor ran the length of the house between the rooms and the garden. One could enter the house either through a wrought iron gate leading from the street directly into the garden and then into each room, or through the door of the front room that opened on to the street. The front room came to serve multiple purposes. It contained a sofa of very dubious pedigree, an arm chair that had seen better times and a very large chest that contained, in happy disarray, just about all of my mother's personal possessions. Over it hung an equally large mirror that gallantly but vainly tried to give the cramped room the sense of space it didn't have. All of this might have qualified the room as a living or sitting room, but for the fact that in one corner stood my parents' high brass bed, giving it the unmistakable air of a bedroom. But whether bedroom or sitting room, this was also the room where my mother did business with her clients, including their fittings, and thus the mirror.

Next to it was our bedroom, with four assorted beds in a row — as in an old-fashioned public ward in a hospital — and a free-standing wardrobe against the opposite wall, next to the glass door to the garden. Since there were no built-in cupboards anywhere in the house, this amazing wardrobe contained the clothes of all six of us in silent stoicism. A small wooden box at the foot of my bed served to store everything else I owned, from my underwear to my toys and school books. I shared this bedroom with my three brothers until I turned fifteen, when my need for privacy and for a space of my own became overwhelming.

The area beyond our bedroom was actually divided into three small sections: a tiled sunroom, in effect just a wide corridor with glass walls and door to the garden, a small bathroom, which had no bath tub or running hot water, and the maid's room, a tiny cubicle with only a narrow bed and a chair.

The corridor led directly into the dining room, the only place in the house furnished according to its intended purpose, with a full dining-room set. There was a round table and six chairs to match, a buffet and a side-board and, hanging on the wall opposite the glass door to the garden, there were even two original oils on silk that one of my Josseau aunts had painted herself. Ironically however, this, the only complete and proper room in the house, was rarely used, and then mainly to entertain my mother's guests for tea or for the occasional birthday party. But except in the winter, when this unheated room was too cold to bear, I did a lot of my homework on the round dining-room table.

I am at a loss for words to qualify the next room in simple terms. Let me just say that it was the room where just about everything happened and where my mother reigned supreme for thirteen years or so. It was her workshop, the place where she did all her sewing, from the initial cutting to the final touches, by hand, of all the dresses, coats, suits and skirts that she made through those years. But it was also the place where she kept all the materials and tools of her trade, including fabrics and spools of thread, garments in progress, fashion magazines and, above all, paper patterns, dozens of them, stuck to the main uninterrupted wall with pins or thumb tacks. A large, second-hand, and slightly warped ex-dining table with massive legs sat towards the near end of the room, in front of the glass door to the garden. Its far end was invariably covered with the ironing pad made up of old blankets and sheets. On this sat the iron, plugged rather precariously into a socket attached to the one electric wire dangling from the ceiling in the middle of the room. The one single bulb that lighted the room after dark was also screwed into this socket, making for a movable and uncertain source of light when the iron was in use.

All the hand-sewing by my mother and her assistants was done around the rest of this table, where every afternoon at around four o'clock they also had tea. When any of my aunts or of the three or four close friends my mother had at the time came visiting, they also had tea there, so that my mother could go on working. Confidential conversations however, and these appeared to me to be frequent, took place in the front room, behind closed doors. I often wondered about what all these women discussed in such secrecy, but I didn't find out until much later.

Next to this table, by the glass door, sat my mother's already legendary sewing machine, the one she had bought by herself in Punta Arenas, when she was fourteen years old. Its two small drawers to the right of the knee hole were the only drawers in the whole room, so that everything in the room was exposed, creating an appearance of constantly changing clutter. Beyond the big table, but in line with it, there was a smaller square table where we had all our meals. And next to it, by a window, there was a small, decrepit, and also slightly warped desk, which had lost its two drawers long before we had acquired it, leaving two conspicuous gaping holes. At this desk my brothers and I took turns to do our homework. The chairs in this room can best be described as a collection of floor samples in a third-rate second-hand furniture store. I don't think that any two of them were alike and when they broke — rather frequently as I recall — my father would fix them coarsely with an odd piece of wood and some nails.

For many years the only source of heat for this room in the winter, when the mean temperature is about 8°C but it often freezes at night, was a brazier. Even though this contraption is a most inefficient source of heat it made the room in question the warmest in the house and thus the gathering center in winter. But I could never stay there for more than at most an hour at a time because, no matter how well lit, braziers are also highly effective generators of carbon monoxide and other gases, which invariably gave me very severe headaches. We also had a small portable two-element German electric heater, but because of the cost of electricity it was used sparingly, in the front room for my mother's fittings, and to take the chill off our bedroom at night.

Some years later, my father got a cast-iron wood stove, something like a Quebec heater, and had it installed in this most important room of the house. This was a fantastic improvement because it heated the whole large room uniformly and because it did not produce any noxious gases. It had, in addition, a flat top on which my father assiduously nursed his beloved pot of coffee whenever he was at home. So, more than ever before, this became the room, especially during the three or four cold and damp winter months, where my mother worked and entertained her close friends and relatives, where my father read the morning, noon and evening papers by the stove, where we all had breakfast, lunch, tea and dinner, and where the four of us played, fought, read and studied. It was a room to remember.

Not so the kitchen, a square room at the end of the house where, although my mother ruled, the maid followed orders and generally made it her domain. It had a gas stove, a sink with cold running water but no counters, a small free-standing cupboard where the everyday dishes, cutlery and such were kept, a scrubbed table to prepare the food and at which the maid ate, and one chair. It was in this kitchen, pretty well out of bounds for my brothers, that my mother taught me the rudiments of cooking and baking from very early on, just as she was gradually teaching me to sew in the big room. Tacked on to the kitchen, but with access only from the garden, there stood a small cubicle with the maid's toilet, and room for nothing else.

What I've been referring to throughout as the garden hardly deserved the name, except for the fact that it was separated from the beautiful and ornate front garden of the landlord's mansion next door, by a very short and rather inconspicuous wire fence. This, of course, allowed us full view of their garden and of all the goings on next door, not only from our garden but from every room in the house. Our garden, which was at most three meters wide, stretched for the length of the house and for a few meters beyond it, where the fence turned right to fully enclose our space. Roughly half of it, going from front to back, had a tall iron arbor with black grape vines entwined all over it. Below it there were a few flowering bushes of which I can now visualize only the jasmine, probably because of the amazing fragrance of its flowers, a phenomenon which enticed me at least once into trying to make perfume - with rather disastrous results!

Except for some bamboo bushes, the rest of the garden was simply a small dirt yard where I once tried to grow lentils with as much success as my lamentable perfume industry, but at the very end, beyond the kitchen, there was a marvelous large plum tree. This tree, besides its lovely blossoms in the spring, came to play quite an important role in my young life on at least two counts. First, it was a great source of jam that my mother and I would make every fall. I would help by picking and washing the plums, removing the pits, and cutting the fruit into small pieces, and my mother would take care of the rest. The resulting jam was a very special treat because we couldn't afford to buy ready-made jams or even fresh fruit with which to make them. It was only when my grandmother or one of my aunts gave us apricots or peaches from their back yards that some variety was introduced into our jam menu.

Second, and perhaps even more important to me than the jam, was the fact that this tree became in due time my main refuge from my pesky brothers and sometimes even from my mother, when I knew she would soon be after me to help her with the chores or run some errand for her. I had become quite a proficient tree climber in La Estrella. So, when I discovered the plum tree in our new back yard I explored it thoroughly and found the perfect spot at the juncture of several large branches. The perfect spot to sit there and read, without being quite visible from the ground. I would use this as a retreat, sometimes for hours on end, until I grew too big to climb trees anymore.

The house was owned by Señor Carlos del Campo and his wife, Señora Elena who, as I've already said, lived in their sumptuous three-storey mansion next door. The proximity of these two utterly disparate houses is explained by the fact that ours had originally been intended for their chauffeur. This is why it stuck out so incongruously in the midst of millionaire and embassy row.

Don Carlos, a self-made millionaire, was an engineer who had made his fortune during the heyday of the nitrate mines in the north of Chile - just as Esteban Trueba did in *The House of the Spirits*. Don Carlos, who was probably in his mid to late fifties at the time, ruled his estates and their inhabitants with an iron hand and uttered his orders and commands in a stentorian voice that made all four of us run for cover whenever he got near our house. Whatever tenderness or sweetness there was in him appears to have been reserved exclusively for his once beautiful wife whom, it was quite clear, he simply worshipped. She, always leaning on a cane because of her severe arthritis, regularly surveyed her gardens, and these were the only times when I recall talking to her, across the low wire fence, because we were never asked to visit. Señora Elena, with her grey hair up in a bun, her Edwardian ankle-length dresses, a choker around her neck, and unforgettably a huge bundle of keys dangling from her belt, would occasionally stop and ask me a few questions about school, and then she was gone, like the Queen in one of her walk-abouts.

They had a butler, a maid, a cook, a gardener and a chauffeur, and a presumably mad aunt locked up somewhere on the third floor. They gave formal dinner parties with some frequency and it was then that I would peek over the fence to get a good look at their elegant guests, the men in white ties and the bejewelled women in their flowing silks and furs, making their entrance from the front gate to the front door, through the garden. The rest was all pure fantasy since I didn't know for sure what went on inside the house which I had never visited. Until one Sunday afternoon, when I was about twelve, and Rosita, their maid, invited me in because the del Campos were away.

Whatever I had imagined beforehand was immediately replaced by my first impression of the house: it was huge, it was opulent, it was somber. Since I had never seen anything like it before — not even at the movies, because I had seen only one or two up to that time — I had no point of reference and no knowledge or understanding of what exactly I was in the presence of. Come to think of it, I'm no better equipped today than I was then to do justice to the decor and furnishings in the del Campo house, because I've never, to this day, been in a private place like it. I immediately noticed that the parquet floors were all covered with silky rugs, probably Persian; that at least in the main rooms of the ground floor the tall windows were attired, like wealthy and noble old ladies, with heavy velvet or brocade drapes, in addition to the translucent curtains between them; that at night the light didn't come from a single bare bulb dangling from a wire, but from glittering crystal chandeliers; that the furniture in every room not only seemed to fit its overt purpose but to be in some sort of harmony both with itself and with the rest of the house; and that what appeared to be important paintings, enclosed in ornate gilded frames, hung on the walls everywhere. It was quite clear to me that none of this was either Spanish colonial luxury or Punta Arenas comfort, and so I asked Rosita for an explanation. She said that the del Campos had acquired most of the furnishings of the house in Europe, especially in France and Germany, where they had travelled widely in search of a cure for Sra. Elena's arthritis.

The second floor, including the bedrooms and Sra. Elena's morning room, was more of the same, but less somber than the first. Rosita didn't make any move to show me the third floor and I, sensing that it would be imprudent of me to ask, didn't say anything either, thus keeping the mystery of Sra. Elena's mad aunt inviolate. She then took me to the servants' quarters on the back and dark side of the ground floor. This section of the house included the large kitchen and pantry, as well as two or three small bedrooms. The overall memory I have of it is that it was all dark grey, gloomy and extremely spartan, but clean and neat as a hospital.

But then, and to my utter amazement, Rosita showed me how all the food cupboards and drawers in the kitchen and pantry were locked, and told me that only Sra. Elena was in possession of the keys, thus explaining the large bundle of keys that always dangled from her belt. When I asked how the cook managed in such circumstances, Rosita explained that every morning Sra. Elena came to the kitchen and, after discussing with the cook the menu for the day, she would take out of the cupboards and drawers exact amounts of whatever was needed, with precise instructions that nothing be wasted or eaten by the servants without her explicit approval. The servants' ration, Rosita further explained, was completely different and separate from their masters' menu, consisting mainly of cheap ingredients, such as beans, corn and cheap cuts of meat.

At home, of course, our maid ate exactly the same fare that we did. Whether this was due to my mother's deep democratic instincts and sense of fairness or, perhaps more plausibly, to the fact that there wasn't one cupboard or drawer with a lock in the whole house, I cannot tell. Neither can I tell, retrospectively, what thoughts and feelings these strange discoveries about the lives of the rich evoked in me at the time. I doubt very much that any thoughts of the exploitation of the poor by the rich, of class struggles, of the unfairness of the distribution of wealth in my country, or of the rather absurd fact that five people were required to keep only two in elegant comfort, crossed my mind at the time. All I knew for sure was that Don Carlos, whose origins were presumably modest, had had to work very hard to put himself through engineering school, and that it had been his good luck to be working at the nitrate mines of the north before World War I, when the Germans invented a synthetic process to make nitrates which significantly decreased the demand for, and therefore the value of, the natural product. And I also knew that my father, whose origins were not nearly as modest, but who had also worked very hard as a young man, had had the misfortune to lose everything in an ill-conceived business deal. It seemed to me that luck, good or bad, had a lot to do with peoples' fortunes, and because of it things tended to be unpredictable. There were no guarantees, not even for the Del Campos. But at the time of my only visit ever to their home they were rich and powerful and we were not.

From my point of view they were powerful in at least two important respects. The four of us children had to behave and control our natural rowdiness, especially when Don Carlos was around, or we would be ordered to leave; and, even more importantly, the rent had to be paid exactly on the first day of every month or we would be put out in the street without any further ceremony. The rent was paid religiously, sometimes at the expense of other basic necessities, and when we finally left that house, many years later, it was because of our own decision to move to a larger and better house but which, ironically, was also owned by the del Campos.

I have described this house at 166 Vicuña Mackenna in great detail because it turned out to be the place where I grew up, and where I've lived the longest, except for the house where I now live in Toronto. It was the physical and social setting in which I changed from a nine-year-old second grader to a twenty-two year old undergraduate university student, who was already holding a part-time responsible job in the Faculty of Medicine.

Discarding Some Career Options

Coincidentally with these family moves, my school had also been moved from its original site north of the Mapocho to an old building south of it in Vicuna Mackenna, a mere block away from home. It was then that I felt really identified with my school and all that went with it. It was an integral part of my territory, we belonged to each other.

Half way through third grade, in the middle of the winter, I got sick with influenza, as all four of us did every winter. This time, however, the flu' or "grippe" turned into a severe middle-ear infection from which it took me more than two months to recover. Treatment had been purely palliative, since in 1929 the sulfonamides, let alone the antibiotics, were some years away from being discovered. When I got back to school, after this long absence, I had the first intellectual shock of my experience, a real blow to my pride at being quick and clever and of learning anything that came my way with the greatest of ease. Arithmetic was the culprit. At the time I had taken sick, two months earlier, we were learning to add and to subtract, exercises that I found extremely easy and at which I was very good. But by the time I came back the class was busy multiplying and dividing, and I was completely baffled. I could not understand how it was possible to obtain a result from two numbers which, instead of being neatly piled up in columns, were side by side on the same line. I was panicky and thought that I would never, ever, graduate from grade three. This time it was my father who came to the rescue and helped me catch up because, having completed grade ten, he was well ahead of my mother in school matters. It is obvious that I must have caught up very quickly because, at the end of that year, I was promoted to grade five, skipping grade four altogether.

By now, for the first time, I was at par with my classmates in age, but not, alas, in height. I still stood half a head taller than everybody else and was invariably seated at the back of the classroom. This, to my mind, arbitrary and unfair rank assignment made me restless and unhappy because I felt that nobody, especially not the teacher, ever paid any attention to me. This led to behavior problems: I was distracting, I moved about too much and, worst of all, I talked too much. I didn't solve this problem until grade seven, when I requested and was granted the privilege, in most classes, of sitting up front, to one side of the blackboard. In the meantime, however, my marks in behavior were very low, bringing down my mark average quite considerably.

My peculiar brand of memory is such that up to this moment, the beginning of grade five, I cannot put faces or names on any of my classmates or teachers. But in grades five and six my teacher was Sra. Eva Page, a sweet, kind, but very serious woman who seemed to think I wasn't all that bad, and who consequently got almost the best out of me. Of the ten years that I spent in that school there is only one picture extant, and that is a snapshot of Sra. Page surrounded by her brood, including me. Soon after moving on to high school we learned, sadly, that she, who was then a comparatively young mother, had died of cancer.

By the time I reached grade five the school had moved yet again, this time almost right across the street from my home. Since the schools did not own their own buildings, these frequent moves must have been made in search of better accommodation or, most likely, simply more space. As it was, we were always cramped in small, poorly lighted, unheated, and poorly ventilated classrooms, and played in skimpy yards, because all these buildings had formerly been the huge private homes of the wealthy, rather than schools *per se*. If I had identified with my previous school, I virtually appropriated the new one, since it was practically in my very own front yard, which in fact existed only in my imagination because we didn't have one.

Whether it was because I had finally caught up with my own age group, or because I liked my teacher, or because of the physical proximity of the school, my love affair with the *Liceo* No.5 had begun, and it was to last until the end of high school. At this point, aged ten, I loved school so much that even in the dark, cold, rainy mornings of mid-winter I would cross the street and sit on the door step for an hour waiting for the front door to be opened. This sort of madness, however, lasted only until puberty, in grade nine, when getting out of bed in the morning became a minor daily ordeal, a problem I have had to deal with ever since.

My love for school was quite genuine, not in the sense that I enjoyed studying itself, but rather learning, knowing and in the end mastering new things. To that extent every school day was a new adventure, but not the only one. I also loved school because attending classes all day and playing with the other girls during recesses had become, in addition to their intrinsic merits, a wonderfully legitimate reason to escape home and all its problems.

My father, who never gave up altogether the idea of grand and profitable business deals, would, between dreams, hold jobs of one sort or another, and when he did, material things as well as the atmosphere at home were reasonably good. But he never seemed to be able to hold on to a job - insurance salesman, worker at the city abbattoir, truck driver - for more than a few months at a time. He would quit, usually in a state of great indignation, because his employers, he claimed, were invariably crooks, incompetent, just plain stupid or, worse still, displayed all three attributes combined, in random proportions.

The intervals between jobs ranged from a few weeks to several months, when he often went mysteriously away, leaving my mother alone to fend for all of us. My own feelings about these periodic absences were mixed, to say the least - highly ambivalent. It wasn't so much that I missed him because, as I was growing older, our relationship was gradually becoming more distant and increasingly silent. It may be that as I was acquiring, step by step, imperceptibly, the traits of an adult, he began to feel that I too was crooked, incompetent or stupid. What I missed, rather, was the comfort, the stability, the support that, from my point of view, his presence at home signified to all of us, but to my mother in particular.

A direct consequence of the fact that my mother could not count on my father's reliability was that, beginning at this time, when I was about ten years old, she began to count on me, in the sense of expecting me to provide the help she needed to the degree that I was capable of. In addition to helping with some of the chores at home, I began to be sent on errands related to her sewing, such as buying supplies or delivering things, but mainly she would send me to buy special supplies such as coffee, meat or drug store items that she felt she couldn't entrust to the maid. I enjoyed these modest shopping expeditions a great deal more than helping around the house or with the sewing, and I invariably ran or skipped my way to and from the stores with great speed, trying to break my own records and, of course, trying to impress everybody around. Far more subtly, however, she had also begun to confide in me some of her other problems, especially those related to her economic situation, as well as those related to the behavior and education of my brothers. In this sense she was increasingly making me feel that I was gradually beginning to fill the vacuum left by my father's absences.

Then during that winter, or perhaps during the following winter of 1931, Raúl, the blue-eyed twin, got very sick. Like the rest of us he contracted the flu, but instead of recovering from it without any further complications, this time he developed a severe case of pneumonia. He hovered at the edge of death for days on end during which my mother, who had once again turned nurse, cried a lot, and my other two brothers and I tried as best we could to be quiet and keep out of the way. He had been transferred to the front room and I think I was sent away to stay at *tía* Luisa's to make room for my mother in our bedroom. One evening, coming home from *tía* Luisa's when it was already dark, and knowing that the doctor had given up hope, I was feeling a very strange and troubling mixture of sad apprehension and exhilaration at the imminent prospect of Raúl's death. I knew that if the light in the front room was off Raúl had already died. If it was on, there would still be some hope. When I turned the corner onto Vicuña Mackenna and looked at the house, the light was on and I felt relief, of course, but at the same time a sort of vague disappointment that the drama of which I was a part was dwindling, petering out rather than reaching its inevitably dramatic climax.

Raúl did not die, but he didn't recover either. The acute pneumonia developed into a serious case of pleurisy for which he was finally hospitalized because surgery was required to drain his chest. As a result he spent the following two months in a public ward of the children's hospital, until he was discharged in good health but very thin and frail. At first, when we learned that he had to go to the hospital, the mood was dismal at home because at that time and place the prevalent view was that being sent to hospital was virtually a sentence of death. This drastic but apparently inevitable measure would serve little purpose except for prolonging Raúl's agony. Although the hospital was about an hour away from our house by street car, my mother went to see Raúl every afternoon for the duration of his stay there. She prepared special treats for him every day because he hated the hospital food, and also took her work along to keep up with her obligations and still be able to spend more time with him.

In the circumstances, coming home from school every day that winter was a sad and dismal affair for me because my mother, who ordinarily went out very little, had unquestionably become the essence of "home", its very core. So my two other brothers and I anxiously waited for her every day, sitting on the front step of the house, trying to discern her figure in the oncoming street cars.

I am quite sure that the overall home situation which I've just described contributed substantially to my perception of school as a refuge, as a great and anxiety-free place in which to spend my days. The lessons, the homework, the periodic tests, the marks and the discipline, were all challenges commensurate with my ability to cope, so different from the bewildering family problems about which I was utterly powerless.

A very different kind of education for me went on in parallel but independent of school during that year of 1930: religious training in preparation for my first communion. For a period of many weeks I went every day after school to a convent nearby, where the nuns taught us the Catholic dogma and catechism, and tried to inspire us to the same levels of ecstatic faith that they themselves had achieved. But once again I was late, in fact three full years behind everybody else in my religious class, since first communion was usually taken at age seven. And once again I was conspicuously the biggest and the most educationally advanced child in my group. I wonder whether my mother ever considered what all of this was doing to my tender and impressionable mind!

At any rate, the dear nuns succeeded beautifully at first. I was docile as a lamb, followed every rule of conduct to the smallest detail, and by the day of my first communion at the beginning of December, and for some time thereafter, my faith had reached the level of ecstasy. I mean this literally, since I can still picture in my mind the image of the Virgin Mary formed by the street lights on the branches of the trees that I could see through our bedroom window, when the light in the room had been turned off and I was supposed to be sleeping. The feeling that went with these visions was something utterly different from anything else I had experienced up to then. If school was fun and a challenge, this was more akin to passion, to being in love, as I was to discover many years later. And like most passions it wasn't to last very long, but in the meantime it seemed to me that becoming a nun, a status which I assumed guaranteed permanent religious ecstasy, was the highest and best possible vocation for a girl. My decision had been taken. I would become a nun.

Therefore, when the nuns asked me to stay on and become an instructor to the younger children, I accepted gladly and kept on going to the convent every day after school. This was to be the first step in my initiation into my religious career. I was good, although quite strict as a counsellor, and my conduct in the circumstances was, or so I thought, impeccable. Until one day, when I took to the convent a copy of a children's magazine called *El Peneca* (The Kid), of which my affluent cousin Milena periodically passed on to me the numbers she was through with. I was reading an illustrated article on the women of the South Pacific, Samoa I think, when one of the nuns took it out of my hands, had one quick horrified look at the pictures of bare-breasted women and then, after tearing the magazine in half, flushed it down the toilet in a state of outraged indignation. Not only was I corrupt and undeserving of my exalted position, but I would poison the innocent minds of the poor children in my charge for ever. I argued vehemently that these women were real people who, though they lived in far away, different lands, were the children of God just as much as she and I. And at any rate, that she had no business flushing my precious magazine down the toilet. I suspect that my own indignation at this act of vicious and arbitrary authority was far more intense and fateful than her own.

For me, it was the beginning of the end, the Church was never to be the same again, as my fervent passionate desire to become a nun came to an abrupt end. If this ignorant woman in a nun's habit was to be my model, I would have none of it, ever. Despite this incident I was not demoted or expelled from religious school, nor did I quit the Church at that point. But my interest, and above all my faith, gradually dwindled during the following five years — a process undoubtedly aided and abetted by similar subsequent experiences — until the final break in 1935.

I have dealt at some length with my short religious career in general, and this episode in particular, because it either set the pattern or perhaps, more plausibly, it reflected an already established pattern of questioning, more than defying authority. This pattern was to become a sort of trade-mark, not only of my life, but of my studies and career in particular. There always was, and still is, some ambivalence in the defiance, a curious blend of cockiness and fear, coupled with the uncompromising resolve to withdraw from, to abandon, beliefs or situations that failed me, either because they had been based mainly on my own illusions in the first place, or because they were inherently inconsistent in themselves, as the nun's episode illustrates. This deeply ingrained attitude has caused me some deep satisfactions but also considerable grief.

School, though, continued to be my main source of stimulation and excitement, much as life in the country had been three years earlier. It was also a major source of rewards, even though I was not an outstanding student, mainly on account of my restlessness and general surfeit of energy. Nothing especially worthy of note happened until the end of grade six, when I graduated from primary school and was ready to enter high school.

So by the end of primary school, at the ripe old age of twelve, I had closed the doors on three possible careers. Fate had decided that I wouldn't become a sheep rancher, or a rancher's wife. A variety of factors, including my obvious lack of talent, had decided I would not become a musician of any sort. And my experience with the nuns at the convent had determined that the religious life was not for me.

The Year of the Lamp

I entered high school in March of 1933, at the depth of the Great Depression, an event that was to have as much of an impact in Chile as anywhere else in the world, and which had a direct bearing on the fortunes of my family. We remained broke to the end of my high school years in 1938. High school was not a carefree, comfortable preparation for three or four years of college, but rather a period of training and qualifying, year by year, for a job in case the family needed an extra breadwinner. I do not mean to imply that the curriculum was so geared, because it was in fact purely academic in its orientation, called *Humanidades* (Humanities) but that the particular circumstances of my family made me feel that I might be called upon to leave school and go to work at any time before completing high school.

The transition from primary to secondary school was marked by a number of important changes, sufficient to confer upon it the feeling, if not the formality, of a rite of passage. In the first place, many children at that time dropped out of school altogether at the end of grade six, so that there were far fewer high schools than primary schools. The funneling of those students who chose to go on with their education into a smaller number of schools inevitably conferred upon them the status of an educational elite. One proudly wore a sort of invisible badge that said: "I am a high school student."

Secondly, there was yet another move to a different building, because the primary and the secondary schools were separated. The Liceo No. 5 proper was a large building on the Alameda Bernardo O'Higgins, the wide main

48

thoroughfare of Santiago, running east to west, and therefore perpendicular to Vicuña Mackenna, my very own street. To get to school now, 1 had to walk eight blocks, four north to the Plaza Baquedano and four west, towards downtown Santiago. My cocky sense of school proprietress disappeared *ipso facto*, not only because of the distance, but because this was truly the big time. Grade seven students or, better still, first year of the Humanities students, as we were in fact referred to, were at the very bottom of the hierarchy - the youngest, the smallest, the most ignorant, the least sophisticated, just beginning the awkward transition between girlhood and womanhood, a process that preoccupied many of my classmates far more than educational pursuits.

But not me, not yet. Everybody else in school, from grade eight to twelve, appeared to me as paragons of achievement, of accomplishment in every sense — physically, socially, academically — whom I envied and resented, but also secretly tried to emulate. All of this became painfully real in the person of my cousin Milena, who was a year ahead of me. Although she attended another Liceo, parallel but more socially sophisticated, we saw each other frequently and, imperceptibly but resolutely, I turned her into my model, or worse still, my idol. From then on, until the end of high school, I strove to achieve her level of excellence in everything.

In my view, Milena was impeccable in every respect. She and her family lived in a new and beautiful — or so I thought — three-bedroom bungalow in the Barrio Alto which they owned outright. For a couple of years or so, Milena shared her bedroom with Nora, her older sister, but became the sole owner of this amazing room as soon as Nora married very young. This, coupled with the fact that Milena had clearly acquired from her parents an almost excessive sense of order and tidiness, turned the setting of her domestic territory into the exact opposite of mine, and her into a princess in her palace. And the princess, as neat and well groomed as her bedroom, behaved accordingly. She was haughty and distant, and towards me in particular she was carefully condescending, probably because of her higher status in every respect. She was older, prettier, better dressed, more educated, and far richer. I don't think there was anything malicious or deliberate in her attitude towards me. The differences between us, all in her favor as I saw it, were simply there, stark facts that she dealt with in a kind of dignified aloofness that hindered much warmth.

In the circumstances, it is no wonder that almost all contact between us occurred as a result of my visits to her, hardly ever the other way around. I covered the distance between our respective houses, probably twenty blocks or so, by street car when I had the change, but more often than not on foot. This would happen mostly on Sunday afternoons, when I knew I would find her doing her homework and readying her immaculate uniforms for the beginning of the school week. There was a ritual in her meticulous preparations, but also perhaps a more exalted kind of ritual in my witnessing of them — the priestess and the worshipper. I would then go back home sanctified, but with barely enough time to make my own preparations for school the next day.

When we were just small girls we hadn't had a chance to play together much because of living in different parts of the country. But later, as adolescents, we weren't each other's confidantes either, and yet I valued her as my best and in effect only friend. While my admiration for her was boundless, to the degree that I indignantly refused to hear any criticisms of her — especially from my brothers — she mainly tolerated me, and then only for as long as I kept out of the way. She never introduced me to any of her friends and never asked me to any of her parties. I was, I suppose, a potential source of embarrassment because I was younger and awkward, a feeling that to some degree I understood and even condoned, but which became increasingly hurtful as we grew older. This rather lopsided, if not sado-masochistic, relationship continued throughout my high school years and no doubt had a great deal to do with the evolution of my values, standards and life aspirations. I owe Milena a significant debt, but unfortunately the question of what if anything I meant to her remains unanswered.

Grade seven ushered in a drastic change in the way subjects were taught. There was now a separate specialized teacher for every subject, or category of subjects, such as mathematics and physics. I had lost my one, kind, all-knowing Sra. Page and now had to confront a group of women of various ages, capabilities, personalities and the rest. Despite my mild nostalgia for the warmth and comfort of a sole teacher — a mother surrogate, I suppose — I soon realized that the new set-up had its advantages, in the sense that there now was choice. If I didn't like or get along with one or another teacher, there were others. And if a subject seemed dull and boring when taught by one teacher, it might become alive and inspired when taught by another. It may well be that my current tendency to perceive everything as potentially interesting had its roots then, when I learned to teacher-shop in search of excitement.

One teacher, however, assigned to each class from above, had closer contact with us than all the others, and she was called the class's chief teacher, or is it teacher-in-chief? Besides coordinating all matters related to her class, she kept an overall eye on the progress of each student and made contacts with parents or guardians as required. A big bound book was kept on the teacher's desk during classes, with daily columns to enter such information as marks, attendance and, most dreaded of all, at least by me, conduct. This last column was labelled "Observations", but I'm sure it never included anything positive, just our own personalized misbehavior. Up to the end of grade eight I was a regular and consistent contributor to that column. Just as there was a teacher-in-chief there was also a student-in-chief, or president of the class, selected by the former and in charge of the class in the absence of a teacher. This mostly honorary and symbolic position was to become significant for me some time later, in grade nine.

Our teacher-in-chief, from grade seven to ten inclusive, was our French teacher. It is a remarkable and significant fact that I cannot recall her name despite the fact that she played a major role in our school lives for several years, and that I remember the names of most of my other teachers. I'm almost certain that this selective memory lapse is connected to a disagreeable episode that happened in grade ten and to which I shall return. I shall refer to her simply as Mademoiselle X.

From grade seven to nine the curriculum was comparatively simple and straightforward: reading, writing and grammar in Spanish, of course; one foreign language (choice of French, English or German); history, geography and mathematics; and then there was a miscellaneous group of disciplines which included calligraphy, drawing, gymnastics, music — which consisted only of choir singing — embroidery, knitting and, later on, cooking, which dealt exclusively with the preparation of hors-d'oeuvres and desserts. We were clearly on our way to becoming accomplished young ladies, or señoritas, if you wish. All subjects were mandatory except for the choice of one foreign language up to the beginning of grade ten, when two foreign languages became mandatory.

The time had come then, at the beginning of grade seven, to make my first, perhaps fateful, decision. I chose French without the slightest hesitation. First, it was part of my ancestry, of which I felt inordinately proud; secondly, everyone *knew* that French was and would forever be the reigning international language, without which one would be a cultural non-entity, or worse; and thirdly, more than any other language I had heard, including my own, it rang like music in my ears. As things turned out, of course, I would have been wiser to major in English. But how could I have predicted, in 1933, the collapse of France only seven years later, and the subsequent ascent of the English-speaking U.S.A. to international preeminence? Not a very wise child, I'm afraid, but to be forgiven in the circumstances. I shall explain later how I made up for this mistake to the point of being able to write in English without much difficulty, sixty years later.

In this setting, my passage through grades seven and eight was quite unremarkable, except for the fact that at the end of grade eight I stood second in my class. This was unquestionably some sort of achievement, especially in view of the fact that my conduct still left a lot to be desired, according to my teachers, but not, of course, according to me. Naturally, I had no access to the class book with its column of ominous "observations", but somehow or other I got hold of one of them in grade eight, which read something like: "Oriana Josseau disturbed the embroidery class by changing into her gym clothes during that period." This is an example of the sort of thing I did that got me constantly into trouble, rather than being mean or truly naughty.

Then, in 1935, came grade nine, a sort of landmark year in several important respects. First of all, the class was huge, fifty of us to be looked after by one teacher at a time. Keeping such a large group of rowdy teenaged girls under control in one room evidently became a major headache for Mademoiselle X, who was a stickler for order and discipline. Then, in a moment of uncharacteristic but inspired desperation, she appointed me, the most restless girl in the class, as student-in-chief, or in effect her lieutenant. This veritable stroke of genius transferred me virtually overnight from the ranks of the rebellious troops to the officer corps, albeit at the lowest possible level. In one stroke Mademoiselle X had made her most troublesome student vanish and had acquired a powerful ally.

As a result, my own attitude and behavior changed far more profoundly than my formal change in status. I felt so appreciated, valued and important, that I lived up to my new role scrupulously, transferring all that boundless energy from aimless restlessness to a well structured exercise of authority, lowly as it was. The net result was that my poor conduct, and the accompanying low marks, ceased to be a problem for good and, for the first time, I stood first in my class, a ranking that I was to maintain to the end of my high school years. The end-of-the-year certificate, signed by the Principal, doña Josefina Dey, included a handwritten commendation to the effect that it was hoped I would continue to strive for the same level of excellence in the years to come. But that was to be my golden year, the year of my best and most consistent performance, except, perhaps, for my final Ph.D. exams many years later. Too many extracurricular interests and a certain cocky arrogance, to the effect that I didn't really need to work very hard to excel, explain, I think, why I didn't do quite as well later on, especially during my college years.

The other significant event of 1935 was the introduction into my life of two new teachers who, although poles apart in most respects, were to become potential role models for me, or at least whose traits and personalities I found far more intriguing than those of any of the teachers I had had up to then. For that reason, both of them had a far more profound impact on my subsequent development than either of them, or even I, realized at the time. If teachers only knew how far and how powerfully they broadcast all sorts of messages which have little to do with their purported conveying of simple knowledge!

One of them was the formidable Sta. Maria Elena von Delitz, who taught mathematics and physics from grades nine to twelve. Her reputation throughout the school and beyond, as the most capable, demanding, strict, and even terrifying teacher around, was awesome. Her severe face and demeanor are so indelibly imprinted in my memory that I cannot recall the faces or names of anyone else who taught me mathematics before her. It was said that if she took any liking to you, or if you showed any talent at all in her courses, she would demand blood, nothing was ever enough. If you didn't deliver, you were doomed. She was said to be more knowledgeable and demanding in her disciplines than many university professors.

It was, therefore, with great trepidation, if not overt anxiety, that I waited for what I pictured as her inaugural address rather than her first class in advanced arithmetic for grade nine. But when she finally appeared, holding a pile of books against her middle-aged bosom, she didn't look or sound as formidable as I had anticipated. She was of medium height and her mature but not heavy figure was invariably clad in plain black, navy or grey frocks which were clearly designed to conceal and protect, like a shield, rather than to reveal anything. All of this was crowned by an impressive head with fair but incipiently wrinkled complexion, scrubbed clean and framed by limp, thin, ashen blond hair.

But it was through her eyes that one really met Sta. von Delitz's unique personality. Those keenly intelligent small grey-blue eyes which let nothing go unnoticed and which, when the occasion so required — from her point of view, of course — could cut through one's mind and soul like a sharp dagger. They could indeed be frightening, but also fascinating, and one could read them more easily than her words. And her words were lucid, economical and to the point. The logic of her mathematical reasoning was clear as spring water if one was able to keep pace with her. If one couldn't, and fell behind, nothing but impatience and contempt came flying out of those cool blue eyes.

Since I was able to follow her reasoning, at least through grades nine and ten, I was not only spared the contempt but quickly became her star pupil. This meant that I was constantly singled out, in the sense of being regularly called upon to respond when the rest of the class couldn't. I felt immensely flattered, considering Sta. von Delitz's reputation, but also somewhat uneasy and embarrassed because it became gradually apparent to me that my exalted position was at the expense of my classmates. But this ambivalence on my part did not come to a crisis until much later, in grade eleven. In the meantime, I mostly enjoyed my demanding but highly privileged situation.

My status of star student was further enhanced by the relationship that developed between me and our biology teacher, the second of these two women mentioned above, and the very antithesis to Sta. von Delitz. Victoria

Mora was an easy-going, elegant, married woman whose expectations of us, academically at least, were as undemanding as those she had of herself.

Biology in grade nine didn't go much beyond taxonomic zoology and botany, subjects which did not require much intelligence or effort to be mastered, just some systematic memorizing. Sra. Mora's impact on me, therefore, had much more to do with her personality and looks than with academic accomplishments. She was a brunette, probably in her middle thirties at the time, with no single distinctive or salient physical feature to explain her beauty. It was perhaps the symmetry and regularity of her features, coupled with impeccable grooming, that explained her outstanding — to my naive and inexperienced mind — good looks. She dressed beautifully, mainly in black, and was unquestionably the most elegant teacher in the whole school. More than elegant, she was chic. And as if by design, she had one small physical flaw that, instead of detracting from the whole, seemed to underline, to call attention to the near perfect harmony of her appearance: one somewhat deformed thumb, with a scar, that not even the obligatory nail polish could conceal. Sra. Mora's flawed thumb was the subject of much discussion and conjecture among us students, but it remained a mystery forever, adding even more to her glamor.

After a while it became quite apparent to me that Sra. Mora's expectations of me were rather different from those of Sta. von Delitz. Rather than taking for granted that I was there to learn what she taught, she seemed to assume, at least part of the time, that I already knew the course, treating me more as a junior partner than as a student. On one occasion, for example, she arrived in a great hurry, called me to the front desk and asked me, quite matter-of-factly, to give the scheduled class in her stead because she had to attend a meeting. When, in my astonishment at this request, I explained it was impossible because obviously I did not know the material yet, she said something like: "Well, in that case do anything, but keep the class occupied." I don't really remember what I did, but it must have worked, because nothing untoward happened, except for my puzzlement at her attitude towards me.

She consistently singled me out in a variety of ways, including an invitation to tea to her home, on at least one occasion, but the instance that sticks most clearly in my mind was an ostensibly minor one. She arrived one day carrying a newspaper clipping in her hands, and promptly asked me to come up front and read it to the class. It was Marie Curie's obituary. Madame Curie had died in France but, as Eve Curie was to write in the biography of her mother some years later: "The event escapes from the silence of the sanatorium, and spreads throughout the whole universe ....". Indeed, reaching even our distant and modest class, and making an unforgettable impression on my young mind. Not because her death had any particular significance for me, since I had never heard of her before, but because Sra. Mora went on to tell us something about the life and achievements of this remarkable woman, that suddenly opened new vistas, new horizons for me to dream about. Women didn't have to be only mothers, or nuns, or teachers, or poets. They could, clearly, become famous scientists as well, and be mourned around the world when they died. Thanks to Sra. Mora, this was an important widening of options, but it was the mere beginning, the first glimpse into science as a life vocation. I did not make up my mind until much later, when many other factors intervened.

I came to love Sra. Mora. I suspect that I secretly wished she was my mother. But I never had for her the respect that I had for Sta. von Delitz on academic matters. If only I could have blended the two into one perfect model with the intellectual brilliance of the one and the human and esthetic qualities of the other! But to this day, I consider myself immensely fortunate to have had such interesting teachers. And this is not all. Just wait until I introduce you to Laura Vargas, my psychology and philosophy teacher in grades eleven and twelve.

The question of being singled out, which naturally gave me a sense of being special and apart, was not confined to the mathematics and biology classes. One episode, in a way an omen of things to come, will illustrate the point. On the occasion of the 18th of September (Chile's independence day) of that year, celebrations involving the whole school and lasting a full day had been planned. In mid-afternoon of the day before the event, my history teacher came to me with a book in her hands and asked me to write a speech on the life of Bernardo O'Higgins, the liberator and first President of Chile. The book was, of course, a biography of the man with that characteristically delicious Chilean name, and I was being asked to read it, and write a speech based on it, in less than twenty-four hours. When, after a desperate fit of swallowing, I told her I didn't think it was possible to prepare such an essay on such short notice, she said she knew I could do it, and that she would be counting on me.

She was right on both counts, but there was a hitch that neither she nor I had anticipated. The next day, with perhaps a couple of hours to spare, I was seized with sheer terror at the idea of having to read the benighted speech to the whole student and faculty body assembled in the improvised auditorium for the occasion. And so it was that one of my classmates, who had a great voice and a flare for reciting poetry in front of a crowd, read it instead of me, while I tried to make myself invisible, hiding in the last row of the choir, at the very back of the large crowded room. There must have been applause, I suppose, and some sort of recognition for my efforts, but I remember nothing but the panic and the shame that went with it, feelings that I have re-experienced, although in a much attenuated form, right now, as I write.

That was the first remembered and clearly recognizable panic attack of my life, but the story would repeat itself time and again throughout my student and professional lives. At the time, however, the incident was dismissed by everybody involved, including myself, as mere shyness. I think, however, that this episode illustrates most aptly the interpretation suggested to me by my last psychiatrist to understand the genesis and dynamics of what eventually became my protracted and pathological state of anxiety. Here I was, confronted with a demanding and difficult assignment and simply with no time to do it justice. I know that then as now I felt immensely uncomfortable and embarrassed at the sole idea of preparing a biographical essay based only on a hectically read single source, without even time to have it checked out by anyone else. I'm quite sure that what I was really afraid of, rather than just a big crowd, was being booed and rejected, and of losing the admiration and approval, if not the affection, of my classmates, but even more so, of my teachers. Irrational perfectionism had already raised its ugly head.

But it wasn't only school that turned 1935 into a sort of landmark year for me. In a way it was the year of my emancipation, especially from my brothers. The year during which — at least from my point of view — I came of age. In the presence of all the bodily and emotional changes of adolescence, the sharing of the bedroom with my brothers had become quite intolerable. In addition to the completely obvious lack of privacy, I had to contend every night with their merciless teasing and making fun, not only of me, but of everything I did. In this respect Orlando, the brown-eyed twin, was the master, because he seemed to have an inborn talent for clever sarcasm, a talent that as a grown man he developed into a veritable art. Because by now I was no longer capable of fighting all three of them physically and winning, as I had done when we were all smaller, I felt besieged and quite defenseless against their merciless attacks on everything I was or stood for.

Since there was no extra room in the house to turn into my bedroom, my mother agreed to let me move my bed into a corner of the dining-room, an awkward arrangement, but nevertheless my nightly refuge for the following seven years. Almost simultaneously Milena's parents, *tío* Antonio and *tía* María, had decided to redecorate their pleasant house in the Barrio Alto, and offered us a few of their discarded furnishings. These included a bath tub, a radio and a night table lamp. Why anybody in his or her — more likely the latter — right mind would have wanted to replace these fine objects for no apparent good reason was completely beyond my ability to comprehend. But the fact that I thought this was all plain foolish extravagance on their part did not prevent me from being enormously happy at our new acquisitions.

The bath tub, an old-fashioned four-legged affair, had a gas water heater attached to it. This meant that, for the first time since I could remember, I could have a hot bath now and then. No more washing piece by piece with a wash-cloth while standing in a basin in an otherwise cold and nearly empty bathroom.

The radio, which was quite ceremoniously installed in the dining-room, a.k.a. my bedroom, was a contraption the likes of which I've never seen anywhere else. It consisted of two sections: an octagonal speaker, about a foot in diameter, which normally sat on top of the radio proper, but which could be placed anywhere else within reach of the connecting wire; and the radio itself, an oblong metal box finished to simulate mahogany, about three feet in length and a foot tall, which must have weighed a ton, or so it seemed to me. From this rather ungainly contraption there emanated an amazing assortment of sounds, enough to satisfy anybody's taste or whim. One day, shortly after its arrival to our home, I was fooling around with the tuning dial looking for something, anything, to listen to, when I heard some marvelous orchestral music hitherto totally unknown to me. I liked it so much that I stayed with it to the end. It was, the announcer said, a piece called Islamey by the Russian composer Balakirev. That was, as current parlance has it these days, a defining moment. I had been seduced and converted to "classical" music, although the piece in question is as romantic as they come. But I was hooked for good and the radio became a companion, but in a way also a rival, to my beloved books.

I think that the lamp, a salmon-pink colored Art Nouveau specimen of most uncertain origin, slightly dented at the base, became even more important in my life than either the bath tub or the radio. Up to this point my reading in bed at night had been strictly limited by the fact that my mother would turn off the one light that hung from the middle of the ceiling of our bedroom at a specified time every night. No amount of pleading or excuses ever got me anywhere because my brothers' going-to-sleep time had to be protected. But now, God-like, I could think "Let there be light" and there it was, to illuminate the pages of Alexandre Dumas père – I then thought that The Three Musketeers was a work of sheer genius, the greatest novel ever written - Conan Doyle, James Oliver Curwood, Charles Dickens, and an assortment of lesser known Spanish and French authors of romantic love stories. The saddest and most tragic among them was something called The Incurables by Virginia Gil de Hermoso. But now, duly shielded from the scorn of my philistine and insensitive brothers, I could cry disconsolately throughout, while thinking that this too was the greatest novel ever written. All in all, I read forty books during that year of untrammelled tears and excitement - the year of the lamp.

Causally or coincidentally, it was at about this time that what might have turned into my first romance took place. A few houses over to the south of us there lived a boy called Tadeo. His Italian mother, a widow who ran a boarding house for a living, was on mildly friendly terms with my mother, so that I had been at their house occasionally. Tadeo, who must have been all of sixteen years old, was rather short for his age, but had a nice fair face, crowned by a very thick mass of ash-blond hair. I don't remember having had any significant contact with him prior to the day when he came to my house, boldly rang the bell - a real bell, by the way, attached to a string that could be pulled from the gate - and asked me to go out with him.

I must have been so astonished that I can't remember where we went or what we did or talked about, until we were at his house, standing in the middle of his very spartan bedroom. Even though he had left the door to the large central hall open, he came close and gently kissed me on the cheek. I didn't feel, even remotely, any of the things I had been reading about and further embroidered in my fantasies. But there was instead a keen sense of excitement and turmoil because a boy had found me grown-up and attractive enough to ask me out and to kiss me, if only on the cheek. The fact that I didn't find him at all attractive, or that he didn't in any way inspire in me the feelings of the heroine of The Incurables, was of no particular concern to me at the moment. What really mattered was that I had inspired him, thus providing unassailable proof of my incipient but in my mind still questionable status of full womanhood.

After reflecting about this momentous event for some time, thus allowing the immediate turmoil to subside, I reached in addition the very disturbing conclusion that having allowed a boy to kiss me, while we were alone in his room, was a sin. A sin that I had to admit to and confess at the earliest opportunity, lest I die and go directly to hell. As I further pondered on the exact nature of my sin, however, I became increasingly convinced that the notion of sin, applied to my actions, was at best unfair and at worst ridiculous. Tadeo and I had simply engaged in an innocent and harmless act, completely in accordance with the laws of nature. Hard as I tried to reason with myself, and logical as my arguments seemed to one compartment of my mind, the other one kept on nagging: You have sinned, you have sinned, you have sinned!

Unable to resolve the conflict on my own before my next confession, I had little choice but to mention the incident to the priest next time I went to church. He, a little grey-haired old man who was not at all tormented by such sophisticated theological arguments, left me in no doubt that I had indeed sinned, grievously, especially in view of the fact that I had not told my mother about the happening. The intensity of his response, coupled with the severe penance he imposed on me, as well as his demands for repentance, evoked the same kind of indignation in me as the nun had produced five years earlier, when she shoved my magazine down the toilet. The Church, by virtue of being against innocent nature, was in the wrong. At any rate, that particular priest not only resolved my conflict of the moment, but in the process destroyed whatever little faith I had left. I have not been to church since, except as a tourist, to admire the art and the architecture.

As for my sinful romance with Tadeo, it too petered out rather quickly, if for no other reason than that I kept on growing taller and taller while he stayed the same. I don't think I ever told him about the fateful consequences of our small encounter. I never saw him again until I heard a couple of years later that he had died of meningitis.

Some time during this year, that I see in retrospect as far more eventful than I realized at the time, my father left yet again for what I most likely thought was a routine one or two month trip. He was going to Puerto Aysén, a small town two-thirds of the way between Santiago and Punta Arenas, in the middle of the islands and the fjords, and in a way the last Chilean unexplored frontier. Whether he had a specific business project in mind or was simply in pursuit of one of his elusive dreams, I do not know. Neither did I know, when we all went to say goodbye to him at the railway station — as we always did when he went away — that we wouldn't see him for the following three years. He wrote to my mother with some consistency and sent money now and then, but never really enough to dissipate our chronic economic anxieties.

As if the year of 1935 needed a suitable finale, I too went on a trip all by myself, during the summer holidays between grades nine and ten. *Tía* Luisa, the oldest of my Josseau aunts, and her family, *tío* Carlos and their three small children, had moved from Santiago to Valparaíso some time earlier. Now they invited me to come and visit them. Most residential areas of Valparaíso are built on the rather steep hills that form a semicircle around the port itself and the busy and crowded business sector between them. The hills (*cerros*) are roughly rated from poor to rich according to the economic class of their inhabitants, the richer ones being equipped with quaint but efficient lifts. As for the rest, one has no alternative but to climb on foot up the steps of the sidewalks on either side of the narrow cobblestoned road. Carlos García and his family lived modestly but decently on the Cerro Yungay, one of the hills without lifts.

And so it was that one day in the summer between grades nine and ten, my mother took me to the railway station, with a brand new five peso bill in my purse, and sent me on my very first trip all by myself. Big adventure indeed since, in addition, I was now only a short distance away from the sea, the Pacific Ocean, which I had never seen before. Remember that our trip from Punta Arenas, itself on a strait rather than on the ocean coast, had carefully avoided the open Pacific.

My uncle, a charming Chilote (a native of the southern island of Chiloé) who was a court clerk at the time, met me at the station and took me home, where for many reasons I spent a splendid month. Their children were small. Sergio, the oldest boy, was only five or six years old, so that again there was no one my age to keep me company. But no matter. I made the best of it. *Tía* Luisa, then in her early forties, was a very French-looking woman, a characteristic that I can spot almost instantaneously, but which I am at a loss to describe. But, paradoxically, her excellent cooking, based mainly on the abundant and enormously varied sea food of the coast, was as Chilean as her husband, and very different from the Yugoslavian-European cooking of my mother. I enjoyed it all with great gusto, but drew the line at the hot chili peppers that seemed to me to accompany every meal except breakfast, as a side dish.

For me, the biggest treat of all was breakfast, because of the bread. There was a bakery at the foot of Cerro Yungay where one could buy the best square buns in the world. They were called *colizas* and were made of white flour and enough lard to form a dough reminiscent of that of a croissant, but not quite as light. I soon developed the habit of running down the hill to the bakery every morning before breakfast, and then of running back up the hill with my precious cargo of shiny golden-brown and still-warm *colizas*, right out of the oven. These daily errands of mine caused such a delighted reaction from my aunt and uncle that I soon turned them into a contest with myself. I ran faster and faster every day in an effort to keep my *colizas* as warm as possible, but also, no doubt, to impress my hosts with my physical prowess. I'm sure I've never been more fit in my life, and that I could then have beaten the best Kenyan or Ethiopian runners, such was the effort that I put into my up-hill sprints.

My aunt, who kept house very efficiently and looked after her three small children without the aid of a maid, rarely went out. During the month that I spent there, it was I who did most of the shopping and other errands, as I was used to doing for my mother. After lunch, when all the chores had been done, she used to read the papers and then turn to the equivalent of the present-day Harlequin romances, and cry quietly about the sad fate of her heroines. She read to me aloud on more than one occasion, when we would both cry, sharing in the romantic and tragic plots of her stories. She would then confide to me that her husband, my uncle, although a good man in many ways, was the exact opposite of her romantic and dashing heroes. He not only drank too much red wine, but was earthy and coarse by comparison, caring only about food and the flesh. It is true that he drank too much because I remember that every day after work in the evening, he would stop at a tavern or pub to drink wine with his pals, and then he would stagger up the hill to come home for dinner. Even so, I liked him a good deal because he was very kind to me, and he was also charming, amusing, intelligent and, having studied law at the university for several years, better educated than most of the men I had known up to that time.

I particularly enjoyed a sort of game he used to play with me, the gist of which was to test my knowledge and maturity in whatever subject was occupying his attention at the moment. I did pretty well overall, and was very proud of his obvious approval, until one day at lunch. He was reading the morning paper when he stopped, looked at me and told me some piece of news about Claudio Arrau. When I innocently asked who that might be, he burst into a good-natured but very righteous diatribe, the likes of which I had never been exposed to before: "You, at fifteen, a first-class student, about to enter grade ten, and a citizen of this proud country of ours, have never heard of Claudio Arrau? How is that possible? What do they teach in school these days?", or words to that effect. After he explained who Arrau was, I fell speechless in my defenseless humiliation and vowed never to forget. And I didn't. When, several years later, Arrau came to Chile to give a series of concerts, I made damned sure I would attend them all. And so it was that I heard him play all of Beethoven's thirty-two piano sonatas in eight consecutive concerts. I had paid my debt of ignorance in full, I thought, but more than that, it had been a musical experience never to be repeated or forgotten. Thanks for the lesson, *tío* Carlos!

I had discovered, immediately upon my arrival, that I could get a good view of the port from the window in the kitchen at the back of the house. Even though this wasn't the most comfortable observation tower imaginable, since the plane of the window was not parallel but perpendicular to the line of the coast, I was still able to spend many hours there, twisted like a pretzel, watching the big steamers and the ships of the Chilean navy come and go out into the vast ocean. I soon learned to identify them by name, thus keeping the family fully informed of all these comings and goings. I dreamt of the day when I would get on board one of them and sail to far away lands.

But I still hadn't seen any of the grand waves of the ocean breaking on the sandy shores, something I had so often imagined but never seen. Not until, on the first week-end of my stay, *tío* Carlos took his two older children and me to the Torpederas. This was the only public beach around — no entrance fees charged — and for that reason there were vast crowds of working class people, all vying for a place in the sun. Even though the beach was cramped, the sand coarse, and the water badly polluted because Valparaiso's garbage dump was just around the corner, I was thrilled to finally be able to stick my foot in the mighty Pacific, and generally fool around in the waves which, in that particular location, were not as huge and impressive as I had imagined them. We went there by street car every Saturday and Sunday afternoon, my first experience of a seaside resort.

But not the only one. Nora, Milena's older sister, who had been married for about a year to Eric Cheetham, a prosperous and very English businessman, was also living in Valparaíso at the time. They had a very attractive apartment on Cerro Alegre, the most affluent of Valparaíso's seven major hills and which, of course, was equipped with a very efficient lift. Nora, who was a very good-looking young woman - just twenty at the time - and also impeccably groomed, was lonely, very lonely, she told me. Consequently, as soon as she found out I was in Valparaíso, she contacted me and invited me frequently for lunch or tea. The Cheethams' looks — they could have just stepped out of a Hollywood movie, I then thought — their home, their car and their way of life, everything seemed to me to belong to another world. Eric, a tall and very handsome young man, had been born in Argentina of British parents. Probably for that very reason, he was more English than the English, a trait that imparted an air of Britishness to everything around him, from his neat grey flannels to his young bride who was then studying English very seriously. This was, no doubt, in order to communicate with her mother-in-law, the formidable Mrs. Cheetham, the spitting image of Queen Mary and who, despite a life-time in South America, could not speak a word of Spanish. So, once or twice a week, I had to make radical switches from the lowly smoked mussels, chili peppers and red wine of the very Chilean Garcías, to the tea and cucumber sandwiches of the Cheethams.

The latter further enlarged my horizons by inviting me a number of times to El Recreo and Concón, two of the beautiful beaches north of Valparaíso, and the playgrounds of the affluent. On one occasion, on a Sunday morning, they even invited me to a regatta in which Eric was participating. These outings would invariably end by having coffee and Viennese pastries at some fashionable cafe nearby — a treat even more transcendent than the warm *colizas* in the morning — and then driving home in Eric's car. (There was a road around the tops of the hills that connected with the up-and-down streets below). Despite my still childish and awkward age and my immaculate but modest clothes, I would then feel on my way to the top of the world, a proto-debutante in training, something like Eliza Doolittle at the beginning of her indoctrination by Professor Higgins.

I felt ambivalent, very ambivalent, caught up between the two worlds in which I found myself living. In the last analysis, I'm quite certain that I preferred the savor, the color and the complex warmth of the Garcías to the order, the elegance and the reserve of the Cheethams. But then there was the question of their respective social status. I must admit that I was very much impressed by the higher social position and manners of the Cheethams, and by the doors that they seemed to open, and I made every effort to fit and be accepted. As subsequent developments will show, I succeeded, because eventually I became much closer to the Cheethams than to the Garcías, but the ambivalence remains, as does a sort of nostalgia for that other part of my family.

Friendships in School

All in all, it had been an enriching and very enjoyable holiday, quite in keeping with my academic achievements and other life experiences of my fifteenth year. Not so my sixteenth, which pales by comparison, and during which I completed grade ten. I didn't meet any new teachers of note that year, and as I recall, the only new subjects were algebra and geometry, and of course English, which I was to study for the next three years, as well as taking my fourth year of French. Despite the moralistic and utterly uninspired Mademoiselle X, I loved French and wanted to get ahead on my own. So, at the end of that year, when one of my aunts came to our home carrying a beautiful leather-bound two-volume set of *Anna Karenina* in French, I borrowed it. Since my spoken French, then as now, was virtually nil, and my reading skills severely hindered by my limited vocabulary, trying to read Tolstoy in French was an act of sheer temerity, if not of outright foolishness. But I began to read anyhow. At the end of two chapters I had no idea what the book was all about, but I went on anyway, without even the help of a dictionary. However, by the end of the very sad story I was not only thinking, but even crying, in French. A strange way to learn a language, but it paid off because I have continued to read French quite fluently to this day. Come to think of it, I've even translated a whole volume from French into English not so long ago, but I'm getting ahead of my story.

English was all right, but at the time it hadn't quite aroused in me the fascination that French had. That was to come later, and for very different reasons. I suspect, in retrospect, that our high school teachers of foreign languages did not speak them fluently. They knew, I'm sure, all the rules of the game, grammar, literature and the rest, but not the spoken word. This was made dramatically clear to me after my return to Chile from Canada in 1948. 1was walking along a downtown street one day when I saw Miss Carvajal, my last English teacher in school, coming towards me. I immediately thought this was a golden opportunity to show off, on the one hand, and to please her enormously on the other, and so 1 greeted her in my very best and most polite English. To my everlasting dismay, she turned red as a beet and answered in Spanish. 1 am sure that 1 was even more embarrassed than she was, but 1 think that my faux pas was understandable. Sorry, Miss Carvajal. 1 shall never do that again!

It was during that year that my polite but rather distant relationship with Mademoiselle X came to a sad end as a result of an incident involving one of my classmates. Minerva (I am not kidding, that really was her name) was a very sexually precocious girl with a reputation to match among our teachers and parents. 1 cannot tell exactly what happened to her in grade ten, but there was a big hush-hush scandal involving her boyfriend, as a result of which she disappeared from the school for good, probably expelled. Although 1 never knew all the details, and have conveniently forgotten much of that episode, 1 know that Mademoiselle X was directly involved and that my own judgment of the situation was completely at odds with hers on moral grounds.

It is quite possible that 1 thought her judgment of Minerva unfair if we consider that Mademoiselle X was a rigid and devout Catholic and that 1 had already parted with the Church on the grounds of moral arbitrariness. I must have expressed my opinion in no uncertain terms because Mademoiselle X cut me off completely. From then on, to the end of high school our interaction was cold to say the least, and strictly limited to business. The fact that I couldn't even remember the name of this very important teacher, and the mild pangs of guilt that I feel every time I remember her, suggest that I probably did her an injustice, and that my conscience is still uneasy, because at some level of my mind I know that I hurt her deeply.

Shortly before the beginning of grade eleven three distinct events having a bearing on my future education happened. First of all, my father was still away in Puerto Aysén. He was to remain there for another two years without notable success. His monetary contribution to the upkeep of the family was irregular and inadequate, and my mother, who had become a full-time dressmaker by now, was the main, if not sole, provider. Despite her talent as a dressmaker, and her very long working hours, she did not make enough to keep us comfortably. We lived mostly from day to day, never sure that there would be enough money to pay the rent at the end of the month.

In these circumstances, our wealthy landlady introduced me — I suspect through my mother's intervention — to an old friend of hers who lived across the street, presumably to see if this lady, who was very well connected in Santiago, could help me in some way. Despite the fact that we had been neighbors for more than six years by then, I knew very little about Sra. Puelma, except that she was a widow and that twice a day, every day, my landlady's gardener had to go across the street to help her butler carry her in her wheel chair from the second to the first floor of her cheery house, and then back up. She was an old, white haired, very wrinkled, tiny woman who had been severely crippled by arthritis for a long time, but whose charm and keen mind were intact. My initial fear at having to meet someone whom I thought would be a formidable figure dissipated instantly when finally confronted with this tiny creature, as alert and quick as a hummingbird.

She received me in her study, a large airy room with huge English style windows on two sides and floor-to-ceiling bookshelves on the third. She was sitting at a very large table which, to my amazement, was covered with the latest issues of all kinds of magazines and journals from everywhere in the world and, naturally, in several languages. I had never seen anything like this, not even in the National Library that I used to frequent. When I expressed my amazement she just told me she was interested in many things and liked to keep up with cultural and scientific events. You couldn't do that if you didn't know at least some foreign languages. To my regret, she soon changed the subject and asked me all sorts of questions about my school work, my interests, my plans for the future and, of course, about the financial situation of my family. When she was satisfied we had covered all the angles, she said there was an organization in Santiago called The League of Poor Students, with which she was somehow connected and to which she would recommend me because I seemed to qualify for their help.

The main qualifications were high marks in school and demonstrable poverty. The ultimate decision would, of course, rest with the League. She then told me something about her only son, a young physician who had died of typhoid fever in Germany where he had gone to do post-graduate work many years before. When I subsequently inquired whether the hat, overcoat and umbrella that I had seen in the entrance hall had belonged to him, the answer was yes, and much more. She had kept his room, as well as all his belongings, intact and his bed was changed regularly, exactly as it had been before his departure! The most dramatic example of denial I've ever encountered.

That was the first, and I think only, meeting I ever had with Sra. Puelma. During the years that followed I often thought of going to see her, because I had found her quite fascinating and also because I thought she might have liked the company of someone young and as eager for knowledge as she was. I never did go, because I was afraid she might interpret my genuine liking and interest in her, as self-serving interest in what she could do for me. I have always regretted that decision.

Sra. Puelma's recommendation worked because, after due process, I was accepted by the League of Poor Students. Ascertaining my grades was easy, but not so my status as a "poor" student. Among other things, the League sent a social worker to my house, which she inspected thoroughly, in addition to interviewing my mother and me, singly and together. After some hesitation on the social worker's part we passed the test, but by then I almost wished we hadn't because I have never before or since been so humiliated. I am sure that it was the neatness and cleanliness of our home, together with our appearance — we never looked "poor" — that gave the social worker pause. Be that as it may, I finally got the darn scholarship, which I was to keep, secretly I may add, to the end of college. It consisted mainly of materials for my clothes, especially my school uniforms at first, some school supplies, and free lunch and tea at school. This doesn't sound like very much at this distance, but it was materially of some help to my mother, and it relieved me of at least some of the unease, if not guilt, that I felt about the sacrifices she was making to put me through school.

Oriana as a high school student, but not in uniform!

It was at that time also that, to further alleviate my mother's burden, I began to work part time as a private tutor for students who, for one reason or another, needed supplementary help. Some were little kids who had difficulty learning to read and write, some were simply slow and needed a push, and some, probably the most interesting group, were foreign students who needed a crash course in Spanish or simply guidance to catch up with the Chilean educational system. I liked this work which sometimes turned out to be immensely rewarding. The prize example was the mentally retarded or, to be politically correct, the mentally challenged fourteen-year old Venezuelan boy, Andrés, whom I tutored for a couple of years. His older brother had come to complete his studies at the University of Chile and Andrés had come along for the ride, while both were being looked after by their aunt. Although no one explicitly told me anything about Andrés' specific problem, I caught on to his needs and level of understanding rather quickly and adjusted my mode of teaching accordingly. Surprisingly — at least to me — we got on very well indeed and Andrés, although much slower than my other children, made considerable progress. This, which was barely enough to satisfy me, was clearly seen as a remarkable achievement by Andrés himself, whose shy, even taciturn, expression had changed into a charming smile and an almost disarming loquacity by the end of our relationship.

But when their stay in Chile was up and I went to say good-bye, Andrés broke my heart, when he refused to appear and sent his older brother instead. Andrés had asked him, the brother said, to tell me that I had been the only person in his life who had made him feel intelligent and worthwhile. Despite the rewards though, I didn't make much money. Just enough to pay for my books and other small expenses, but it also helped my mother a bit and, perhaps most importantly, it put me on my way to appreciating the meaning of economic self-sufficiency, my first taste of the significance of economic independence.

Eight years had now passed since I had entered school looking forward so much to joining a group of girls my age, among whom I would surely find some friends. This of course happened, or didn't happen, depending on one's definition of friendship, a concept that has fascinated me all my life, but with which I'm still grappling. If I were to follow the conventional dictionary definition of "friend" (a person with whom one establishes a mutual relationship of affection and regard), I would have to conclude that I had in fact had several friends during those years. They were the girls next to whom I sat in class, with whom I played during recesses, with whom I walked to and from school, and whose homes I had the chance to visit with some frequency. Although a degree of "mutual affection" developed between some of them and me, however, I cannot honestly remember any of them as "friends", except for Wanda. The fact is that I can scarcely remember their faces, let alone their names. The reason is simple. These relationships lacked the closeness, the sharing of common interests, values and feelings, and the tacit mutual trust that in my judgment a relationship must have before it qualifies as friendship. Since, for whatever reasons, I was shy, reserved, and unable to share my small but all-important preoccupations with ease, or with just anyone simply because they were there, I kept most of my classmates at a distance. It was all right to play, or talk with them about school matters and games, but not about my feelings, my dreams, and most of all my family.

As I've already said, only Milena was my friend, albeit in that lopsided way I've already described, until Wanda appeared sometime during grade nine or ten. Interestingly though, the same dynamics that characterized my relationship to Milena applied here, but in reverse.

Wanda and I became friends, but she was consistently more my friend than I was hers. The feelings of friendship were mutual, but not equal. Soon after meeting her in school we discovered we were also neighbors, as a result of which we promptly began to walk to and from school together. Because her house was on my way to school, I frequently stopped at her place to pick her up and thus became more or less well acquainted with her family and domestic surroundings. Wanda was Italian. In fact, more than Italian she was Roman, a fact of which she was inordinately proud, even though it had left an indelible mark in her accent.

Her father was the owner of an ornamental iron foundry nearby, and her mother a typical Italian mama who fretted over her husband and two children — Wanda and an older red-haired brother called Mario — even more than my mother did about her brood, and who, in addition, cooked beautifully. Her Milanesas (Wiener schnitzels) were without question the best I've ever had. The family lived in a very large duplex with huge high-ceilinged rooms, commodiously furnished with first-class furniture, including a quarter-grand piano which seemed more ornamental than functional. Wanda, of course, had her own room, something that I passionately envied. These people, especially her mother, were all very good to me, but I have the sneaking suspicion that at some level they feared that I, with my bookish ways, would make their precious only daughter deviate from her pre-ordained path towards an early marriage to an affluent and eligible young man, to — heaven forbid! — an intellectual career of some sort. They had overestimated my powers of influence, and underestimated their own daughter's drive in the desired direction.

Wanda no doubt looked up to me academically, but otherwise there was no competition. She was not outstandingly beautiful, but pretty, attractive and, above all, vivacious, coquettish and, in the last analysis, intensely passionate and expressive, befitting her ancestral origins. Her mother needn't have worried about her interest in boys and in marriage at that point. I remember one occasion when she and I were sitting on a bench in the Parque Forestal, going through some home-work, when a tall good-looking young man approached us, introduced himself — he was a law student — and promptly became engaged in a very animated conversation with her. Feeling completely ignored and excluded, I left them alone to their fate, to find out the following day that, before making a date with him, she had — after somehow securing his address — gone to see what sort of house he lived in, to make sure he was a young man of the right social class. Apparently he was, because they dated for a while afterwards.

I was astounded. Such calculating shrewdness was so alien to my underdeveloped mind that I could hardly believe it. At any rate, Wanda and I continued to be friends for the rest of our school years, during which time she kept on confiding in me and wanting to know my judgments and opinions about her affairs and other matters, while I, for the most part, played it close to my chest and didn't disclose nearly as much, if for no other reason than that there wasn't very much to disclose.

By the beginning of grade eleven, when we had dwindled from the fifty students we had been only two years earlier to about twenty-five, my class got very excited at the news that a new girl from Limache, a small agricultural town halfway between Santiago and Valparaiso, had come to join us, the old troopers. When we further discovered that the girl in question, called Fusa Sudzuki, was of Japanese extraction, the excitement turned into a sense of total adventure. Imagine, a Japanese girl, an Asiatic among us! I suppose we had imagined her as a petite and demure girl with thick straight black hair combed up and kept in place by fan-like combs, and who would, of course, be wearing beautiful silk kimonos and dainty slippers. It was, therefore, with an appropriate blend of disappointment and relief that we met the real Fusa at the beginning of grade eleven. She naturally wore the same uniform we all did instead of the fanciful kimono, and her hair was fine, silky, dark brown and cut short like that of the rest of us. There was enough of a slant to her eyes to suggest an Oriental appearance, but otherwise nothing in particular distinguished her from many of us.

As it happened, our initial excitement should have been only one-half of what it had in fact been, because we soon found out that she had been born in Chile to begin with and, perhaps more importantly, that she was only half Japanese, her mother, now dead, having been of English extraction. In this sense she was not exotic at all, but the prototypical Chilean, a blend of whatever races, effortlessly adapted to the main stream. However, and probably because there were very few Japanese in Chile at the time, the combination of her name — everybody wanted to know what Fusa meant — and of her attenuated Oriental looks conferred upon her the glamor of the exotic, perceived not only by us then but also by many other students later on in university.

During that first year of our acquaintance, Fusa lived with her older sister Gladys, a medical student, in a boarding house in Vicuña Mackenna, only a couple of blocks away from my home. This proximity, as in Wanda's case, greatly facilitated our daily contacts and thus we too became friends. In this case, however, the relationship that developed between us was far more even and balanced than those with Milena or Wanda, even though I think that Fusa was also two years older than me. Despite some notable differences in background and temperament, we then shared enough traits and aspirations to make for a satisfying and certainly interesting relationship. We both took our studies very seriously and, even more importantly, we shared the same kind of commitment and aspirations to a university education and eventual professional career.

But we were very different with respect to our extra-curricular interests and skills. Fusa was a little busy beaver who, regardless of whatever else was happening around her, always kept her hands busy when we were together. She would invariably keep sewing, or embroidering, or knitting to make progress in whatever project she was involved with at the time, or drawing those immensely detailed and skillful drawings of hers, while I talked and talked and talked, expounding on my engrossing ideas or theories of the moment with as much conviction, certainty and immaturity as I do today. Oh, how I wish I had at least one audio-tape of those encounters that invariably took place in Fusa's room! Although obviously there was considerable overlapping with respect to our interests and skills, basically she was the doer and I the thinker, or at least the talker. And from these shared differences we both drew a great deal of enjoyment and, who knows, perhaps inspiration and strength.

Halfway through grade eleven another new arrival to our class was to have considerable impact on our school-girl lives. This time, and for a change, we are not dealing with someone sporting an Italian, Japanese or French name, but a true honest-to-goodness Spanish one. I refer to Irma Veliz, a girl from the north of Chile whose family had just moved to Santiago. It was unusual for anyone to join a class in mid-term and even more unusual for our teachers to take some of us into their confidence with respect to another student's problems. But this is exactly what happened soon after Irma's arrival. Fusa and I were called by our chief teacher to tell us that Irma had some very serious family problems and to request that we not only befriend her, but help and assist her as best we could. This was not an easy task since the language used to convey the request was at best euphemistic and at worst confusing.

To translate into contemporary terms, Irma was an emotionally disturbed adolescent whose problems seemed to stem from the fact that her step-father had been or was still abusing her, I presume sexually, although this, to the best of my recollection, was never overtly stated. Such a situation should clearly have been within the jurisdiction of a social worker, a school psychologist or both. But in 1937 in Santiago, that sort of professional help was not available in the schools. I can't talk for Fusa, but I remember that I was not at all clear as to the exact nature of Irma's problems, and she wasn't saying very much either. I suppose this was in part due to my own naivety in matters of this sort and even more to the utter lack of openness with which everybody, including figures of authority such as our teachers, spoke when dealing with matters of sex, especially aberrant sex.

Irma was beautiful. Irma was a poet. And Irma, if not disturbed in the strict clinical sense, was a very unhappy and tormented girl. To us the most obvious sign of her current frame of mind was that despite her luminous large green eyes, her lovely light brown wavy hair — I would have given my right hand for such hair — and her smooth, flawless complexion, she stank. She exuded that pungent and peculiar odor of sweat that decades later I would come to associate with states of profound emotional disturbance through my own personal experience. The difference was, however, that Irma didn't wash or change her clothes often enough, so that being in her presence was offensive and embarrassing. But, if Fusa and I felt rather helpless about the source of Irma's emotional conflicts, we thought there was something concrete we could do about her personal hygiene. Though we tried in various subtle ways to present her with the problem and with suggestions to correct it, we met with very little success. Pressed by our teachers to do something effective about this, I felt quite at a loss, because my own domestic situation precluded any chance of offering Irma any material help. So it was Fusa who came to the rescue. She and her sister had moved to a new boarding house, this time quite far away from my home, where she had a lovely large room all to herself. In the circumstances, she was concerned and generous enough to invite Irma to join her and share her room and the expenses with her, and it was thus that my two new friends became room-mates.

There was no question but that Fusa, who in keeping with Japanese traditions was the essence of neatness and cleanliness, would set the standards. And so she did, but not before running a daily struggle with Irma which often drove Fusa to distraction. She would then confide in me about hairs in the basin, rings around the bathtub, clothes scattered all over, and all the other ways with which a slob can torture neat people. My only contribution, alas, was to give Fusa all my moral support, to reinforce the merits of her standards every time I visited, which was rather frequently, and to share with Irma not only a concern for her problems, but also her interest in writing, in poetry and in literature as a whole. I am quite sure that she enjoyed my company a great deal more than Fusa's exercise of authority, but in the end the victory was Fusa's. Despite a shaky start, in due time Irma became quite presentable, more beautiful than ever, and, though still tormented by her own brand of demons, far better able than at the beginning to concentrate on her studies. We too remained friends to the end of high school, when she no longer shared a room with Fusa.

So, even though because of my own make-up and family circumstances I had been somewhat of a loner through my childhood and early adolescence, I now had friends. Friends and peers who, precisely because they were so different from me and from each other, satisfied different facets of my emotional, intellectual and spiritual needs and aspirations during those last two years in high school, when difficult definitions had to be made and even more difficult decisions had to be taken.

Laura Vargas

We all waited for the beginning of grade eleven with some anticipation because our psychology teacher was going to be Laura Vargas, without doubt the most popular teacher in the whole school. I soon found out that her reputation was fully deserved, and then some. At thirty-four she was married and the mother of two small children. She was so timelessly modern that I have no difficulty at all in taking her out of the time and place in which I met her and transferring her to my here and now, where she would have fitted perfectly. She was tall and dark, and neither elegant nor dowdy. Instead, she had a flair for casually striking clothes which seemed to blend seamlessly with her easy and happy, but at the same time serious and impressive, personality.

We soon discovered that at the beginning of each class she would take five or ten minutes out of the curriculum to discuss with us anything and everything that she felt we should be enlightened about. The topics covered everything from current affairs to sports, from sex to art, from music to grooming, from how to choose a man to how to keep him interested. Suddenly, through these mini-talks, all doors were opened, so that I went from feeling like the awkward and nearly irrelevant school girl that I was, to feeling in and of the world. These exchanges with Laura Vargas — notice that I do not refer to her as Sra. Vargas — taught me more, far more, than the formal classes that we had to get through. But in addition to that, the way in which she related to us was unique. Alone among all my teachers she gave me a sense of being her friend, her equal. Instead of limiting herself to imparting her knowledge, her wisdom and her enthusiasm, she was eager to share them with us, with me.

And yet, despite having left me with this wonderful feeling, she, as opposed to so many of my other teachers, never singled me out overtly. It was *I* who singled *her* out as a remarkable woman who, during the very short time that I knew her — just a year and a half — had more influence on me than anyone else in school, and under whose spell I still am. Some years ago, in 1980, when I published my thick volume on *Alcohol and Drug Problems in Women*, I thought of dedicating it to her. I knew then, I still know, that she would have approved, because although we never discussed feminism as such, her concerns for and interest in women's and children's issues were patently obvious, a fact further reinforced by her active participation in the left wing (Socialist) political activities of the country. A small anecdote will serve to illustrate both this point and the important influence that her mini-talks had on me. She arrived one day to tell us, most enthusiastically, about an art exhibition then on view at the Instituto Pedagógico, and to encourage us to go and see it. It was, she said, a wonderful show of drawings and prints by Käthe Kollwitz, the German expressionist artist famous for her portrayal of the misery caused by social injustice and war. We should not miss this rare opportunity to see the work of this great artist.

And so it was that Fusa and I went to see the Käthe Kollwitz show, and I've never been quite the same since. At this point — I was just sixteen — I knew virtually nothing about art, not even what I liked, since our one-hour-a-week classes were almost exclusively confined to the rudiments of drawing, such as perspective, but not a word about art history and no teaching tools such as slides, or even art books. Needless to say, there were no pictures at home or at the homes of our relatives and friends either. In the circumstances, therefore, my response to the Käthe Kollwitz show was almost exclusively a response to the contents, to the message of her prints, and it was very intense. Squalid men, old defeated peasant women, poor young mothers rejoicing in the undernourished smiles of their little children. The prints were simple and powerful, I thought, and how wonderful it would be to be able to draw like that. But I knew I didn't have the talent to draw or the imagination to capture from my surroundings important, or beautiful, or powerful things to put on paper or canvas for the illumination and enjoyment of others. My own drawing exercises up to this time were abysmally monotonous and pathetically deprived of originality in both form and content: a one-story adobe house, a tree or two next to it and, of course, the mountains as a background, the whole illuminated by a brilliant sun above.

I suspect that at least some of this enormous artistic poverty had more to do with what I thought my teacher expected of me than with a genuine lack of skills and imagination, because towards the end of grade twelve I found myself spending many Sunday afternoons — when there was nobody home — doing some charcoal drawings completely outside of this stereotyped pattern. These were portraits of famous people whom I admired, done from pictures I had found in books and magazines. The list included Leonardo da Vinci, Pierre Curie (I didn't do Madame Curie; instead, I tore her portrait from Eve Curie's book, had it framed and hung it over my bed), T.E. Lawrence (of Arabia), Beethoven, and myself. Except for Beethoven these sketches were quite good. Good enough to be the only things from that period that I kept for many years and even brought to Canada, only to lose them, or at least misplace them, later on. The problem with Beethoven was that his mouth defeated me. Everything else, the hair, the forehead, the eyes and the nose were fine, but hard as I tried I could not capture the essence of the mouth and chin.

As for my self-portrait, it was a rather horrifying picture not of my physical face or head, but of what I then thought of my spirit, of my soul. A veritable monster, quite at odds with the girl I have been portraying in these pages. My very own Picture of Dorian Gray, even if I had not heard of Wilde's book yet. I am as puzzled today by that sketch as I was then, and for that reason I wish I could find it so that I could reappraise it. Except for a few close friends, I have never shown these sketches, especially mine, to anyone else, and most certainly not to my art teacher who, incidentally, told me on my last exam in grade twelve that my work was competent but derivative, lacking in originality, a judgment with which I fully agreed, annoying as it was!

Whether or not there was some causal connection between my private drawing exercises and the Käthe Kollwitz show, I cannot tell. Be that as it may, I soon abandoned these timid artistic activities and have never gone back to the drawing board since. But my interest in art never ceased and my involvement with Käthe Kollwitz in particular endures to this day. One of her pictures — not, alas, an original print — of a little boy happily wrapping his skinny legs around his mother's waist hangs on the wall of my study at the present time.

Besides, I am quite certain that Käthe Kollwitz, the first artist with whose work I came in close and real contact, and whose work has such a powerful social message, played a highly significant role in my subsequent, but fortunately transitory, thinking about art as fundamentally an instrument of social change rather than primarily a means of esthetic expression. The fact that as a woman she was an artist of international reputation had no impact on me at the time. Why should it, considering that my mother, as virtual head of the family, my piano and religious teachers, and equally importantly, all my highly diverse school teachers were women? It is no wonder that in late adolescence I came to think that if women didn't quite rule the world all by themselves, they certainly shared with men a good deal of the power, more than half anyway. The fact remains, however, that it was Laura Vargas who introduced me to art in an immediate and meaningful way and that the artist involved was very much a woman.

On another occasion Laura Vargas and Sra. Mora took my class on a one-day trip to a small town on the outskirts of Santiago to visit and entertain the poor children of a public school. My main and almost only recollection of that outing is my surprise and delight when after lunch, in the afternoon, Laura Vargas pulled her guitar from under the table and began to sing popular Chilean songs. I was immensely impressed by this feat because neither the guitar nor the kind of songs she sang were part of my cultural patrimony or of our singing repertoire in school which, in the hands of the hearty Sta. Benke, ranged from Palestrina to Brahms. These were the songs of "the people" (*el pueblo*) from which we, young ladies of the middle class, had been cut off, if not protected. It would take another generation or two before this kind of music became fashionable among the cultural elite, and its creators and performers, such as Victor Jara, veritable heroes. Once again Laura Vargas had been way ahead of the crowd.

I don't know how well she sang or played the guitar, but it sounded wonderful to me and, yet again, Laura Vargas had enlarged and widened my range of experience quite beyond the rigid boundaries of our official school program. When I now evoke in my mind the picture of this handsome, earthy, dark woman singing to those deprived small children, I know that my subsequent leftist political leanings had at least to some degree their origins in Laura Vargas' vision and understanding of things. Curiously, though, I do not remember much at all about the formal psychology course that she taught us in grade eleven. For some reason it did not make much of an impression on me, although I was sufficiently interested in psychiatry during grade twelve to, at the initiative of an older friend, attend a university course on the subject designed for law students, and to inquire at the source about a career as a psychiatric nurse. But Laura Vargas' teachings on general philosophy and especially logic was another matter. If I had already learned to reason systematically in Sta. von Delitz's courses, logic, as taught by Laura Vargas, as well as syntax, especially parsing of long, complicated sentences in Spanish taught by Sra. Bocaz, completed the picture. I tremendously enjoyed these subjects and the exercises that went with them, and used them rather shamelessly to shine in class.

Half way through grade twelve, in 1938, Laura Vargas who, incidentally, had replaced Mademoiselle X as our teacher-in-chief, was uncharacteristically absent from school for a week or so. We were told she was ill but that she would be back soon. When the week turned into several weeks I became suspicious and inquired again. This time I was told that she had had a serious operation but that she would be back as soon as she was strong again. I missed her terribly — we all did — and was afraid she might never be back. But after another couple of weeks or so we were told she would be back next day, and not to worry. My hopes that she was really well again, only a little weak, were revived immediately, and I looked forward to a warm and happy reunion the following day.

But when she came in, gaunt and very thin, utterly bereft of her contagious and inspiring energy, and began to talk to us in a barely audible voice, I knew that far from recovering she was well along the process of dying. When this, the saddest of all classes, was over she hadn't said a word about her condition, nor had we asked any questions or made any comments. She never came back, and when a short time later I asked again, I was told that she was very ill, that she had terminal cancer, which went unspecified. I felt that if she had come to see us for what she might have known was the last time, she might welcome a visit from one or two of us and so I asked permission to go. Wanda and I got the permission on condition that the visit be very short and that we not ask any awkward questions or say any inappropriate things.

We were given the address, and when we got there I was surprised to find that she lived in a most modest one-storey house in an equally modest district of Santiago, between the Mapocho and the Cerro San Cristobal, a nine-hundred foot hill which is like a toe of the Andes stretching towards the core of the city, and its most impressive landmark. Her two little children, a girl and a boy, probably four and five years old respectively, were playing in the barren dirt front yard. Her husband, who probably because of his abundant grey hair and the deep sad lines on his face looked to me much older than her, came to the door and showed us in, without uttering virtually a word. Laura Vargas was lying on her back, a white shawl around her shoulders, on a very low bed in this dingy and barely lit bedroom. When we came close and quietly spoke to her, she half opened her eyes for an instant and tried to smile, but couldn't. She looked grey all over. Even her beautifully black hair looked grey and dishevelled, and I couldn't stand the idea that she was almost gone, but she was. We stood there silently for a few more minutes and left her bedroom to find her husband sitting on a low chair holding his face in his hands, the saddest, most lonely man I recall ever seeing. When we left, the children were still playing outside.

A few days later Laura Vargas was dead and we were told to get our uniforms in shape because she would lie in state in the very large room where three years earlier I had failed to deliver my speech on O'Higgins. We, the students of her class, would stand guard for the next twenty-four hours and we would then escort the horse-drawn hearse to the cemetery. And so we did.

Hundreds of people carne to see the open coffin, something that quite amazed me because up to then I had had no idea how well known and well loved she had been by so many people well beyond her family and school circles. I realized then how very little I actually knew about her and regret to this day not having made more of an effort to come closer. But then, I was just a school girl among many and she an important and imposing figure of authority.

On the following afternoon, the day of the funeral, we, twenty-plus students of grade twelve, were lined up on either side of the hearse heading a cortege that slowly wound through the streets of mid-town Santiago from the front door of the Liceo No. 5 to the nondenominational General Cemetery. There was a strange sense of sadness blended with an air of almost military ceremony in this most unusual procession headed by ten or so of us on either side of the hearse, almost proudly wearing our school uniforms consisting simply of a navy blue serge skirt, a white cotton summer jacket and a blue beret. I walked up front on the right, erect and solemn, knowing that I was participating in the most momentous occasion of my seventeen-year-old life. The grief was to corne later and the memory would last for ever.

I mean her memory and the memory of that procession, because I remember nothing about the burial itself, or about the ceremony and speeches that went with it. I can't even remember whether there was a priest in attendance, but if there wasn't I would not have been surprised. All I know is that I was present to the very end, and that when it was all over I met a new friend, whom I shall introduce shortly, downtown and that for the first, and I think only time, he invited me for coffee and cakes. Afterwards, he consoled me as best he could while we strolled through the parks towards our favorite spot at the base of the San Cristobal. Hers was the first important loss of my life, and hers the last funeral I would ever attend.

Laura Vargas was neither beautiful, nor brilliant. She was simply a splendid woman. It is because of that, and because I never had the chance to tell her how I felt, that I wanted to dedicate my volume on women and drugs to her in 1980. But I didn't because I was afraid of hurting my mother's feelings if I did.

A Very Good Year

During my summer holidays between grades eleven and twelve, in February, 1938, I spent a week in Melocotón, a mountain town not far from Santiago. This most modest of holidays, but an unprecedented luxury for me, must have been Wanda's initiative because she invited Olga, a friend of hers I didn't know, as well as me to come along. Wanda's mother, confronted with all the perils that three seventeen-year-old girls would inevitably face in such circumstances, also sent along Mario, Wanda's brother, to protect us, or just for good measure.

After a relatively short train trip up the mountains along the banks of the river Maipo, we reached this small dusty town, where a clean but very modest room in a local pensión had been reserved for the three of us. We soon discovered that the "dining room" consisted of long tables and benches installed in the patio of the main building across the dirt road from our sleeping quarters. This sumptuous setting, surrounded by the ubiquitous poplars, was also the dining room and general headquarters of dozens of chickens who happily pecked at their maize all around us, while we tried to concentrate on our country fare.

It was at breakfast, the following day, that we met Claudio. Besides that fateful encounter, bathing in a nearby creek, hiking on the slopes around the town and sun-bathing wherever we could, I remember virtually nothing about either the place, or the week we spent there. But Claudio made quite an impression on all three of us, if for no other reason at first than appearing for breakfast among the chickens in his pajamas. He must have sensed our bafflement because as soon as breakfast was over he joined us and introduced himself as Mario N., born in Argentina, but long a resident of Chile. The relevance of this otherwise rather indifferent piece of information became immediately apparent to us when he explained, quite seriously, that wearing pajamas for breakfast, even in places other than one's home, is a most respectable custom in Argentina, or at least in Buenos Aires, where it is very hot and humid in the summer.

Having been somewhat reassured that we were not dealing with a dangerous eccentric or worse, I had a second look at him. He was tall, slim, dark and pale, probably twenty-five. His dark straight brown hair was parted on one side and combed backwards and flat, as was then the fashion in Latin countries. He wore glasses, a pince-nez I think, and carried a pack of cigarettes in the breast pocket of his pajama coat, and a camera dangling from a strap on the opposite shoulder. He was serious - studious, perhaps? - and impeccably polite, projecting an aura of sensitivity, even of romantic fragility.

As soon as it became apparent that we would be companions for the duration of our stay, the issue of his name arose. Since Wanda's Mario had seniority in the group, by virtue of being her brother, he would keep his name. Mario N., on the other hand, a stranger and newcomer, could easily be renamed so as to avoid confusion or cumbersome explanations every time the name came up. Mario N. seemed quite amused by all this, and even eager to become someone else temporarily. I think it was I who suggested Claudio as a possibility, simply because I loved the sound, the music in the name. Little did I know at the time about notorious Roman emperors or fictional Danish kings, and even less that the name in Latin means "lame". Apparently nobody else did either, because it was immediately agreed by all that Claudio was a fine name, which Mario N. accepted most graciously. From then on Claudio became our constant escort and companion, often impressing us with his apparently vast knowledge of literature, art and music, and of course photography. He took pictures of us, of the chickens, of the poplars, of everything around us, leading me to believe that this was a very affluent young man. Except for one of my well-to-do uncles, I didn't know anybody who owned a camera. It was also quite clear to me from the start, that if seduction was in his mind, his target was Wanda, the prettiest and most coquettish member of the trio. Otherwise his attitude towards us was protective, even paternal.

By the time we returned to Santiago we had all exchanged addresses with Claudio — I don't think that even Wanda, the most affluent of us, had a telephone at that time — with earnest promises of keeping in touch. I had learned in the interval that he was not as old as he appeared, he was just twenty-two, that he was Jewish and, most important of all to me, that he was a medical student, although he was taking the year off for economic and other reasons. This was important because at the beginning of grade twelve, when medicine was still one of my career options, Claudio could be most useful as a guide. He kept his promise. As soon as we were back in Santiago and classes had started, he came to see me, but it became immediately apparent that his interest in Wanda was keener, and his visits to her were far more frequent than to me. But whatever happened or didn't happen between them was short-lived and of no particular consequence to him because, as I soon learned, he was hopelessly in love with another woman who was never named, only referred to as *Ella* (She). We — he and I — would be friends.

So we began to see each other with increasing frequency, and to correspond. Between March 6/38 and March 2/39 he wrote me twenty-six letters, infrequently at first, and then increasingly more frequent. Judging by his comments, and eventually his pleas for me to write, my letters to him were far fewer, eight in fact. I have no idea what happened to them, which is just as well, but I've kept his for all of these fifty-seven years. In his inimitably elusive, lyrical, romantic, often obscure style, overdone by today's standards, they tell his side of our relationship. It is on them and on my memories that this tale is based.

Despite some original concerns and even objections on my mother's part, Claudio came to see me with increasing frequency. But my home was no place to entertain anybody, let alone a boyfriend. Between my mother's very busy dressmaker's shop, with two or three assistants at a time, the constant visits from her clients, and the comings and goings of my three teenage brothers, there was no peace, let alone space to entertain anybody. So, after my mother's objections had dissipated, mainly because of Claudio's charm and evident integrity, he would call for me after school and we would go out.

Since neither of us could afford it, we never went out to eat and only rarely to a movie or a concert. Instead, we walked. Together, we must have walked hundreds of miles during the year. The Parque Forestal and the Parque Japonés, only three or four blocks away from my house, became the major settings for our blossoming friendship. The Parque Forestal, said to have been designed by Pierre Charles L'Enfant, the French architect and American army major who designed Washington, D.C., is old and stately with its huge trees and elegant avenues, and the impressive Palacio de Bellas Artes to the west. To the east, towards the mountains, is the Parque Japonés (the Japanese Park, renamed Great Britain Park during the Second World War), new and young then, and of obvious Japanese design. We were not alone. The parks of Santiago were traditionally the places for the young to meet, to court and occasionally to study. And, according to a British documentary I saw just a few weeks ago, they still are.

Later on, we discovered a little corner on the slopes of the Cerro San Cristobal, across the river nearby, which we made our own. There, with the city at our feet, we watched countless sunsets illuminating the Andes to the east with a prodigious variety of hues, while we talked. We talked about _War_ and _Peace_, about _Truth_, about _Beauty_ and _Poetry_, about _Understanding_ and _Kindness_ and, of course, about _Us_, about _Life_ and about _Love_. Exactly like that, every one of these lofty words and ideas with capital letters, in italics and underscored, as if we were the first to have discovered them, or at least to have fully appreciated their deepest import.

One evening in early March he read aloud to me Khalil Gibran's "The Prophet". My reaction to this book of purported wisdom was such, apparently, that it left Claudio most impressed, if not frankly ecstatic. The next day he wrote:

> "I want to tell you something. I want to tell you that yesterday I had the chance to listen to your spirit and that what I heard left me with the immense joy of knowing that I couldn't have done anything better than reading The Prophet to you. That the soil that received the blessed seed could not have been any more propitious. Thank you, my friend."

It is implicit in that paragraph that he had already assumed the role of guide, of teacher, and there is no question that I went along with this notion very happily because, compared to anyone else I knew in and out of school, Claudio was, to my adolescent mind, the wisest, the most knowledgeable and the most exquisitely sophisticated person I had ever known. He was in a class by himself. He soon began to lend me the books he had read in the past which had particularly impressed him, as well as those he was currently reading. We would then discuss them as if the fate of humanity depended on our judgments. They were mainly by French authors and we read them in French, a language that we both adored. He must have been much better at it than I because some of his letters are written wholly in French and some of the others contain full paragraphs in that language. Since French was not part of the background of either his birthplace or his family, this was a romantic pretension that fitted well with my own.

The giant among these authors, unquestionably the one with the greatest influence on both of us, was Romain Rolland, the author of Jean-Christophe. It is a novel in ten volumes about the passionate life of the German composer Jean-Christophe Krafft and his great friendship with the young French intellectual and writer Olivier Jeannin. Both Claudio and I were crazy about it. And we weren't alone. Apparently for the nearly three decades since its publication Jean-Christophe had been a major source of inspiration for the young everywhere to have lofty ideals and try to live noble lives, even though sometimes trying or tragic ones.

As far as I was concerned, the most crucial and inspiring of all the ideals expounded by Rolland was his particular concept of friendship. The intense, devoted and unselfish relationship made real by Jean-Christophe and Olivier would become one of my ideals. Since, for obvious reasons, sex and even falling in love were out of the question with Claudio — or so I thought —the reading of Jean-Christophe at that time greatly reinforced my determination to keep and develop our relationship into a great friendship. But because of the difference in age and in life experiences it inevitably developed into a rather lopsided friendship where, as I've already noted, in many important respects he played the role of guru and I of disciple, albeit an endlessly questioning and challenging disciple.

There was another, perhaps even more significant imbalance in our relationship, or rather a complementary nature to our respective personalities and prevalent mood at the time. I had known from the very beginning that he was suffering intensely because of his ill-fated and most unhappy love affair with *She*. But it became increasingly obvious to me that there was more to his misery than this particular feature of his life. In May, for example, he wrote:

"I'm listening to Beethoven, his third symphony, the Eroica .... while listening to the Eroica what I hear, by contrast, is the Coward, with its notes of defeat ringing within myself. This is to break the silence with a greater silence, the silence of nothingness."

Occasionally his letters described moments of great joy such as his nearly ecstatic reactions to Mozart's symphony in G minor, or the burgeoning of nature in the spring, or even a Katharine Hepburn film. During most of that year, however, his mood was gloomy and his general attitude defeatist. It is patently clear through his letters that he found in me understanding first of all, but also the genuine innocence of my very green seventeen years, compassion, tenderness and all the enthusiasm and strength of my then robust constitution, as well as my challenging intellectual restlessness. What I found in him, in addition to the experienced guide and teacher already mentioned, was an exquisitely sensitive and tormented man in need of caring and of uncomplicated undemanding love. This made for a very dynamic and intense interaction between us, in which our respective needs were generously satisfied for many months.

Some time during 1938, three full years after his last departure, my father came back home. As usual, we all went to the station to greet him, and we were happy to see how well, and how well groomed, he looked. What he thought or felt when he saw his four grown-up children, I never knew, but he seemed unusually amiable and happy. I suppose this was at least in part due to the fact that, judging by the gifts he had brought us, this time he had done well financially. It was almost like Christmas when, once at home, he began to distribute presents all around. Among all these things he had brought furs for my mother, and fabrics for her and myself. But unquestionably the most startling present of all, from my point of view, was my wrist watch. A beautiful little thing encrusted with make-believe diamonds, and with an elegant black wrist band. This was my very first watch ever and the first "jewel" I had had since I had been a small child in Punta Arenas. It was one of those moments that call for great effusions of affection and gratitude, commensurate with my delight and his satisfaction. But I don't remember anything of the sort. Only the usual reserved and polite reticence on both our parts. I did, however, wear my new watch to school with enormous pride, and for a long time afterwards felt that strange but delightful sensation of having turned really grown-up and glamorous by the mere fact of feeling this new sensation on the skin of my left wrist.

If my father had acknowledged at some level, by the very nature of his presents, that I was no longer the awkward girl of fourteen he had left three years earlier, he appears to have refused to do so at other levels of his mind. Inevitably, of course, he discovered that there was a young man in my life, since Claudio and I carried on as usual. And when he did, and without bothering to ask me any questions or even to meet Claudio, he immediately jumped to the conclusion that we were lovers. So, not very long after his sunny arrival, our relationship came to an abrupt conclusion when my father and I had a rather brutal confrontation over this issue, alone, in the big room. I explained as best I could that we were just friends, not even in love with each other, let alone lovers. He was so outraged at my presumed lies that he quite uncharacteristically began shouting, and at the top of his voice called me a whore and every other outrageous name he could think of. Until, provoked even further by my protestations of innocence and my persistent denials, he picked up my mother's iron, sitting inertly on the table, and threw it towards my head. I ducked. He missed. He missed for good. I walked out of the room and out of his life, because we never talked directly to each other again, until many years later, when other events broke our respective proud stubbornness.

In retrospect, this miserable episode makes me realize that I not only look, but in many ways am, much more like my father than like my mother.

One of these ways is my temper, and my holding of grudges, sometimes forever. I haven't yet written, and probably will not write, much about this trait of mine, but it is and has always been there, lurking in the background. All I can say in self defense is that my own explosions of temper as opposed to those of my father, that were primarily provoked by his own imaginings, are usually in response to what I consider to be legitimate reasons, such as injustice, inexcusable lack of sensitivity, or outright misrepresentations or lies. And, in serious instances they are, as with my father, followed by very prolonged silences.

Much more, however, was going on simultaneously because, for the first time, I had to make choices and take decisions about my future. This turned out to be quite difficult for a number of reasons. I don't think that the option of marriage, that two or three of my classmates decided upon during grade twelve, ever seriously entered my mind at the time. And even if it had, I never, then or later, saw marriage as a full-time career, or in any way incompatible with an independent vocation of my own. With that out of the way, there were two major factors left to consider. They were my economic situation and prospects on the one hand, and my skills, talents and preferences on the other.

After considering my economic situation quite carefully, I came to the conclusion that a long, heavy course such as Medicine was out, but that a profession that took three or four years to complete was feasible. My main concern was not the cost of a university education *per se,* but the time it would take me before I could earn a living sufficient to support myself and my mother. Although she was doing better by now, she complained constantly about her work, and never let us forget the "sacrifices" she was making to give us an education. But she, as opposed to my father, did want me to go to university. In addition, the cost of a university education for me amounted only to room and board for three or four years, because, as a result of my high academic standing, I never had to pay any tuition fees, either in high school or in university. My own earnings, mainly from tutoring, would pay for most of my modest expenses. The question of what to study, of which path to follow, however, turned out to be much more difficult, and a number of people, in and out of school, played a role in my ultimate decision. As it was, much of my spare time and energy, especially during grade twelve, was spent agonizing over the problem, so that my teachers, mainly indirectly, had a good deal to do with the eventual outcome.

Laura Vargas, who by her sheer presence might have been of great help, was, of course, gone. But Sta. von Delitz's formidable presence was very much in place. However, despite her persistent efforts to keep me involved and excelling in her courses, my own interest and involvement in mathematics and physics dwindled perceptibly, as my interest in the humanities, especially literature, was increasing by leaps and bounds. Although I remained her best student to the end — mainly because the others weren't very good — I resisted her pressure increasingly throughout grade eleven, until a confrontation of nearly dramatic proportions took place halfway through that year.

One day, at the beginning of one of her geometry classes, she presented us with a problem that we were supposed to solve. She went through every student in the class, bench by bench, row by row, demanding an answer that clearly no one could provide, never even attempting to disguise her disgust and her contempt for our ignorance and stupidity. She naturally left me for the end, taking for granted that I would provide the answer, but, for reasons that to this day I do not fully understand, I refused to play her game and, playing dumb, I told her that I didn't know the answer. The fact is that I knew only the immediate next step rather than the full solution, but I refused to cooperate even with that small step.

She called me to the blackboard anyway, where I stood, dumb as a door nail, for the rest of the period. The class was still, the silence deadly, and the tension inside of me mounting to unbearable levels until, ready to surrender, I began to make a move towards the ruler and square to draw a parallel line, when the bell, indicating the end of the period, rang loud and clear, proving the wisdom and precision of the saying beyond any question. I had indeed been saved by the bell, but not quite, not really, because my conscience wasn't clear. When Sta. von Delitz left, after writing something in the class book, my classmates surrounded me with a barrage of questions and comments. Naturally, they all wanted to know whether I did or did not know the answer — I told them the truth — but beyond that they were all very excited about the fact that at last one of us had had enough guts to confront and defy the reigning terror of the school, and wondered aloud about the punishment that would be in store for me.

And so did I, aloud and silently, until I had a chance to read what Sta. von Delitz had written in the class book. It was under the "Observations" column and said: "Oriana Josseau has shown herself to be ill-tempered and badly behaved." At this point I wished to goodness that the world were fair, in which case the class book would have included a column for us students to record our observations of our teachers! But strong as Sta. von Delitz's words were, they were mild compared to what I had anticipated. If that was going to be the only consequence of my unprecedented act of revolt, I was going to get away with it scot-free. Nevertheless, my surprise was even greater the next day when, on looking over the class book I read the following over her signature: "This observation is not valid"! She had retracted. She had, on thinking it over, admitted that if anyone was at fault it was she rather than I.

Elated as I was at what I then perceived as my stupendous victory, I felt compassion for this bitter and unhappy woman who had had the honesty to retract officially. It must have been hard as hell for her to do that. But even though she had cleared me of any wrongdoing, my own conscience still bothers me about my role in this episode. So much so, that about twenty-five years later I wrote a short story about it, called The Geometry Class, in an attempt, I suppose, to clarify, to discover more about my own behavior and my subsequent feelings about it. I have deliberately refrained from rereading my story now, until I finish writing this version of it, to see how faithful or consistent my memory of the event is. It is more clear to me now than then that my quite spontaneous, unplanned act of defiance against Sta. von Delitz had everything to do with my repugnance for and rejection of her unforgivably autocratic methods. I could now contrast her with the understanding, fair and democratic Laura Vargas and there was no contest.

There is no question in my mind that my increasingly obvious loss of interest in the exact sciences that Sta. von Delitz taught was to a considerable degree related to my quite negative perception of her as a human being. Although after the above episode our relationship became quite cold and stiff, she persisted in her attempts to groom me as her heir apparent, but I would have none of it. I did the minimum amount of work to pass with decent but not outstanding marks and ignored her as best I could. But she didn't quite give up. At the end of grade twelve, we and the rest of the high schools of Santiago presented our annual gymnastics show at the National Stadium in front of a huge crowd that included the President of Chile, don Arturo Alessandri. At the end of the show it was announced through a loudspeaker that all participating students would be exempt from their final oral exams. A deafening Hurrah! went through the stadium as Sta. von Delitz spotted me in the crowd of extremely exhilarated students and frantically gestured me to come over. It was to plead with me to ignore the exemption and face my exams, so that I could improve on my marks. And so I did, probably for old time's sake, but I have no recollection of what happened to my marks. If, because of my early success in Sta. von Delitz's courses, I ever seriously considered taking up mathematics and physics as a career, I had lost all interest by the end of grade eleven.

The relative loss of interest and skills in mathematics that I suffered after puberty has intrigued me ever since, particularly because this phenomenon went on in parallel with a sustained improvement of my skills and interest in other areas, especially languages, but also in disciplines such as chemistry and the biological sciences. Somewhere along the way, probably when I was doing postgraduate work in experimental endocrinology in the 1950s, I developed the hypothesis that, since this applied not just to me but, on average, to women in general, it must have some physiological, or better still, endocrine basis. I must confess that it never occurred to me then to think that women's mathematical performance and involvement might have anything to do with environment or up-bringing. I had had, after all, all the encouragement one would want throughout high school, but my performance, and most certainly my commitment, nevertheless clearly declined from grade ten on.

While writing these pages on my mathematical trials and adventures in school, I was intrigued enough by this whole issue to make a brief and cursory search of the relevant scientific literature. As one might expect, I found a profusion of references on the subject, especially during the last two or three decades. What it all seems to amount to is that although there are no differences in mathematical performance between girls and boys prior to age twelve or thirteen, there is a significant difference in favor of boys from then on. And there is a very marked difference in the same direction, in the proportion of boys and girls who are exceptionally well endowed with mathematical ability. Despite the reporting of these empirical findings, however, I failed to fmd any reference to, or discussion of, the possible role of sex hormones in mathematical performance. But I cannot vouch for this because, as I say, my search was anything but thorough and exhaustive. Tempted as I was to follow through and research this literature in depth, I have not yielded because that could easily signal the end of this current writing project.

I further think — just another totally unsubstantiated hypothesis of mine — that the relative decrease in interest and skills in mathematics in girls after the age of puberty is related to the very nature of this discipline, that is, its precision and exactitude. Inevitably there is always only one correct answer to any given mathematical problem. The methods, the pathways followed to reach the solution may vary, but the final answer is always the same, leaving no room for subtleties, nuances or alternatives. I contend that the very rigor, the absolute exactitude of mathematical solutions is anxiety-provoking and thereby inhibitory to the person confronted with the problem. Compare this with writing an essay, dissecting a frog, or discussing the role of Queen Elizabeth I in the arts. No two people confronted with the latter tasks would ever come up with exactly the same product. I further contend that women are more prone to experiencing anxiety than men, or at least that men cope with it in ways that are more effective and constructive than women. Therefore, when girls become women, they tend to avoid mathematics or they don't apply themselves as eagerly as they did before. This is enough to explain not only my own puzzling story, but also the empirical findings cited above. And if this bit of science fiction doesn't fully alienate me from the feminists, especially the authors — all women — of the articles referred to above, nothing will! Nothing I've read so far invalidates my first hypothesis.

At the beginning of 1938, during my summer holidays between grades eleven and twelve, I knew I had to make concrete decisions about my future, but was far from sure about anything except the desire to go to university. If my mother ever entertained the idea of my joining her in her shop, she never pressed me. As for me, having been a witness to her working life and to the meagre income that it provided, and having helped her finish and deliver dresses, especially on Saturdays, the idea was definitely out. I realize in retrospect that dress-making carried to the level of haute couture can be a very creative and a highly profitable enterprise, but not with my mother, who had a passion for resisting any progressive suggestion that involved change. When later on, during my university years, I tried on a number of occasions to help her reorient and reorganize her business, I got absolutely nowhere.

So back to the books and to the greedy acquisition of knowledge. That was fine as far as it went, but the urgent question of what specialized knowledge, what kind of field I wanted to turn into my life's commitment, remained unanswered for most of that year. The problem, as I see it now, was that although I was very good at many things, including sewing, I was not outstanding at any one in particular. And to make matters worse, I was interested in almost everything — except mathematics and physics! Besides, as opposed to many young people, I had no dreams at that stage, no lofty ones anyway. I really admire those children who know from grade one that they want to be a fireman, a ballet dancer, a doctor or a singer, and stick to it with fearless determination for the rest of their lives. I changed my mind, with equally fearless determination, as often as I changed clothes, but for one goal: I would study and I would earn enough to have a nice house of my own with a desk, a lamp and a gorgeous arm chair that would allow me to read in comfortable splendor. Modest dreams, seen from this distance, but outrageously daring at that time. I may add, with just a bare hint of blushing, that I also dreamed of having a wardrobe like those that Katharine Hepburn in *The Philadelphia Story*, Ingrid Bergman in *Intermezzo* and Joan Fontaine in *Rebecca* would exhibit a couple of years later. In summary, my dreams were mostly short-term, readjusted and upgraded periodically, as I progressed through my education, and new vistas opened up.

Some things, however, clearly interested me more than others and among them was literature, especially poetry in Spanish, not to be confused with Spanish poetry. By the beginning of grade twelve we had already covered, more or less, the Spanish classics and subsequent writers, so that Sra. Bocaz, our Spanish teacher, now had the task of indoctrinating us in the beauty of the poetry of the turn-of-century and more recent writers. This was all right as far as it went, but the problem was, for me anyway, that she completely left out of her course the modern Spanish and Chilean poets. Three names stand out like giants in my mind: Federico García Lorca of Spain, and Gabriela Mistral and Pablo Neruda of Chile.

To us, these people were as vital, necessary and popular as Bob Dylan or The Beatles were to become to the young of a later generation in English-speaking countries. But Sra. Bocaz would have none of it, while stolidly and conscientiously sticking to the likes of Ramón de Campoamor and Gustavo Adolfo Becker. The reason for her ignoring our favorite poets was not lack of familiarity on her part, or irrelevance, but rather an active dislike and rejection of their poetry. This inevitably led to a clash of judgments that expressed itself in many vehement and spirited but good-natured arguments in class, especially between her and me, since I was usually the most vocal and outspoken student. I vividly remember the occasion when, looking at me quite intensely, she said: "Gabriela Mistral's verses sound to me like an ox-cart rolling over a cobblestone road." And then she added that if I felt so keenly about Mistral's poetry I should write an essay on the subject not only for her benefit but for the benefit of the whole class as well.

I accepted the offer but didn't quite know how to go about it. There wasn't much literature about Mistral yet since, at forty-nine, she was still comparatively young, and she herself was, as usual, abroad on some kind of diplomatic mission or another. I found out, however, that a close friend of hers, the sculptress Laura Rodig, was in Santiago teaching at the Palacio de Bellas Artes and so decided to ask for an appointment to interview her, which was granted. When the time came, however, I chickened out right at the front door of the building and asked Wanda, who had come along with me, to go in my stead. I sweated it out, my heart racing and the palms of my hands moist, until Wanda came out to tell me all the things Rodig had said about Mistral. But by then I had lost all interest in the project and could think of nothing but my humiliating defeat. I don't know whether I then connected this episode with my last-minute failure to deliver my speech on O'Higgins in grade nine, but I certainly do now, when I can see a picture emerging.

I never wrote my essay on Gabriela Mistral, and that would have been the end of the episode but for a fortuitous encounter with Sra. Bocaz some four or five years later. While I was still her student, and à propos of the heated discussions described above, she had said to me on one occasion that she wished we could meet five years hence when, she was certain, I would have changed my mind and agree with her judgment of my favorite poets. Lo and behold, some four years later I was going into a coffee shop — where one could get the best chicken salad sandwiches in the whole world — when we met quite accidentally. She invited me to join her and we reminisced over coffee. She told me, among other things, that we were very much missed, that there had never been a class as exciting as mine since. When I reminded her of her prediction she just smiled and graciously accepted the fact that I had not, after all, changed my mind. Especially since by then I had had the golden opportunity of seeing all of García Lorca's plays on stage.

Margarita Xirgú, the foremost Spanish theater actress of the time, had fled Spain after Franco's victory and had come to Santiago with her company in search of a hospitable place to settle in. That would eventually become Buenos Aires, but not yet. She produced and acted in all of García Lorca's plays, some of which I believe he had written specifically for her. The beauty of the language, the intensity of the passion, and the superb acting were enough to turn my head to such a degree that, in order to gain entrance to the top balcony, the cheapest seats in the house, I even pawned two fine gold chains I had owned and cherished since my early childhood, and which, naturally, I was never able to retrieve. I felt very badly about this cavalier lack of consideration for my patrimony, but I had seen the great Xirgú and nobody could ever rob me of that. Let me note, in passing, that García Lorca, still a young man of thirty-eight, was executed by Franco's troops in 1936, at the beginning of the Spanish Civil War, that Gabriela Mistral won the Nobel prize for literature in 1945, seven years after my spirited defense of her, and Pablo Neruda twenty-six years later, in 1971.

My interest in literature, however, was not confined to a few very popular poets. My records show (I've kept a list of all the non-professional books I've read since I was fifteen years old) that during that year I read fifty books. Two of them stand out in my mind because of the deep impression they made upon me: Isadora Duncan's My Life and Eve Curie's biography of her mother, Marie Curie. The impact, however, of these two lives on my own was completely different. Isadora Duncan personified for me the revolutionary artistic innovations of a beautiful dancer who, untramelled by the conventions of her day, danced and lived across the stages of the world with exquisite freedom and abandon, in tune with nature, with the natural. That her life and death were poignantly tragic, only added to the pathos. I admired her from a very long distance, knowing only too well that I had none of the attributes required of such a creative artist. I therefore neatly confined her to my day dreams as a possible role model, and turned to more realistic goals in my real life.

Madame Curie's life and achievements, on the other hand, seemed somewhat closer to my own potential, at least to the degree that she was an inspiration, someone I could, more realistically, aspire to emulate. I am not saying that I had any illusions about my genius or even my talent for a brilliant career in scientific research. I'm only saying that an infinitely more modest degree of achievement in science seemed attainable in my circumstances, and that Madame Curie had become the catalyst, the spark for such dreams. Even her initial struggles against poverty and loneliness as a young student in Paris, and the equally miserable conditions under which she and Pierre worked in the early stages of their career, seemed familiar to me, even comfortable. The other two crucial factors in the equation of her success — her genius and the level of scientific thought and research at the Sorbonne at the time, compared to that prevailing in Santiago — I would put aside for the moment, in order to keep my dream alive.

Paradoxically, however, none of the books I read during that year, except for Madame Curie's biography, had anything to do with science. The list is a random selection of authors and titles that pretty well reflects the eclectic and unsystematic nature of my interests. Among a roster of obscure Chilean and other Latin American writers it also includes such notables as Gabriele D'Annunzio, Khalil Gibran (I read The Prophet then, long before the hippies rediscovered it), Rabindranath Tagore, André Malraux, Thomas Mann, Romain Rolland and, of course, Mistral and Neruda, everything they had published. Judging by the number of titles — four each — Neruda and Romain Rolland were my favorites, although the latter was soon to be replaced by Thomas Mann.

I am intrigued by the fact that despite spending virtually all of my spare time reading this sort of book and, judging by my marks in school, my clear proficiency in languages, I don't remember ever even entertaining the idea of pursuing that field as a career. In effect, writing per se was not a career but an avocation, since no one but the very famous made a living at it. I knew, for example, that Gabriela Mistral had been a school teacher and was now a diplomat, and that Neruda was then the Chilean consul in Madrid. Chile, incidentally, had a long tradition of appointing writers and other artists to the diplomatic service.

The only choice at the University of Chile to pursue a career in languages was the Instituto Pedagógico, designed exclusively for the training of high school teachers, because the university did not have faculties of liberal arts and sciences. In fact, I didn't even know of the existence of such departments until I came to Canada. So the question of majoring in languages didn't even arise, because I had earlier determined I would not become a teacher, despite all the role models around me. I think that even if I didn't articulate this thought very clearly in my mind at the time, I wanted something that at least potentially would be more creative than exclusive dedication to teaching.

And finally, and perhaps most importantly, I never thought, and no one ever told me through my school years, that I had any particular gift for writing. If some of my essays were singled out for special praise it was usually because of their originality of thought, or even their outrageous revolutionary content, rather than because of the quality of the writing. Further, I remember vividly the intense sense of frustration I then used to experience at my inability to translate into the written word the thoughts and images that went through my mind. I was, however, quite confident of my ability to think straight, to reason systematically, to stitch things together in such a manner as to produce a convincing and coherent whole. But that ability applied even more to the sciences than to the arts, so that my eventual choice makes some sort of sense.

Thus, by the end of grade twelve, I had eliminated all of the humanities, as well as physics and mathematics, from my list of options. There were only chemistry and biology left. The only place to pursue the biological sciences in full was the Faculty of Medicine, and that option, although still vaguely entertained, was for all practical purposes out, for the reasons already stated. And so it was, that almost by default, at least superficially, I turned chemistry into my vocation, but not before a great deal of exploration of all the practical angles, of careful weighing of the external influences being exerted upon me, especially by Claudio, and of tormented and laborious soul-searching. In effect, I did not make my final decision to register in the Faculty of Chemistry and Pharmacy until March of 1939, just before the beginning of the academic year.

Nothing about my school experience or performance suggests any particular interest in chemistry, except perhaps for the impact that the biography of Madame Curie had had on me. That reflects the facts quite accurately because chemistry, as taught to me in school, was as interesting as anything else, but most certainly not a discipline fascinating enough to exclude everything else. What made it interesting, even fascinating, was the fact that in the context of the University of Chile at the time, it seemed to be the only scientific discipline that offered at least a hint of a possibility of a career in scientific research, eventually,... maybe,... perhaps. All I knew then was that scientific research had to do with discovering new things and perhaps laws of nature hitherto not understood. I knew it meant long and arduous work, most likely in poverty and obscurity. I knew that to come to fruition, this work required prolonged and intensive training, since a prerequisite to discovering the as yet unknown was to know the old, all of it. I knew that to succeed one had to know how to ask the right questions instead of just stumbling upon the truth as one might accidentally discover a wonderful new friend. I knew, intuitively, that the thrill of discovery surpassed most other thrills in worth and in splendor. And I knew, vaguely, that scientific research, as opposed to many other creative vocations, required costly material facilities, such as laboratories and equipment of wondrous variety.

This lofty ideal of becoming a scientist was clearly only the romantic dream of a schoolgirl in search of an exciting future, because it had precious little to do with any sober evaluation of the reality about me. In fact, up to this point my understanding of the sciences, and especially of chemistry, primitive as it was, was almost purely theoretical, since the Liceo No.5 had no teaching laboratories of any kind, except for a dingy cubby-hole full of dusty old instruments which we visited at most a couple of times throughout our last two or three years in school. But the dream, romantic and unrealistic as it was, became the big magnet, the real focus of my very uncertain plans.

In addition, and I am sure crucial to the outcome, there was the undeniably powerful influence that Milena by example, and Claudio by seductive persuasion, were having on me. In 1938, when I was in grade twelve, Milena was already a medical student and had met and become involved with Fidel García, the man who would become her husband. Fidel García was the son of Guillermo García Latorre, professor of general chemistry at the medical school and of analytical chemistry at the school of pharmacy, himself a graduate of the latter. Fidel, with four or five years of medicine behind him, had already dropped out and was spending all of his time teaching the laboratory course to his father's students. In effect, this turned him into the boss, but also the sole occupant of the chemistry lab because his father, like the rest of the faculty, except for the staff of physiology, came to the premises only two or three times a week, to give lectures.

So Fidel reigned supreme in this subjectless land where he presumably divided his time between teaching and doing research. He was, as Milena gave me to understand, a highly idealistic young man, fully dedicated to his work with nearly complete disregard for economic or material advancement. I must admit that when I finally met him at Milena's I was impressed. His physical appearance matched perfectly the image of the romantic and idealistic young scientist that I had visualized. Even more strikingly, though, he looked, like Pierre Curie, right out of the Edwardian era in his dark grey suit, high buttoned vest and high and stiff shirt collar. All of this crowned by an imposing and, for his age, mature face with keen dark eyes and an impressive mane of dark hair. There was not the slightest question in my mind that I was in the presence of a man duly impressed with himself. Neither was there any doubt that he had already succeeded in seducing Milena into nearly total submission. His conversation, totally devoid of small talk, as if afraid of being diverted, even for an instant, from his high minded preoccupations, was exclusively about science and the role he was planning to play in it, and the role we should all play in it if we could only be persuaded. As I say, I was impressed, but not seduced, or even fully converted, because there was an air of unreality, perhaps even the suggestion of phoniness about both him, with his strange old-fashioned looks, and his nearly obsessive preoccupation with his one grand topic. Needless to say, he and Milena would dedicate their lives to scientific research.

However ambivalent my judgment of Fidel García may have been, he and Milena, who seemed to me to have become little more than his echo at the time, exerted quite an influence on my eventual decision to go into science, and for some time afterwards. This is not at all surprising since he was the first and only real flesh and blood "scientist" I had met, and whose ideals and beliefs neatly meshed with my own juvenile dreams.

And then there was Claudio. By the beginning of November, with a little over a month left before my graduation from high school, my idealized image of Claudio as a young man of tremendous spiritual integrity, moral character and lofty ideals, received its second blow in as many months. The first had been his admission to me that he had a woman with whom he shared nothing but sexual lust, something that seemed to be in flagrant contradiction with his professed ideals. He now confessed that he had never been a medical student. He went on to explain that for three years he had consistently attended the lectures and laboratory courses of the program, had shared all the interests and concerns of the regular students - including "She" - with them, and had studied as if he had been one of them. If he had formally registered from the beginning he would have been in fourth year by now. But he had been unable to do that, partly for economic reasons and, more importantly, for some very unpleasant reasons that he did not care to discuss. What he most regretted now, he added, was that because of this lie — the only one, he insisted — I would not trust his word in the future.

Whether I did or did not trust his word from then on is a moot question. But my view of his moral authority had been severely damaged, as had his authority as an advisor on matters of academic choices. These revelations brought him precipitously down from the pedestal on which I had placed him with his full cooperation, if not complicity. Because I'm convinced that, despite his protestations to the contrary, he too desperately wanted to believe in the reality of the fictional image I had built.

Since academically he had brought himself down almost to my level, and spiritually he had revealed himself to be a man like any other, the dynamics between us changed radically. My understanding and compassion for the friend were more or less intact, but not my almost unqualified admiration. I was no longer in awe, he was no longer my prophet, not even my teacher. He clearly perceived that something was amiss because, after hinting for some time that he was afraid I would leave him, give him up as a friend, he wrote me a forty-five page letter telling me the story of his relationship to a woman he once tried to save from emotional depression and physical deterioration, only to have her fall in love with him and make demands that he couldn't or wouldn't satisfy. She, like all other women before her, had failed him by not understanding the true nature of his love. There was a time, he wrote, when I responded to his song and understood.

What I understood then, and still do, is that he was referring to some sort of love that goes beyond the selfish love between two particular individuals and transcends it. He had told me this long and intimate story now, he said, because he was afraid that I would want to say good-bye to him, and that he dreaded the thought. His fear, therefore, was not that I had failed him, like so many others, but that, having once understood him, I was now withdrawing. He was partly right. Some of Claudio had indeed died in me, but not all of him. I still needed him as my friend and thought I had clearly understood his message of New Year's Day.

Imagine my surprise, therefore, when at the end of that same month he wrote that on that very day he had posed an "important, capital, definitive, decisive" question to me. He interpreted my failure to respond immediately to mean that I had fully understood the significance and import of both the question and the answer in terms of the future course of my life and of his life. Since he didn't reiterate the question in writing and unfortunately I do not remember its verbal version, I can only surmise its nature from the context. After reading the biography of Madame Curie he had fully identified with Pierre Curie, a figure not only familiar to him, but someone he had always known. He had found in the life and achievements of Pierre and Marie Curie his own life-long dreams and aspirations fully realized, come to fruition. His question to me, he said, was something arrived at after "cautious and careful analysis ... on the basis of our understanding and knowledge of each other." The letter ends: "I wait for your word ..."

If this was not a marriage proposal, it was at least highly suggestive. Otherwise, it could have only meant that we live together to embark on a joint course of studies which would eventually lead us to a career of scientific research. But considering my puritanical upbringing and the time and place of which I write, such an idea was completely out of the question. To say nothing of the practical considerations, since neither of us had a penny to our names or any prospect of making a living until after graduating from the university four or five years later. Because he talked and wrote in riddles, and I was probably afraid of offending him with my crudity and lack of sophistication, or perhaps because I wanted to avoid facing the issue in the open, I never confronted him with any direct questions. The result was that I was thoroughly confused, but also very tired, because I had just faced my high school graduation examinations in December.

As I've said before, I was exempt from most of them because of my participation at the gymnastics show at the end of the year, but faced a few, including mathematics and physics, at Sta. von Delitz's request. At that point something unusual, and for which I wasn't at all prepared, happened. I was so self-confidently - or was it cockily? - ensconced in my top standing that I didn't notice, until someone pointed it out to me, that there was a serious contender right behind me, threatening to dethrone me. Ana Fregneaud, also fair and blue-eyed, had appeared seemingly from nowhere in grade twelve to challenge my God-given — or so I seemed to think — preeminent position. This so intrigued the class that our classmates soon took sides, turning Ana and me into their respective leaders, to the point of espousing not only us but our heroes as well, such as our favorite writers, composers and the like. I can't remember who her favorite writers were — old fuddyduddies like Shakespeare and Cervantes, I'm sure — but I do know that Mozart was her favorite composer, while mine was, of course, Beethoven. The cult of personality, daring to intrude into the pure and innocent domain of teen-aged girls! The politics involved were real, though, so that at exam time the generally demure girls of grade twelve were rooting for one or other of us as if their own fate depended on the outcome.

I didn't budge, however, sticking to my decision to ignore the final exams and let the chips fall where they may. Doing otherwise would have been an admission of a thirst for glory and power that I was not willing to admit, not publicly or openly anyway. As it happened, it was just as well, because although Ana came close, she didn't quite make it, and I exited from grade twelve with my crown, my pride and my record intact. For the last time, however, because, for reasons that will become apparent later, I never achieved the same status in college and such measurements of academic worth did not apply in postgraduate work. In addition, I had to prepare for and pass the tests for my baccalaureate degree, a university entrance examination, in the middle of January. It goes without saying that my decision as to which academic path to follow, now further complicated by Claudio's intrusion into the picture, was still pending.

So, when the opportunity arose to go and spend a month on the farm at La Estrella, where I had had such a splendid year when I was seven years old, I took it. I left Santiago at the beginning of February, before making any decisions, or even attempting to clarify what appeared to me to be a flagrant contradiction between Claudio's feelings and thoughts at the beginning and at the end of January, or responding to his puzzling suggestions. I needed a break and I took it.

It is a remarkable fact that, hard as I've tried, I remember virtually nothing about that month. I have only a vague recollection of being in the train with Sra. Inés, my hostess, and of sharing with her all the goodies of the picnic basket she had prepared for the occasion. But I must have luxuriated in the wonderful food of La Estrella because when I got back to Santiago, at the end of February, I could hardly get into my city clothes. I guess the moral is: When in doubt, eat.

What I do know absolutely for sure, because I have the physical evidence to prove it, is that I received eight letters from Claudio during that short month, while, according to him, I wrote only two. Shortly after I had left Santiago he had moved from his parents' home to a small modest apartment over a garage that some friends of his, a couple, had lent him while they were away on a trip. From the context it is quite clear that he was no longer working at the printing shop where he had had a job for the best part of that year. He had no money, and following a quarrel with his mother he had stopped going home for meals. As a result, he was subsisting on tea with milk, on the peace and tranquility of his new quarters and on his dreams about the future, about which he wrote profusely. He had thoroughly investigated the various university schools in Santiago and elsewhere that offered comprehensive programs in chemistry. He wrote most enthusiastically that a five-year course in industrial chemistry, I presume at the University of Chile, was by far the best, and was already spending most of his time studying algebra and inorganic chemistry in preparation for the beginning of the academic year in March.

He loved the charm and the independence that his temporary dwelling provided and, he said, he kept thinking about me and what a wonderful life we could enjoy together in a little oasis like that one. It would be an invitation to study and to love, he thought, and he would dearly like to know what I thought.

He had to wait until the middle of February to receive my answer, and even then I played dumb and was obviously non-committal. I almost blush now, when I realize that, instead of responding directly to his clear, but to me still ambiguous "invitation", I wrote asking for his help in finding my own personal and individual solution to the problem of my future studies. His response now was as clear and precise as Claudio would ever get. What he had offered me was not his solution but our solution, and that he was offering me everything, body and soul. He felt I should neither be surprised by any of this, nor respond with an "ironic smile" because his words were not a product of the moment, but had been clearly foretold in all his pain and in every one of his letters. And a week later, in French, came a florid and impassioned plea for my answer.

During the first ten months or so of our relationship I had been so thoroughly convinced of its inviolate platonic nature that I still was not fully sure of the exact meaning of his words, and was consequently very afraid of "failing" him through my own misinterpretations. I did, however, write to him at the end of February, just before arriving back in Santiago. The next day, March 1, I received an uncharacteristically brief, business-like and terse note, asking me to be at his place at 6:30 p.m. either that day, or the following day.

I went to see him that very day, uncertain and apprehensive in general, but knowing very well that something concrete and definitive was going to happen. And then, perhaps perversely, I made sure I would be wearing my best summer clothes, a white, light-weight pleated skirt and a checked taffeta jacket in reds, oranges and white, which followed the contours of my figure quite closely.

He was waiting for me at the front gate, and then we walked along a grape-covered wrought-iron arbor and up some stairs to the small apartment above the garage. Physically he was a wreck. No doubt because of his recent diet of little more than tea and milk, his constitutionally slight frame now looked simply emaciated, accentuating even further the darkness and the sadness of his brown eyes, and the slowness of both his movements and his speech. So, in addition to the problem between us which had brought me there in the first place, I soon became fully conscious of the clear and uncomfortable physical contrast between the two of us: tanned and well fed, I looked the picture of health and energy. After showing me around and offering me a pathetic small dish of fermented strawberries - the only thing he had to offer and which I declined - we sat on the edge of his bed which he had placed by the wide-open window overlooking the arbor.

We talked. We talked at length about the issue he had raised in his recent letters, about us, about the future and about my surprise at what appeared to me to be a contradictory turn of events in his feelings about me. Until it was dark and the moon began to light the small room by the garden — there was a full moon that night. I said no. I couldn't accept his proposal or his plans because, as he should have known, that was not the way I had loved him, and there was no chance at all that it ever would be. While he persisted in trying to persuade me I was telling myself, inside, that I didn't even want him as a friend any longer, because Claudio was indeed dead in my mind. There was only Mario left, and he was a stranger. It was at that point that he tried to touch me, to hold me, for the first time ever. I didn't let him, I couldn't. So I stood up and left him, alone with the moon, and walked into the street free and sure. But not quite. Not yet. The following day I received Claudio's - or was it Mario's? - last letter. It was a wrenching lament, a pitiful plea for me to come back. Moved as I was, I did not respond and I never heard from him again.

Two weeks later, while waiting for a medical examination with a group of students at the University, I saw him sitting alone on a bench quite some distance away. He had grown a beard and was wearing a white summer jacket. Although he was looking at us, there was no attempt to make contact. Several years later, when I had graduated or was about to graduate from the Faculty of Chemistry and Pharmacy, I saw him walking vigorously towards the entrance of the school while I was on my way out. I don't think he saw me, and when I later inquired, I was told he was a second year student. That was the last I knew of him until many years later, when my mother wrote to me in Toronto that she had met him in downtown Santiago. He was very well, and was now a married man and the father of two sons. He had, she said, asked about me and my doings with great interest and affection.

Seventeen. It was a year of turmoil. It was a year of discovery. It was a year of decision. It was a very complex year. It was a sad year. It was a very good year.

University

By the beginning of March, 1939, with only a couple of weeks left to make a definite decision, I was far deeper in limbo than I then realized. Our schools, good as they were from a strictly academic point of view, lacked any counselling facilities whatsoever, or any serious means for the professional assessment of our aptitudes. As a result, our choices were haphazardly determined by whatever preferences and talents we appeared to have developed in school, by our rather rudimentary understanding of the structure of the university and of the options it offered and, finally, by the influence of the chance connections and friends we had made up to that time. Possible careers outside the university, say in business or the arts, including writing, never even crossed my mind at the time.

As far as I was concerned, Claudio, with whom I had been able to discuss career options in almost excruciating detail, was gone. I had lost track of Wanda and Irma for the time being and, at any rate, their interests then appeared to have precious little in common with mine. Fusa, with whom I shared a great deal more, and who had already decided to enrol in the School of Agronomy, was as usual away at her father's place in Limache. In the circumstances, the only friends left to help me weigh the pros and cons of various options might have been Milena and Fidel García. But this introduced its own complications.

During that summer, when Milena had finished her first year in medical school, to my utter astonishment she decided to give up her studies. When

I asked her why, she simply said that it was because of emotional problems, but didn't elaborate any further. I didn't understand then — I still don't — whether these were problems related to her medical studies, to her relationship to Fidel, or to a combination of the two. What I did understand, however, was that when I most needed her as my strong and highly principled role model, the idol I had so faithfully built up in my imagination was crumbling down with precipitous speed. Not only because of what I perceived as her dramatic academic defeat, but also because in my view she was surrendering to Fidel's domination to such a degree that she was virtually disappearing under my very eyes. Although the Milena that was disappearing was of course largely a product of my own idealization, the real flesh and bones Milena did in fact largely disappear from my life, as well as that of the rest of the family, not too long afterwards. She had married Fidel — despite her father's strong objections because Fidel was a divorced man — and, for reasons that I never understood, the two of them largely withdrew from any family contacts for the several years that their marriage lasted, and during which they had a daughter. I think I was at their apartment once during all that time.

By the middle of March I finally made my decision, virtually alone and almost by default, to enrol in the School of Chemistry and Pharmacy. But I was very ambivalent, if for no other reason than that I knew that if I ever graduated I would emerge from my studies as a "pharmacist" rather than as a chemist. In society at large, the label of pharmacist for such graduates was partly due, I suppose, to historical reasons, and partly to the fact that the most visible of them run all the pharmacies in the country. These were noble and respectable institutions that never dispensed anything but pharmaceutical and cosmetic products. Never, ever, cigarettes, candies or bacon and eggs.

However, a careful inspection of the four-year curriculum clearly indicated to me that the bulk of the program covered virtually every branch of chemistry except, alas, biochemistry, while only two courses, pharmacognosy and Galenic pharmacy, dealt directly with the pharmaceutical sciences. There was inorganic chemistry and mineralogy in the first year, organic and analytical chemistry in the second, organic chemistry again and physical chemistry in the third, and food chemistry and clinical chemistry in the fourth. Other courses of interest to me included physiology, pharmacology and bacteriology. In view of all this, and with all due respect to my pharmaceutical colleagues, I still can't understand why I would, if I survived at all, become a "pharmacist" rather than a "chemist". "0, be some other name! What's in a name?" Everything, I dare say.

The University of Chile, a venerable institution almost one hundred years old at the time I joined it, had not been built around a unified campus, as North American and British universities tend to be. It consisted, rather, of a conglomeration of professional schools whose buildings were scattered all over Santiago, usually a fair distance from the central core, except for the central administrative building, the Casa Central, which was located in the Alameda Bernardo O'Higgins, right across from the periphery of the commercial core of downtown Santiago. The School of Chemistry and Pharmacy, believe it or not, occupied a moderate sized and relatively modem building right at the beginning of Vicuña Mackenna, where it meets, at right angles, the Alameda Bernardo O'Higgins. So here I was again, spending the best part of my waking hours a mere four blocks away from home. Had it not been for my dashing and irrepressible sense of adventure, that often took me downtown or to the Barrio Alto, I could easily have spent all of my life within four blocks of my home until I was twenty-two years old.

The building had very nice front and back gardens packed full of duly labelled botanical specimens of pharmaceutical interest, and the bust of Professor Gigliotto who, the legend had it, had discovered that zinc was a normal constituent of the body. This was, to the best of my knowledge, the one and only claim to fame that our School had in terms of scientific discoveries. The one-story building had an ample central tiled corridor along its whole length, with two branches at right angles to it, some distance apart. The entrances to the teaching laboratories all opened onto these corridors and at the end of the main one there were two lecture rooms, one on each side. Although some meager research was carried out in the teaching labs — mainly by undergraduate students after the end of the fourth year of the regular curriculum — there were no research laboratories proper or research facilities of any kind. Since I'm looking at this picture retrospectively and in the light of a long research career in Chile and abroad, this fact seems to me crystal clear now. But I doubt very much that it registered then, when my understanding of what research was all about was vague and naive in the extreme, based as it was only on the reading of perhaps a couple of books, rather than on any direct observation or experience.

Quite in keeping with the dimensions of our school, our class was small, just twenty-four or twenty-five students. Contrast this with the two-hundred-plus students making up the freshman class in medicine. Further, and also in contrast with medicine, the majority in our class, two-thirds in fact, were women. One might have concluded from this that Chemistry and Pharmacy was basically a woman's profession, but one would have been dead wrong. We soon discovered that **all** the faculty were men, without exception, while the female graduates ran the drugstores, often as employees, and some of them manned (!) the junior teaching jobs as assistants to the male professors. No female role models in important positions here, as there had been in high school, where most if not all the teachers and principals had been women.

Remarkably, however, none of this had any impact whatsoever on me at the time. I would go as far as my abilities and my drive would take me, and damn both the precedents and the consequences! The reasons for this were rather simple, I think. Because I had received all my education so far in a girls' school I had no experience of competing with boys my age, of playing up to the standards of male teachers, or of playing the gender games that thrive in coeducational situations. It was not so much a matter of having decided to fight the social norms that generally put women down as it was, at least partly, of being ignorant of them, and therefore of not being self-conscious in matters of the sexual prejudices of society. I simply thought that if women, despite their numbers in the case at hand, didn't occupy the higher positions, it was primarily because they had not been interested enough to try to get there, to do their best, as opposed to any tacit or explicit kind of discrimination. An innocent at home! I was interested and I would try, but not indiscriminately.

Reviewing the first year curriculum, and attending the first few lectures of each course, quickly led me to the conclusion that there wasn't much that was particularly interesting or exciting in the program. I would have to wait for the second year when the two-year course in organic chemistry would begin. Otherwise, I would work hard enough to pass all my tests and exams comfortably, but not enough to excel in everything regardless of the intrinsic merits (or lack of them) of the subjects, and just for the sake of excelling. To some degree this policy of mine, cool as it sounds, may have been tinged with a fair bit of rationalizing because other factors, of which I'm certain I was not fully aware at the time, were affecting my thinking and my attitudes. The most important of them, without question, was that I intensely missed the excitement, the warmth and the comradeship of my last two years in high school. Bluntly put, I was homesick. The subjects were boring, I hadn't made any friends among my classmates yet, and the professors were distant and detached, mostly married men with whom no special relationship of any kind seemed possible.

There was no comparison between my romantic notions of science and scientists and the cold and uninspiring reality of that first year program. What, amazingly, I never realized then, and have become aware of only during the last few years - in the eighth decade of my life - is that I missed the keen involvement with the liberal arts which had provided such lively stimulus for my inquisitive and sensitive mind. I did not know then that with the last few classes in December of 1938 I had closed for good the doors to a structured and formal education in the liberal arts. Sad. One might think that in the circumstances I would have filled in the void with extracurricular reading and other activities. But almost the opposite was the case. As for reading, my records show that during 1939 I read only a third as much as I had during 1938, and that a substantial proportion of those books, understandably, had to do with the history and philosophy of science. I recall having taken a university extension course in French, but no other anecdotes, landmarks or happenings in this area that would put flesh onto the bones of 1939.

My classmates, these young people of both sexes with whom I would spend the best part of my days for the following four years, were mostly a group of decent, average, ordinary students, mainly concerned with getting passing marks and having a good time in the process. The fact of being in a co-educational class for the first time - a concept that I had defended strenuously in high school against the better judgment of my teachers - didn't make much of an impression on me. This was because, nice and even good-looking as some of the boys were, I found none of them attractive or outstanding enough to arouse my interest. This may be unfair or even unjustifiable, but the main memory I have of them collectively is their passionate involvement with soccer. When they weren't playing themselves, they followed the scores of all the amateur and professional teams with the true and rabid zeal of devoted converts. I can identify with them now - although not about soccer - but not then.

Academically, there was no contest between the boys and the girls. The top three or four spots were consistently occupied by the girls throughout the four-year course. It didn't take more than a few weeks to establish the fact that Silvia Fernandez was the number one student in the class. She, a very nice-looking, soft-spoken, unpretentious girl, got top marks in everything from the dullest and most obscure of subjects to the most complex and exciting. Her performance was so consistent and predictable that it soon lost its lustre, while we followed the shifting positions of numbers two, three and four with keen interest. I was one of them, but not before having a very humbling and yet challenging experience.

An experience which can only be fully appreciated after I introduce the redoubtable Dr. Herman Schmidt. He is one of the only two professors that I can remember from that benighted first year, such was the profound impression that the program as a whole had on me. The other was Don Juan Ibañez, professor of botany, as well as the director of the school, and eventual dean when the school became a full-fledged faculty.

Dr. Schmidt was preceded by almost the same kind of reputation that Sta. von Delitz had been a few years earlier, in high school. He, the only Chilean academic that I ever knew to have obtained a Ph.D. abroad, in Germany, was the terror of the school. He was the most important single obstacle one had to surmount to complete the first year, where he taught inorganic chemistry, as well as to exit from the fourth year where he was in charge of the course in food chemistry, his specialty. He was indeed the severe and relentless guard at the entrance and exit gates. Dr. Schmidt, a Chilean of German extraction, towered over all of us with his six-foot-plus lanky frame and his ill-fitting off-the-rack suits, whose trousers, forever at half-mast, invariably revealed his coy white socks. He had short blond straight hair which ended at the top in one of those tufts more commonly seen in eight-year olds, and a robust and equally blond moustache.

A bachelor in his early thirties, he resembled Sta. von Delitz in most respects except for the genius. Punctual, autocratic, disciplinarian and hard-working to a fault, he expected only excellence which, in his terms, was nothing but total recall of the subject as he taught it. And this, as I recall it, was mostly a huge and uninspired mass of details concerning the physical and chemical characteristics of every inorganic compound known to man, the sort of information easily found in reference books rather than in the neurons of one's brain. The theory, on the other hand, the knowledge and understanding of the general laws that govern the behavior of inorganic substances, was cursorily and briefly covered at the top of the course and seldom referred to again. Therefore, the incentive to study and master the subject had virtually nothing to do with substance or meaning, and everything to do with getting marks high enough to satisfy the demanding Dr. Schmidt, and pass. Hard work and memorizing were the only challenges, and the rewards virtually nil, since the memorized details were promptly forgotten. This knowledge was at least partly reinforced during exercises in the laboratory course that went in parallel with the formal lectures.

In the circumstances, I decided to leave my studying-memorizing to a prudent but short distance before the written term exams, in order to avoid going through the same exercise repeatedly, and thus save my time and my efforts. It seems that I had either forgotten or failed to pay enough attention to the fact that Dr. Schmidt made it a practice to quiz individual students at random during the lab courses. So one day, when I least expected it, he called me to the board and asked me to tell him and the whole class all I knew about that obnoxious compound known as hydrochloric acid. He had caught me completely flatfooted. Falling silent after mumbling a couple of clichés about acids in general, I reluctantly confessed that I didn't know a thing about the acid in question.

The tirade that came down to me from the heights of Mount Schmidt was worthy of the performance by Charlton Heston in The Ten Commandments: Did I know what the University was all about? Did I know the responsibilities of a university student? Did I know we were no longer children, to be spoon-fed semi-digested bits of knowledge? Did I know the cost of our education to the society at large? Did I know what I, in particular, was there for? And finally the bottom line, uttered with the flourish of a consummate judge. If I didn't know the answers to any of these questions, as was obviously the case, it would be far better for all concerned if I gave up my academic pretensions and dedicated the rest of my life to the cultivation of the lowly potato. Flattering as the last proposition was — since he had conceded there was at least one creative and constructive thing I could do — I was at first floored and then angry, extremely angry. Worse than angry, I was piqued. My pride had been hurt to the core, but I couldn't tell, in the immediate aftermath of the strike, whether the wound was or was not fatal.

I very soon realized that my anger was directed only at myself for having been caught totally unprepared, rather than at Schmidt who, except for the hyperbolic style, had only been doing his duty. And then, with the mental clarity of someone on the verge of drowning, I also realized that I was no longer a star, pampered and humored, and allowed to get away with murder, as I had been in school only a few months earlier. In effect, I was nobody in my new milieu, a plain student without history, reputation or glamor. I was a nobody, I repeated to myself, and that hurt even more than the immediate and offensive incident which had provoked all this introspection.

So, right there on the spot, I resolutely decided at least two things: I would establish my reputation as a first class student anew, even if it killed me and, even sweeter than that, I would have my revenge. I would prove Schmidt to have been dead wrong. I would prove incontrovertibly to him that while I had no talents whatsoever to grow potatoes, I had plenty to master the inert and arid contents of his inorganic realm. And I did. I passed my term tests with high marks, and on my final exam at the end of the year, I scored twenty out of a possible twenty-one points, or a resounding ninety-five per cent.

This odd set of twenty-one marks was made up of three sets of marks each ranging from one (very bad) to seven (excellent), given by the three professors in each oral exam committee. I always wondered who had given me the six instead of the third seven, but I'm almost sure it wasn't Schmidt. He was positively delighted with my performance, and even flirtatious, and congratulated me effusively on the achievement, especially in view of my abysmal beginnings, as he didn't fail to remind me. I've always felt ambivalent about this outcome because I knew that I had done the right thing for the wrong reasons, namely out of pique and that, in the process, I had sacrificed my own principle of concentrating my efforts on the courses that really mattered and letting the others pass. But, as I've said, there wasn't much else that really mattered during that year when my performance, overall, had been good and reasonably consistent with my own standards. I may add with regret that I've never tried my hand at growing potatoes. I therefore have absolutely no way of knowing what exalted levels of success and excitement I might have reached in life if I had taken Dr. Schmidt's advice more seriously.

Perhaps more significant in terms of my future aspirations during that first year in university was the realization that no scientific research of any sort existed on the premises. All the faculty, except for Ibañez, the director of the school, were part-time appointees for the exclusive purpose of teaching. Otherwise, they all had regular jobs in various institutions corresponding to their fields of specialization, but of a practical or applied nature. In other words, there were no provisions for the funding of either research facilities or full-time research staff. As far as I then knew there was only one institution in Santiago where research in the fields we were studying was carried out, and that was the Instituto Bacteriológico. But its primary mandate was the production of biological materials such as vaccines, and of chemical drugs used in medicine. Whatever research was done there was of an applied nature, to implement in Chile whatever developments in those fields were taking place abroad. As far as I was concerned, that was better than nothing. Besides, I still had at least four years to go before graduation, at which time other opportunities might arise.

If my academic environment had turned out to be anything but stimulating, my social connections were also quite meager. I had made only one friend from among my classmates and this turned out to be an odd and short-lasting relationship. Anne-Marie Gundlach, a dynamic and quite determined young woman of German ancestry, was an average student who spent a good deal of her time divided about equally between her sports activities and her German boyfriend, the first person I had ever known to own a motorcycle. When he once took me for a ride up and down the foothills of the Andes, while I clutched his waist for dear life, I thought that was the ultimate of physical thrills. The second ultimate was doing the same thing on a bicycle, and Anne-Marie provided the opportunity, because she would often lend me the use of her own beautiful black two-wheeler. It had been my ambition for years — ever since at nine years of age or so I had learned to ride on the bicycle of a rich boy next door — to own such a portentous vehicle, but I would have to wait yet a little longer before I could afford such dreamy luxury.

I don't recall her ever coming to see me at home — I seemed to have kept all my friends at a distance from my home — while she often invited me for tea, after classes, and ocasionally for lunch to her house. This was a high-class boarding house run by her robust and hearty mother and her step-father, a meekish, small, self-effacing man. Anne-Marie had, I think, two older sisters who were, to my eyes at least, very glamorous young career women, but with whom I had a minimum of contact. I just admired their elegant clothes from a distance.

They were all German, of course, and spoke nothing but German at home. One day, at lunch, when there were seven or eight people around the table and I was listening helplessly to the very animated German conversation all around me, I was suddenly startled by Anne-Marie standing up and giving to the rest of them what appeared to me to be a very angry but short speech — in German, of course. Without much apology, everybody switched at once to Spanish. Apparently Anne-Marie had scolded them all quite severely, judging by the tone, for speaking German in front of a guest who clearly couldn't.

The experience was somewhat reminiscent of lunches at the Cheethams when the elder Mrs. Cheetham was present and the conversation was carried out in English exclusively. But then Mrs. Cheetham honestly didn't know any Spanish and I could already say, but barely audibly, such brilliant English phrases as: "How do you do", "Thank you very much" and "Good-bye". These experiences, plus the Yugoslavian that I was constantly exposed to at the home of my grandparents, as well as the Italian at Wanda's place, are probably at least in part responsible for my tendency to cosmopolitanism, a trait which has served me well. But they also taught me never to underestimate the power of one's mother tongue as it relates to self-identity.

In Anne-Marie's case this went well beyond language. She belonged to the Deutscher Sportverein, a German country club where she practiced all sorts of sports including field hockey — my first acquaintance with the term "hockey" — and where, no doubt, much of her social life took place. Further, when I once visited her in Concepción, a University town in the south where she had gone to take the second year courses, I found her staying at a German boarding house where everything, from the spartan decor to the food, and the way it was served, was German.

Even though I'm getting ahead of my story, I may add at this point that one evening, while in Concepción, Anne-Marie and her boy-friend invited me out for the evening to — what else! — a German night club. When I realized they might like to dance I told them to go ahead since I didn't mind at all being left alone for a while with my beer. But in a few minutes my solitude was brusquely interrupted by a very tall, blond and handsome young man from a nearby table who, vigorously clicking his heels, asked me to dance. Flattered as I was by his gallant gesture I had to decline in humiliating embarrassment because, as I told him, I didn't know how to dance. This major shortcoming of mine would soon be corrected, but that's another story.

Even though the Second World War had begun in September of 1939, and I knew quite clearly where my allegiance was, Anne-Marie's Germanness had not yet interfered with our relationship. In fact, it was not her Germanness which did, but her Nazism. I don't think we had discussed either the war or our respective affiliations very much until one day when, to my near total disbelief, I found that she had a picture of Hitler in her bedroom. If there was any discussion of the matter — or rather, I suppose, a heated argument in view of our opposite convictions - I do not remember. But I do remember that the incident brought our short-lived friendship to a clear end, even though we were civil to each other for the following three years.

My closest friend during 1939 continued to be Fusa, though our contact now was considerably less frequent than before because the School of Agronomy, where she was a first year student, was very far from mine, at the other end of Santiago. Even so, we would meet in the evenings to compare notes about our doings, or go out on weekends. Through her I regained contact with Leonardo Mella, whom we had both met at the end of 1938 during joint choir rehearsals of his school and ours. He was now studying engineering and because he lived only a few blocks away from me, and had been reintroduced by Fusa, the opportunities to meet were frequent. Eventually he and I became friends, and our friendship a unique and valued experience.

Leonardo was a very handsome and attractive young man of dark complexion and athletic build but, even more importantly, he was charming and extremely intelligent. Since, in addition, we shared all kinds of interests and we were both free at the time, it seems totally logical that I should have fallen madly in love with him, but I didn't. And neither did he with me. Tnis is hardly surprising, since romantic liaisons are anything but logical. However, to the degree that one can be logical about such mysteries, I can invoke at least one powerful reason to explain why I didn't become more seriously involved: Leonardo was short. A good two or three inches shorter than me, who by now had reached the scandalous height, for a Chilean woman, of five feet, ten inches. Glib and superficial as my feelings in this respect may sound - and I do not intend to seek deeper explanations - at this point they were a powerful deterrent to anything but a chaste friendship. Besides, and although the subject never even came up for discussion between us at the time, subsequent developments strongly suggest that he was already emotionally involved with Fusa. Simply put, I wasn't his type either.

However, none of this prevented us from spending a good deal of time together, especially during that first year in university, and we thoroughly enjoyed each other's company. There is no question that for me he filled the void left by the loss of Claudio in many important respects. The big difference was, however, that I never did idealize Leonardo out of all recognition, a fact that suggests to me now that my involvement with Claudio had not been as innocent as I pretended to believe. It would help, wouldn't it, if one were to be born fully experienced!

As with Claudio, Leonardo and I talked at length about our goals and aspirations, about how these were or were not being met by our studies, about our likes and dislikes, especially in literature, and about the other important people in our lives. And all of this, again, took place mainly in the outdoors, walking through our beautiful parks and then, gradually, venturing up the foothills of the "Cordillera", as the Andes were called by everybody. Because neither of us had any money, we would often take an apple each up the hills for a snack, climb the slopes, contemplate the city below while we talked and talked, and then climb down, dusty, tired and content.

He would often carry a book along, usually poetry, and read to me aloud. I remember one specific instance when the book in question was a collection of poems by the famous German poet, Rainer Maria Rilke. The text was in both German and Spanish, on facing pages, and Leonardo read blissfully from both to introduce me to the greatest German poet of the century. I guess the impact was not all that great because although I read some more Rilke on my own he never captivated me to the degree that some poets in Spanish and in French already had, but at least Leonardo provided me with the opportunity. Maybe Sta. von Delitz had been right after all, when she had told us in high school that unless we learned German we would never be able to enjoy and appreciate Goethe, the greatest poet of all time. Oh, dear! We illiterates would have to make do with only Cervantes and Neruda, Voltaire and Baudelaire!

Another deficiency of mine that Leonardo gallantly set out to correct was mathematics, specifically calculus. Himself a wizard at math — at least from my point of view — he was teaching calculus to a small group of people a couple of evenings a week, and he invited me to join in, if I wished. I did, not out of love for mathematics as we already know, but rather out of a sense, reinforced by Leonardo, that unless I became at least reasonably conversant with the rudiments of higher mathematics, I would probably never master science at its higher levels. This noble and well intentioned effort on both our parts turned out to be a failure. In keeping with my experience of the last two years in high school, I was quite unable to get the hang of the subject and so, after what I thought was a reasonable period of time, I gave up for good.

Tne moral is that either Leonardo was wrong, or that chemistry and the biological sciences hadn't yet reached their "higher levels" because, as I subsequently discovered, I was quite able to sail through these disciplines easily without the benefit of higher mathematics. Otherwise, the main pay-off from these classes, which took place in the dingy house of one of the students, at the other end of the world, it seemed, was the trip back home with Leonardo, when we invariably stopped for refreshments at a nearby cafe, to carry on with our friendship.

We continued to see each other, sometimes with Fusa, especially when we hiked in the mountains, for at least another two years. But then, I think it was in 1942, and quite out of the blue, he suddenly announced that he was quitting engineering altogether. He had been offered a very good scholarship to go and study meteorology in the U.S.A., and he had jumped at the opportunity. He said he was going for just one year, at the end of which he would be back to reassess his future plans. I was very surprised at this development. It was out of character for such a disciplined person as Leonardo to interrupt his studies in mid-course, but that is exactly what he did. I think, in retrospect, that his decision had more to do with his frustrated feelings for Fusa, from whom probably he wanted to get away, than it did with any serious change of mind about his career. But he left, and I lost track of him, not just for one year, but for several years afterwards. I was beginning to experience and understand the ease and unceremoniousness with which friendships vanish, if sometimes only temporarily, when compared to other relationships.

The forever evolving, but to a considerable extent more stable and reliable panorama of my family, provided the rest of my social contacts and relationships. If I saw less and less of Milena, I then established close and warm relationships with her two older sisters, Viola and Nora, especially with the latter. The Cheethams had moved back from Valparaíso and by now had three lovely little children, Cedric, the oldest, and the twins Edgar and Jeannette. Their English names were, of course, totally in keeping with Eric's English traditions, now fiercely reinforced by the outbreak of World War II. They lived in a handsome and comfortable house across the street from Milena's and only a short block away from Viola, who had recently married Jorge Skoknic, a very good-looking, happy and charming young man of Yugoslavian origin, who in due time would also become a very successful business man. My grandparents Eterovic and *tía* Catalina, who stayed single and looked after them, lived two blocks away in a much more modest but also comfortable home, where my sweet grandmother tended her vegetable garden in the backyard.

Only we, the Josseau-Eterovics, lived far away from the Barrio Alto, in genteel poverty, amid the splendor of embassy row. A trip to this area of the Barrio Alto was almost a guarantee that I would always find somebody at home. So I often went there, unannounced, since we didn't have a telephone, and made the rounds, but more often than not I would visit Nora who frequently invited me to stay for lunch or for tea. However, even now, as a mature (?) university student, I never rang the bells before peeking through the windows to make sure there were no other guests, such was the power of my shyness. If there were, I would try the other places, or simply go back home, defeated and despondent.

Raquel: How to Socialize a Bookworm

By 1940, however, my life began to change substantially in many respects. Among them was the fact that a group of four or five of us, at the top of the class, had become friends to various degrees. The primary bond was academic, giving rise to endless discussions of the merits or otherwise of the courses we were taking. We soon reached the consensus that organic chemistry, that beautiful science that deals with the composition and structure of all the components that make up living matter, was without question the most interesting course so far. And we also agreed, regretfully, that Professor Castañeda, in charge of the course, was a dedicated but dismal lecturer. These, and similar discussions on the program as a whole, soon resulted in our meeting after school to study together, or simply to socialize.

On one occasion, for example, four of us took advantage of off-season rates to go for a long week-end to the best hotel in Quintero, a fashionable summer resort on the Pacific. We had a splendid time, not just because we were in such elegant surroundings, but because we hit it off so well. I don't remember much about the substance of our interactions, except for two things. One was the laughter. I don't think I've ever, before or after, laughed more than during those three days in Quintero, but I have no idea what all the laughter was about. All I know is that my cheeks were constantly sore, and that recollecting this episode now makes me think that giggling girls seem to be a universal phenomenon, regardless of their academic pretensions, such as ours. Silly as it may appear to others, I can guarantee that it is, nevertheless, a lot of fun.

Secondly, it was probably during that week-end in Quintero that Raquel Rotman and I became interested in one another. We had, of course, known each other for more than a year, since we were classmates, but had not been close friends until that second year in university. She would confess to me many years later that during that first year she had thought I was the most arrogant, opinionated and obnoxious person imaginable. Until she got to know me a little better, when she at least dropped the superlative. She too, I soon discovered, wanted to become a scientist eventually, but like myself, she didn't quite know where or how. This immediately provided me with an ally, someone with whom to share my apparently unrealistic aspirations, and explore and evaluate whatever opportunities would present themselves. In addition, and to my delight, she also loved literature and music. We now were able to exchange not oniy our responses to and ideas about whatever we were reading but, of course, the books themselves. This alone set her apart from most of my other classmates.

But there was a great deal more. During that second year of our studies World War II was raging in Europe. To my utter dismay, and even disbelief, since I had thought the Maginot Line to be the most formidable of defenses, the French had capitulated, and the Battle of Britain would soon follow. Although by 1940 I was totally committed to the Allied cause against Hitler and the German forces, I cannot pinpoint with any precision the particular events or beliefs that led to my very strong feelings. But I am quite certain that the ground had been prepared very early as a result of hearing my parents discuss the role of France in World War I from the day I was born, two years after the Armistice. But these were primarily pro-French and anti-German, rather than anti-Nazi feelings, since Nazism did not yet exist.

As for the latter, all I can say with any degree of certainty is that, while at the very beginning of the Spanish Civil War — probably because my religious beliefs were still more or less intact — I had been anti-Republican if not pro-Franco, by the end of that war, while still in high school, I had switched my allegiance to the Republican side with even greater fervor. I flatter myself in thinking that the conversion occurred when I stopped believing in what I was told, especially by the Church, and started thinking and judging for myself. Although I cannot speak for Raquel, I should think that her commitment to the anti-Nazi cause, probably even stronger than mine, was likely more related to her being Jewish than to any nationalistic likes or dislikes. What is important, however, regardless of the original causes of our respective sentiments, is that this was yet another bond between us, and a very powerful one throughout the War, which we followed with passionate interest and which covered exactly all of our years together in university.

Raquel

We were, however, very different in many ways, but some of these differences eventually turned to my benefit. Although a Chilean citizen, she had been born in Argentina of Russian-Jewish parents. She was tall and of dark complexion, but undoubtedly her most striking feature was that rare combination of black wavy hair and intensely blue eyes. None of this struck me in particular at the time, since I seemed to be fated to have girl friends far better looking than I, but it certainly did strike many of the young men around us.

Temperamentally, she was socially outgoing but fiercely reserved, a reserve which she often camouflaged behind a non-committal but charming smile that in the end revealed very little. This was a significant contrast between us, since my awkward shyness precluded my being outgoing, yet at least with a few close friends I was not nearly as reserved. Even more importantly, my perception was that her involvements and commitments, whether with people or with ideas and causes, were consistently steady and serious in the extreme, while I, although never flippant, was less steady but far more passionate in mine. In other words, we could easily have been cast as the two heroines of Austen's *Sense and Sensibility*. Oh! How I've wished throughout my life to have been good-looking enough and born in the right place so that I could have become a film actress, and deeply moved or stirred not just a couple of dozen people, but millions! But back to my narrow little path which I was so tentatively exploring, as if blindfolded.

Gradually through that year, Raquel and I began to study together, and as a result she often came to my home. She was the first of my friends, male or female, whom I freely allowed into the privacy and the secrets of my unorthodox family. My mother received her warmly and eventually became fond enough of her to write to me, many years later, that Raquel had been the sister I had never had. My brothers, who consistently disparaged and even mocked my friends, conceded that she was all right, perhaps even attractive. And my father, although predictably keeping his distance, surprisingly made no objections.

My reception at Raquel's home was somewhat different. Both of Raquel's parents worked at the cosmetics factory owned by her uncles. But her mother, Sra. Nina, did much of her work, packing and labelling many of their products, at home. As a result, their relatively small apartment, near the factory, always seemed crowded and busy and, as I recall, we never spent much time there. Her father was a strange man who talked loudly and most often completely out of context, so that nobody seemed to pay much attention to him. Her older sister, Lolita, was already married and lived in her own home with her family. And her younger brother, Boris, was still a school boy, quite uninterested in older girls. Although Sra. Nina was invariably civil and hospitable, I never had the feeling of being openly welcome at Raquel's. I learned much later that my feelings had been essentially right since she had apparently feared that I would lure Raquel into a social group of "goyim", and that she would marry one of them, and thus betray her race. Little did Sra. Nina know how wrong she was.

Things turned out to be completely different at the home of her dear aunt Olga, who lived with her family just around the corner from the Rotmans. The Arensburgs - Isidoro and Olga - were, together with his older brother, the owners of the very prosperous cosmetics firm, also located in the neighborhood. They had two sons who were small school boys at the time. Their house, set in the middle of a semi-commercial, semi-residential downtown district, was of recent vintage and completely modern in design and style, the first such dwelling I had yet seen. The ample rooms, the high quality of the modern furnishings, the central heating, the huge tiled terrace and garden at the back, and the two servants, all spoke of taste and affluence. None of this would have mattered much, however, without the warmth and interesting personality of Raquel's aunt. Now in her mid-thirties, she had come from Russia at age twenty, and yet she spoke perfect Spanish, even though Russian was the preferred language at home. She was a wonderful mother to her sons and an impeccable housekeeper, especially in the kitchen where, with the help of her cook, she invariably produced the best of Russian cuisine artfully blended with the best of Chilean dishes. It was at her home that I first tasted and became converted to such things as blintzes and beet borscht, while I listened to them all talk most animatedly about current affairs, but most especially about the War.

She was vibrant, informed and committed, so that there was no way one could avoid being caught up in her concerns and her enthusiasms, which otherwise went well beyond this to encompass literature and the arts, and even gardening. What was most remarkable to my mind was that all of these interests and activities were, seemingly effortlessly, combined with her full participation in the family business, where she worked full-time, and her later branching out into enterprises of her own in the development of sea-side estates.

Obviously, none of these stimulating traits and accomplishments were clearly known to me when, sometime in the early 1940s, Raquel introduced me to her aunt Olga and her family. What struck me, rather, from the very beginning, was her most appealing personality, the warmth and openness with which she responded to this rather awkward but keen young woman, whom Raquel introduced as her classmate and best friend. Physically, there was nothing striking about her. She was short and nicely plump, her features regular but not outstanding, and her grooming was at best modestly non-descript. Consequently, the attractiveness rested almost exclusively in her manners, her obvious intelligence and quickness of thought, her keen interest in others - in this case myself - and in the warmth and charm of her expression. We hit it off very quickly, and soon after a few encounters we had adopted each other in the sense that, having become her new niece, I was to call her "*tía* Olga", just as Raquel did. Thus her husband became "*tío* Isidoro", her brother-in-law "*tío* León", and Raquel either my sister or my cousin. Lo and behold, I had a brand new family, as if I had never really had enough cousins, uncles and aunts.

Through this happy development, my social horizons became significantly expanded and my life correspondingly enriched in the process. As Raquel and I visited frequently, and tia Olga followed our careers, adventures and other relationships with keen interest, she became not only Raquel's confidante but mine as well. There would be many occasions in the years that followed when the three of us would retire to the study after dinner to chat for hours, to the dismay of her growing sons who, despite their valiant efforts to conceal their feelings, were clearly jealous, at least occasionally.

The state of despondency, if not of low grade depression, that I had experienced in the first year at university, now dissipated considerably as a result of these developments, and the process was further enhanced quite significantly when Raquel introduced me to her group of friends. With one or two exceptions, these were all university students of our age, but in other faculties - medicine, dentistry, but especially architecture. At the core of this group was Myriam Weisberg, who would eventually become a very distinguished historian of architecture and win many prizes. Myriam, who lived with her well-to-do parents in a large and roomy apartment, was at first the only one in the group who had space enough to give parties, so that her house became the site of many of our gatherings for the duration of our university years.

The spirited and creative group of friends would gather with some frequency at Myriam's to hold parties of which dancing was the major component, if one takes for granted the huge meals served around a single, large, but very crowded table. Some time towards the end of 1940, or during the following year, Raquel invited me to one of these parties. I declined on the grounds that I didn't know any of these people, that I didn't know how to dance, that I had never been to a party except for family affairs, that my social awkwardness rendered me unfit to attend such sophisticated gatherings and, finally, the most powerful of all arguments — still in my repertoire of excuses, five or more decades later — that I didn't have anything to wear! I did not, of course, admit that all these impeccably rational excuses were concentric circular barricades drawn around my excruciatingly painful shyness to protect myself from the near terror of such exposure.

Raquel, exhibiting her characteristic dogged determination to achieve her aims whenever she so decided, would have none of it. She persisted, calmly but relentlessly, until I gave in and finally made my appearance at one of Myriam's parties. I wish I could say that, Cinderella-like, I turned out to be the soul of the party, a smashing success. But nothing of the sort happened. I sat through the foxtrots, the rumbas, and most especially the tangos, in deep humiliation, thinking that even if I ever dared to try and learn to dance to these complicated rhythms, I would never succeed, especially since the whole exercise involved not only moving in harmony with the music, but with one's partner as well. I knew I could never do that with any measure of grace, as I remembered Nora and Eric doing at their wedding party six or seven years earlier.

But when we all moved from the dance floor to the dining room for a buffet supper, things improved considerably. There was a lot of laughter, but enough conversation between jokes for me to form a general impression of the group. These young people, in contrast to my generally dull and pedestrian classmates, were an interesting, even an exciting lot. The conversation ranged through a wide variety of topics, among which politics and current affairs, both national and international, seemed to be preeminent. I was left with the overall impression that my new friends were highly idealistic and committed, both in terms of their own professional pursuits, and in the affairs of the world at large. There was no question, either, that their leanings were clearly towards the left. Even though some of their interests and opinions naturally differed from mine, I felt comfortable and delighted in the knowledge that I wasn't, after all, as much of a loner as I had believed myself to be up to that point. One-to-one friendships or relationships were not necessarily the only options available to me. This particular encounter seemed to offer the promise of groups with whom I could share some if not all of my concerns and ideals. Were it not for the damn dancing!

However, despite my protestations to the contrary, the bug had bitten me, since not too long afterwards I found myself taking dancing lessons from Raquel and Myriam. They were quite determined, as I followed gingerly and reluctantly their patient but amused instructions, while I kept on uttering all sorts of protests to the effect that I didn't have what it took, that I was ungainly, and that I would look quite ridiculous if I tried to pretend otherwise. They persisted however, until one day, at a subsequent party. I yielded and accepted the boys' invitations to dance. Even if I looked clumsy to an outside observer, I loved the experience and felt terrific, in perfect harmony with both the music and my partners, except for one of them whose eagerness was matched only by his awkwardness.

I discovered, further, that there was more to dancing than just moving to the music and the rhythms. Being held by attractive young men — a first for me — was a novel and exciting experience. Perhaps as importantly, the fact of their wanting to dance with me was sufficient proof of my own atractiveness unless — and the thought, of course, did cross my mind — it was only proof of their kindness. Be that as it may, there was no way to stop me afterwards, and in due time I became, quite happily, a very good and enthusiastic dancer.

The whole experience had even deeper consequences. It became a sort of liberation from my own self-imposed negative physical image. For years this had been reinforced by family members telling me that it was such a pity I looked just like my father, instead of like my beautiful mother. This liberation, which turned out to be only partial, and not particularly stable or consistent, was accompanied at the time by corresponding changes in my grooming and appearance. I gradually began to shed my school-girl looks and to take on something of the appearance of self-confident young womanhood. But not without great difficulties, considering that it was very hard for me to find stockings that would fit my very long legs, and that women's shoes went only up to size nine while my long feet required size ten! There was no problem with the rest of my wardrobe because my mother still made all my clothes.

All of this was a significant, even if limited achievement, since up to then I had consistently felt that only my brains and my academic performance might be attractive, without ever stopping to think that beyond these features I also had a personality which, in all its complexity, might count as much as my looks or my intellect, or more.

My Three Brothers

As I was growing up into an adult, so, obviously, was each of my brothers. The twins, Raúl and Orlando, were now eighteen and Fernando sixteen. Although up to this point I have for the most part referred to them collectively as "my brothers", or "the twins", suggesting some kind of monolithic block opposed to me, the only girl, this was not so. They were, in effect, three very distinct, original individuals. That I saw them as a solid group apart from me, was due to many important reasons, besides the obvious gender difference.

To begin with, all three of them went to an all-boys school, the Liceo Lastarria, which was located several blocks east of Vicuña Mackenna, instead of west, as mine was. Therefore, there was no walking together to and from school, ever. For the same reason, we never shared or even knew anything about our respective schools, teachers, classmates, or anything else related to the school settings in which we were growing up.

Secondly, soon after the family moved to the house in Vicuña Mackenna, we began to play and generally spend our after-school hours in very different ways and, again, in very different settings. As I have already noted, Vicuña Mackenna was a very wide main thoroughfare, with street-car lines in both directions, a lot of traffic, and the site of embassies and large mansions. It was hardly the place to play, especially since we seemed to be the only children around. But the streets perpendicular to Vicuña Mackenna were residential, with lots of children from middle-class homes, and comparatively little traffic.

One such street, the Calle Joffre (named after Marshal Joffre of World War I fame), which was only one short block south of us, was soon adopted by my brothers as their playground and general headquarters. Not only did they play there, mainly soccer as I recall, but inevitably they made lots of friends. Some of these friendships lasted well into their adult lives. I shared none of this, and didn't even know any of the Joffre kids until I met and became close friends with one of them, Gregorio (Goyo) Gasman, many years later, and certainly not because we played soccer together.

A third and crucial reason for my perception of my brothers as a distinct and nearly homogeneous entity, was the attitude of my parents, especially of my mother, towards them versus me. They were boys. I was a girl. They were brought up to be future men and I a future woman. In this we were basically no different from boys and girls in any other family in Chile, or China, or Latvia, or Australia, or probably anywhere else in the world. The boys were groomed to study and train in order to become successful and educated providers. The girls, to attract these successful providers, become their mates and eventually bear and raise their families.

In the concrete setting of my own family, however, this went far beyond the generally recognized division of labor, in the sense that my brothers, for as long as they were in school, were never expected to do anything around the house, or in any way help with family problems or emergencies as they arose. Even my father, presumably their primary role model, often did such things as making the morning coffee, helping wax floors, repairing broken things and occasional shopping. But I don't remember my mother expecting my brothers to do any of these things, while she took for granted that I should help with everything that was in keeping with the example she was setting for me. I suspect that this pronounced exaggeration of the usual norms for the upbringing of males in Chile at the time was partly related to the independent factor that at least the twins had been so sickly at birth that she almost lost them. Perhaps she continued to see them, and Fernando by association, as vulnerable and in need of great care, while she saw me as big and strong, an ally. These different expectations of them and of me as children, and our respective responses, were later, as young adults, transferred to our respective sense of financial responsibility towards the family.

I resented this discrimination intensely and well into our adulthood. I felt this wasn't fair because otherwise, namely in school, the same was expected of all four of us. It was not an even playing field. My resentment, however, was not expressed towards my mother, whom I always saw as a victim of her own circumstances, trying her utmost to do the best for her family, but towards my brothers. In my view, they took their privileges completely for granted and, adding insult to injury, made fun of my own efforts instead of appreciating them. Most of our quarrels, physical at first, when we were small but I the biggest, and verbal afterwards when they had grown taller than me, had their origin in these internal family dynamics. These particular remarks, however, apply mainly to Raúl and Orlando because Fernando had from the beginning been far less aggressive towards me, perhaps even loving. He and I would probably have gotten along famously had it not been for the fact that, as already described, he belonged to the "boys club", from which I was not only excluded but to which I myself had no desire whatever to belong.

In other words, as we were growing up, my brothers as a group spent lives very different from mine in school, in their after-school activities and at home. Different and largely separate, because other than sharing our parents and therefore some of our genes, as well as our regular meals at home, we had and did very little else in common. That is why I have, so far, failed to deal with them as the individual and distinct personalities that they unquestionably were.

Raúl and Orlando, being non-identical twins, were physically very different from each other. Everybody was in agreement that Raúl, Fernando and I were "pure Josseau", that is, that like my father we all had blue eyes, light complexions and light brown hair which had been blond when we were small. Orlando, on the other hand, was clearly an Eterovic, with his darker complexion, brown eyes and dark hair, including his eventual and permanent beard. All three of them got to be six feet or more in height, and generally carried themselves and dressed with a certain elegance which, at least at the beginning of their aduithood, seemed somewhat at odds with their meager wardrobes. Once they had stopped playing boys' games in the Calle Joffre, all three of them became quite sedentary, much preferring to read or to discuss intellectual issues with their friends for hours on end rather than to take part in any physical activity, except walking. As opposed to me, I don't think that any of them ever learned to ride a bicycle, or to climb even ten meters up the Cordillera, forever a temptress in all its majesty, and a veritable magnet to so many young people, including myself.

But all this while, the twins must have been honing their intellectual skills with great precision, because, Fernando tells me, the two of them made a formidable duo at the Liceo Lastarria, where they were renowned for their knowledge and intelligence. The two of them together stood first in their class throughout high school, without any prompting from me or anyone else at home. But, sadly, and despite all of the characteristics that they had in common, they did not get along with each other. Fernando has told me recently that they were just as intransigent with and critical of each other as they were of me. And, to my surprise and amazement, he added that they treated him the same way. The styles, however, were markedly different, in consonance with their different personalities, and perhaps with the different course that their respective lives would soon take.

Raúl was serious, reserved and bitter. He was so serious that try as I may, I cannot recall him smiling, let alone laughing. Up to very recently, I had always thought that his extreme reserve and uncommunicativeness had then been directed more or less exclusively towards me, as a result of our many quarrels, the last of which had led to our not talking to each other for some years. But when I asked Fernando specifically about this point, his answer was: "Raúl was a mystery, an enigma." He apparently loved to talk to his friends about philosophy and public affairs, politics, but never about himself. And at home he talked about neither. When I say that he was bitter I mean that I invariably had the impression that he had a high level of contempt for himself, for his body, and for the human race as a whole.

When the twins turned eighteen, in 1940, they were due for their one year of military service, which was then compulsory for all able-bodied males. I have no idea what Raúl's views were on this matter. Neither do I recall the exact sequence of events. But I do know, and remember with great pain, that it was during Raúl's eighteenth year that he was diagnosed as having tuberculosis. Such a diagnosis in Chile at the end of the 1930s was tantamount to a death sentence, much as AIDS was more recently in some parts of the world. This, coupled with Raúl's difficult personality and with his medical history, was a tremendous blow to all of us, but most particularly to my long-suffering mother, who had already nursed him through two near-catastrophic conditions. He was seen by the very best specialists in Santiago, whose prognosis was at best extremely cautious. It would all depend on Raúl's own attitude, and on following to the letter the regimen prescribed.

My recollection is that Raúl flatly refused to go away to a sanatorium. He wanted his mother to look after him, no one else would do. And so it was that once again, when she might have thought that her grown-up son might be a comfort and support for her, she had to contemplate the very real possibility of losing him altogether. Life at home became quiet and somber, as if we were all tip-toeing for fear of disrupting what we perceived as a very precarious equilibrium. As for myself, I did everything I could to answer my mother's questions on medical matters, and to help her with her new and added burden as best I could. Since there was not much else that I could materially do, I went on with my life and did not let this new problem interfere too much with the new horizons that were opening to me in my university life.

Military service for Raúl was clearly completely out of the question. But so were university studies and for that matter a steady job of any sort. He was simply not well enough or strong enough to assume any responsibilities or work of this sort. Instead, he stayed mainly at home and began to read profusely on philosophical and political themes, and eventually to write. Needless to say, I never saw any of his writings, but I have been told by outsiders that he was brilliant.

Other than overt ill-health, the major exemptions for military service at the time were lameness, short-sightedness, and being the son of a widow. Poor Orlando! Much as he hated the military as a whole, and the very idea of playing soldier for a whole year, he most certainly didn't qualify on any of these counts. And so one day he picked up his suitcase and left for Valparaíso with a cryptic smile on his face. Why Valparaíso? I'll never know! But he had gone to register in whatever regiment he had chosen to do his military service in. We all had expected a post-card, a letter, or even a visit in resplendent uniform in due time. Imagine our surprise and puzzlement therefore, when he reappeared at the end of forty-eight hours wearing his civilian clothes and sporting a triumphant smile on his face. He had beaten the system, squarely but not fairly I thought, just cleverly. After registration he had donned his white summer uniform and cap and had gone to perform his first assignment, which consisted of painting a tall outside wall from top to bottom. After placing the ladder in the appropriate place he had picked up his pail of paint and his brush, and had spent hours going up and down the ladder, never making even a slight mark on the wall. Whoever made the diagnosis of terminal mental deficiency was clearly extremely astute! Be that as it may, he had been discharged before the day was over, on the grounds of mental incompetence. But not before having his picture taken, proudly wearing the uniform of a private in the army. Did he ever think of later showing it to people while saying such things as: "When I was in the army... " or "During my military career ... "? It would not have been beneath his wry and sarcastic sense of humor.

But my father was not the least bit amused. Among the very few things that he admired in the country were the army, where he had done his own military service with great pride, and the military in general. This was the one institution that did teach unruly or sissyish young men the virtues of discipline, respect for authority, and generally all those things that would turn them into real he-men. To have a son who had shown such cavalier contempt for this venerable institution was not only not funny, but itself contemptible.

After growing a beard that he would never again shave, maybe as an alternative expression of his own masculinity, Orlando spent the rest of that summer agonizing about his future plans. He had narrowed down his options to two by the time he had to make a firm decision. He would either enter a seminary to train for the priesthood, or study law. Neither option was a surprise to anyone in the family. Among the four of us he was the only one who had remained a practising Catholic from childhood. Now in his late teens, he had already become the profoundly devout believer that he would remain for the rest of his life. There was no question about his aptitude for the law either. He had a brilliant and keen mind but, above all, he was immensely skillful and agile with words, especially complex or even convoluted arguments. And the latter were invariably tinged with his inimitable sarcasm, or at least sense of irony, that was the dismay of his opponents, especially me. He would have made a brilliant and devastating courtroom lawyer, I'm certain.

Orlando (far left), next to mother, and Fernando (far right, back), with Eterovic uncles and aunts

I don't know the exact nature of his struggle to choose between such disparate careers or vocations. But I do remember vividly that when the last day before the deadline came in March, he was still completely undecided. So much so that he spent the whole of that last night awake, pacing up and down, tormented by his doubts. It was a great relief to hear, the following day, that he had enrolled in the Faculty of Law. I was particularly happy, not through any great love for lawyers or the law, but because the mere notion of having a priest for a brother seemed rather outlandish to me, to say nothing of the fear of having someone in the family, so close by, assessing and reminding me for ever of all my sins and transgressions. To no one's surprise, Orlando became a brilliant university student. I didn't know this until recently, when Fernando told me that Orlando's own professors were scared of him. Apparently he had made a point of studying the historical background of the contemporary laws he was being taught — back to Roman times ! — in the process becoming far more knowledgeable than his own teachers.

Fernando's story is substantially different from that of his older brothers, and from mine, for that matter. He had been a beautiful child, unquestionably the best looking of the lot, and now, as an adolescent he was clearly becoming a very handsome young man. Although rather cryptic about some personal things, he was never as serious or reserved as Raúl, or as aggressively sarcastic as Orlando. Instead, he had a much more open and friendly disposition and a great sense of humor. At the risk of betraying my bias, I must admit that I always thought he was charming and loveable, and that he eventually became a very attractive man. There is no question that he was as intelligent as anybody else in the family but, by the time he was in grade nine, at age fifteen, his school marks had become alarmingly poor. In fact, he didn't even have passing marks in most subjects.

Since I had never meddled with my brothers' studies and, frankly, wasn't in any way involved with their activities or concerns, I was most surprised when my mother called me one day and showed me Fernando's school report. It was very bad indeed, and unless something was done about it immediately, he would, against the best family traditions, simply flunk. My mother, extremely upset about this development, and knowing that I had quite a bit of experience at tutoring students in trouble, asked me to help. I tried, and I failed, abysmally. Knowing very well that his failing marks had more to do with lack of application and hard work than with any intrinsic lack of ability, I was firm, stern and demanding. Against my very own tenets of trying to motivate the student first and foremost, I was so firm, stern and demanding that I only succeeded in putting Fernando off, permanently. It was not long after this unhappy episode — still a landmark in my list of painful failures — that he dropped out of school altogether.

With the help of our cousin Eric Cheetham, he got himself a job as office boy at the Santiago headquarters of the Esso Company, where he apparently did quite well for some time. But that was not where his heart was. While still in school he had become interested in the theater as a result of joining a small group of players in a seminary, under the direction of a priest who was a friend of Orlando's. So, when at the age of seventeen he learned that Margarita Xirgú, the greatest Spanish actress of her time, had opened a drama school in Santiago, he promptly enrolled in it. He worked during the day and then spent three hours every evening at the school for the following three years.

An interesting feature of the school was that Xirgú blended it with her own highly renowned professional company, so that many of the students, including Fernando, got bit parts in the plays she was producing. The intermingling of the students and the theory on the one hand, with the hard practice among professionals on the other, thus made for an invaluable learning experience. Partly because of my selfish concentration on my own interests and activities, and partly because Fernando himself was not particularly communicative about his doings, I did not know then as much about his developing involvement with the theater as I know now. Imagine then my surprise when, attending one of García Lorca's plays at the Teatro Municipal, I suddenly saw my kid brother, all dressed up as a page, at the back of the stage! I couldn't judge his acting abilities on the basis of this particular performance because I don't think it called for any lines, but I most certainly thought that he looked great.

Fernando as a young dramatist.

Sometime later Fernando also took a correspondence course on cinematography from the U.S.A. He tells me now that the experience was invaluable to him much later, when he spent some years in Mexico as a successful screen writer. However, his main love was unquestionably the theater. When the Xirgú company left Santiago for Buenos Aires some three years later, Fernando joined the Teatro Experimental, the Experimental Theater of the University of Chile. This outfit, which had just been created, and would become immensely successful for many years to corne, was also a combination of drama school and professional company. At this time, when Fernando was already twenty or twenty-one, his interests were clearly focusing on writing and directing, rather than on acting. In view of the fact that the Teatro Experimental was perhaps too small to include a course in directing, Fernando found himself having to learn the hard way. He was put in charge of staging Clifford Odets' play *Waiting for Lefty*, which had been written and produced to great acclaim in the U.S.A. only five or six years earlier. Fernando passed the test with flying colors, but failed to gain a certificate so attesting, precisely because there was no formal course in this specialty. He did, however, get a letter of high commendation from the director of the Teatro Experimental which, regrettably, has been lost. And thus began his basically autodidactic career as the famous and successful playwright, director, script-writer and short story writer that he became.

These were my brothers at the beginning of the 1940s. Or, far more accurately, this is how I now recall what my view, my perception of my brothers was, more than five decades ago. If each one of my three brothers could now write about our home and our parents, about themselves, and about their own relationships to their other three siblings at that very important time of all our lives, we would most certainly end up, Rashomon-like, with four very different, but equally valid stories. This one is mine.

Of Three Firsts: A Scientific Discovery,
a Job and a Brand New Biycle

Raquel and I had found the subject of organic chemistry, even if not the course itself, such an important and interesting discipline that at the end of the year, in December, we felt that we had not done it justice. Consequently, we decided to postpone our exams until March, when anyone who had failed in December, or who for whatever reasons had not tried, had a second chance. This way we would have most of the summer to study at leisure and in depth. This is exactly what we did, and when the time came we both passed with very high marks. More importantly, however, we had now prepared a solid ground for the second part of the course in the third year.

In the meantime the School was full of rumors and excitement concerning Professor Luís Cerutti. Just a few years earlier, Cerutti had been the child prodigy among professors when he had been appointed to the chair of Organic Chemistry while still in his twenties. Everybody had agreed that he was brilliant, but after a couple of years or so he had been let go, presumably because of his alleged communist political beliefs. Apparently things on the political front had calmed down some and Cerutti now was being reinstated. This was great news for us, but for the fact that, since the course was spread over two years, we would continue to be taught by Castañeda, while the students in the first part of the course would get Cerutti. But nothing could stop Raquel and me from at least attending his inaugural lecture.

We did, and we were overwhelmed. He had chosen aspirin as the subject for his lecture and, for two solid hours of the most energizing and inspiring discourse, to say nothing of the prodigious energy with which he wrote formulas and equations on the quickly movable blackboards, he told us everything known about this amazing compound and about its equally amazing virtues. And all of this in the simplest, most lucid, most unaffected of styles. Every time that a new property or medical application of aspirin is reported these days, I think of the almost prophetical involvement of Cerutti with aspirin, and conclude that he would now need a whole semester of classes to do it justice, instead of the short couple of hours that we then heard. But they were marvellous, and as a result Raquel and I sat in on his first half of the course — a second time around for us — as well as on the second half in third year. He did not disappoint us. He was exactly what a university professor should be, inspiring instead of deadly.

We were almost equally lucky with physiology in the third year because Dr. Samuel Middleton was also a dynamic and lucid lecturer, although compared to Cerutti he lacked the spark. But there was something unsatisfying about this course which, dealing with all the normal functions of the body, should have been fascinating almost by definition. It would literally take me years to discover that the problem was not with the intrinsic merits of physiology itself, but rather with our inadequate background. Surely, to understand properly how the heart pumps blood almost miraculously through the body, or how food is propelled along the intestine, broken down and eventually absorbed into the blood, or how the brain sends commands everywhere, one should first know the shape and structure of the heart, the gut and the brain. But we didn't. As opposed to the medical students, we had not taken any courses in biology, anatomy and histology, and were thus like a sailor without a compass and a map. Even so, I found the subject matter of physiology intrinsically fascinating, and when the time came for my final exam I did very well indeed.

I took the rest of the courses of the whole program as they came, and I did very well in many of them, sometimes through sheer good luck. At the end of the second year, for example, I got one 18 and three 20s because in each of them I had to discuss precisely those topics that I knew best. I got only passing marks in the remaining courses, those that in my view didn't count. And yet in one of these courses, analytical chemistry, I had an experience so unusual and so transcendent that it stands out in my mind with all the clarity of a revelation. We were in the laboratory, and under the supervision of the demonstrator we were doing experiments related to an analytical process called, if I remember correctly, the progression of the elements. At that point our task simply consisted of adding an acid solution to a series of test tubes containing solutions of various kinds. By doing this we caused an insoluble salt to be formed, which appeared in the tube in the form of a solid called a precipitate. Most of them sported brilliant colors, such as yellow, or green, or orange, so that the experiments were also a lot of fun as well as yielding quite beautiful results. Just imagine, mixing two transparent, colorless liquids and getting a tube-full of brilliant orange! So there I was, holding my tube full of this gorgeous orange stuff when, looking again, I saw nothing, just water. I stared at this thing like a dummy and, before saying anything to anybody for fear of betraying my own stupidity, I repeated the experiment, paying close attention every step of the way. I got my orange precipitate all right but, as I kept on adding the acid solution drop by drop, lo and behold, the whole thing disappeared once again.

By now, quite excited at this turn of events, I ran to the demonstrator and described what had happened. As we were doing the test again for his benefit he explained that a number of these compounds did form complex water-soluble molecules in the presence of excess acid, but that, to the best of his knowledge, the phenomenon had never been described for this particular one. "You mean" I said, barely containing my excitement, "that I have made a discovery?" "So it seems", he said, understanding nothing of the wonder of it all. I dropped my tubes, nearly ripped my lab coat off, and carrying my coat and my books, as if struck by an earthquake I ran out of the building and into the nearby Parque Japonés.

I was in a sort of agitated but most pleasurable trance, a high the likes of which I've never had, before or after. I remember meeting a young poet I had only met once or twice before and, instead of stopping to greet him, I just shouted: "I can't talk to you now, I've just made a discovery!" I wandered through the park for quite some time, letting the whole thing sink in, in nearly complete awe of the sheer splendor of it all, of the beauty of the world around me and, above all, of having the good fortune to be in a position to penetrate its secrets. Until, slowly, one by one, the doubts began to creep in. Could this be possible? Had I heard the demonstrator right? Was this all just a bad joke? And, worse still, did he know enough for me to be sure of the accuracy of his statement? I hate to disappoint. But I also hated him for having sent me on such a wild-goose chase because, when I went back to check with him once more, he sang quite a different tune. Well, he had looked into the matter in more detail and yes, this was a well known property of this type of inorganic compound. No, there was really nothing to get very excited about.

No matter. He could deny his original claim until pigs flew, he could consult all the books on earth to deny the originality of my observation, he could go to hell, for all I cared. But he could not, ever, no matter how distinguished his sources or authorities, rob me of the experience itself. Of knowing the incomparable thrill of discovery. At least qualitatively I had now, while just a modest student among thousands, joined the select, that unique community of scientific researchers united, never mind their origins, in that most exciting of all endeavors, the spiritual search for the truth!

All mockery aside, my experience with my colorful but disappearing compounds made a deep impression, or I wouldn't be writing about it now. But, once I had returned to the real world, I had to confront, once again, the ordinary grind of lectures, of exams, of qualifying, step by step, in order to get somewhere. But the question of where, precisely, still remained unresolved.

Until one day, when Don Juan Ibañez, the Director of the School, called me into his office. I didn't have the faintest idea why he wanted to see me. I was quite sure I hadn't done anything wrong but, on the other hand, I hadn't done anything outstanding either, especially in his own courses, botany and medicinal botany, in which I had not distinguished myself particularly. To my considerable surprise, he wanted to know whether I was interested in the position of demonstrator in the new physiology course. Dr. Middleton had asked him to recommend a student and he had thought I would make a very good candidate. (Years later he told me that, other factors being equal, what had most impressed him about me on the day of that interview had been the fact that I was carrying a book by the famous British astronomer, Sir Arthur Eddington.) In response to my questions he explained that this was only a part-time job with a commensurately small salary, but nonetheless an opportunity, an opening door to a department dedicated exclusively to research and teaching. I thanked him profusely and immediately accepted the offer, while silently harboring all sorts of conflicting feelings.

This was not chemistry by any stretch of the imagination. It was a medical or biological science and as such it made me feel quite inadequate and ill-prepared. As far as I knew, all the people in Physiology were M.D.s or medical students. My nearly complete ignorance of their fields would make me stick out like an ignorant and sore thumb. But, on the other hand, it was a great opportunity to be associated with the only research outfit for miles around and, therefore, have the real chance of seeing at first hand what research was actually like. And, finally, this was my very first chance at a real job with a real salary. Since, after all, I wasn't signing a contract for life, if Dr. Middleton accepted Ibañez's recommendation, this last factor was probably the one that unequivocally convinced me I was doing the right thing.

When Dr. Middleton called me for an interview, following Ibañez's recommendation, he described my duties and responsibilities, my schedule and my benefits, as well as my salary. Beginning with the next term I would assist him with all the class demonstrations. There was no physiology laboratory course for the Pharmacy students, but each formal lecture was accompanied by actual experiments intended to illustrate the theory. I would familiarize myself with these techniques as we went along, and generally by spending some time at the Institute of Physiology watching the staff work. In addition, I would be present at all term written exams to maintain discipline and answer questions from the students, and I would also attend the final oral examinations as an observer.

At this point I felt most uncomfortable, if not actually terrified. After three years of chemistry and related topics I was quite familiar with much of the theory and very comfortable with most of the gadgets and instruments used in the labs. But I knew very little physiology after just the one short course. And, worse still, I had no practical knowledge at all of the techniques and instruments to conduct physiological experiments. I had only seen them once from a distance in the lecture room and hardly knew their names. To add further to my terror, the lectures were conducted in the Medical School, miles away, instead of in my by now thoroughly familiar School in Vicuña Mackenna. This was a completely different setting populated by M.D.s and medical students almost exclusively. Would they, as their reputation had it, look at me condescendingly from the heights of their lofty self-image? If so, would I, resorting to my own considerable height and "arrogant" personality, protect myself by responding in kind? Or would I, using my sense instead of my excessive sensibility in matters of self-esteem, clearly define my territory as that of a chemist, but add to my expertise all I could to perform my duties as an assistant physiologist competently? The answers to these tormenting questions lay naturally in the future. In the present, however, I would very soon collect my first salary.

In my circumstances, this became an event of very considerable importance since, for the first time ever, I would have a steady and reliable income, instead of the scattered and unpredictable bits of pocket money I was still making as a private tutor. Further, I would be paid year-round, and generally enjoy all the benefits of a public servant. One would think that such being the case, and having the memory I appear to have for minutiae of all sorts, I would remember the size of that very first landmark monthly salary to the last cent. But, most regrettably, I don't. Probably a few hundred pesos, not nearly enough for a single person to live alone, for example. However, in the context of the family's meager economical situation, it was clearly enough to allow me to make two outstanding financial decisions. One, I would pay the rent at least for that first month. And two, I would pay the first instalment on the bicycle I had been dreaming of for years.

Our salaries were paid in cash — only the wealthy had bank accounts — contained in a sealed envelope with all the pertinent details neatly filled in on the form printed on the outside. When late one afternoon I left the Medical

School with my precious loot in my little red purse, as well as my books, I decided to go straight home to give my mother the money for the rent. I sat in the dilapidated white bus, with my books and my purse on my lap, extremely excited and proud at the very idea of finally being in a position to help my mother in a truly significant way. The rent, or the ability to pay the rent, had, through all those years of struggle, become the very symbol of survival. And here I was, carrying not just a symbol, but the concrete means with which to relieve my mother's anxieties for at least one more month!

I jumped off the bus at our stop, just half a block from the house, and dashed through the gate and into my mother's work-room to discover in one horrendous instant that my purse wasn't there, only my books. I traced back my steps to the bus stop, but found nothing. There was nothing else to be done. Chilean buses and street-cars being what they were, amply populated by pick-pockets, there wasn't a ghost of a chance of ever recovering lost valuables. My mother, being actually more upset at my distress than about the loss, and perhaps because she was, if not inured, at least used to misfortunes, took it in stride, and reassured me that one more month of waiting wouldn't be that terrible after all. But I wasn't that philosophical. While trying to reconstruct all my actions.and movements during that ill-fated trip, I could only conclude that when I got up from my seat to leave the bus, I had been so excited and deeply immersed in my day-dreams, that I didn't notice dropping my little purse. Unless... unless somebody had skillfully taken it from my lap! Either way, I felt immensely stupid, downcast, let down, disgusted, but above all angry, intensely angry with myself. Another full month of waiting, of nothing but day-dreaming about affluence, seemed like an eternity in hell.

The month passed, however, and I survived to put my plans into action for a second time. When the time came, I gave my mother the money for the rent all right. I think I could have swallowed the envelope with the money in it if that could have prevented another loss. My mother was, of course, very pleased with my contribution and, I suppose, even happier when I told her that from then on, for as long as I would have a job, I would give her a portion of my salary, as well as pay for all my own expenses, thus relieving her of that burden.

I felt immensely powerful, especially when I finally went to a specialty shop and selected a bicycle from the large array on display. After inspecting, comparing and assessing all sorts of features, and discussing prices, I settled for an English bicycle. I think it was a Raleigh but I'm not sure about that. Even though the bicycle of my dreams — and even of a short story that I wrote some twenty years later — was red, the one I now chose was black, simply because they were all black. There were no color choices. It was black and shiny like a new Rolls-Royce, and it had a mesh on the back wheel to prevent my skirts from getting caught and causing an accident that would put an end to all my dreams, not just those of riding with all the effervescence of a young filly. And it had a rack for my books, and a lamp up front. It was perfectly beautiful. What more could anyone want! I made a down payment, signed the required papers committing myself to an X number of instalments, and left with the feeling that the seat of my bike had suddenly, through some miraculous transmutation, become the top of the world.

Owning a brand new bicycle, a dream of mine ever since I could remember, was for me then what owning a brand new car would be here and now for a young woman of twenty-one. It was freedom. It was speed. It was empowerment. It was independence. It was wonderful. I could now dispense with the humiliation of having to beg and borrow in order to experience the fun of a stolen ride now and then. So, sitting on top of the world, I rode to school every day and, increasingly as the months passed, to the Institute, which was far away and required a long ride in two bus lines. This was of course my rationale. I would save so much money in bus fares that I would soon have paid for the whole cost of this luxury, this exorbitantly expensive toy. Because, despite my rationalizations, this is exactly what my beautiful bike was. A terrific toy which now would allow me to indulge freely in joy-rides anywhere and at any time I pleased.

The most memorable of these expeditions was undoubtedly a trip to Llolleo and Santo Domingo with Fusa and Leonardo Mella, which we organized shortly before he left for the U.S.A. Llolleo is a summer resort some eighty kilometers south-west of Santiago, on the Pacific. So, one day in the summer of 1942, we packed our knapsacks with food and clothes for three days, and headed first south and then west along a narrow but paved two-lane road. What a trip! After five or six hours of steady pedalling in the hot sun we reached a sandy beach at Llolleo and set up camp. But the latter consisted only of a very small decrepit tent and of a fire improvised over some stones with a few sticks we found nearby. As it turned out, Leonardo's tent was something to behold. It was a pup-tent minus the front and the back, so that when we finally settled down for the night, I found that part of my feet stuck out at one end and the top of my head at the other. Both Fusa and Leonardo were short enough to be fully covered.

We spent the following day happily swimming or just fooling around in the big waves of the Pacific, and generally exploring the surroundings and nearby resorts either on foot or on our bikes. After another night exposed to the gentle but penetrating spray from the ocean we packed our rather primitive belongings and started on our six-hour trip back. Fortunately for us, the traffic, as on the trip down, was rather sparse, consisting mainly of transport trucks. But our small caravan of three young cyclists wearing shorts, red as beets from the relentless sun, and carrying back-packs, was a show-stopper for the truck drivers, clearly a sight they had never seen before. Every time a truck came within shouting distance, it would slow down, the driver would lean out, wave most energetically, and whistle in clear recognition of what they probably saw as outlandish provocation, or at least of dashing daring.

Oriana at the seashore, seen through Fusa's eyes and camera

It is a fact, that I can especially recognize in retrospect, that such activities for Chilean women of the 1940s were extremely rare and therefore somewhat shocking, if not overtly disapproved of by the society at large. But we, as university students, were not at all conscious of, or particularly affected by, the general standards of behavior, since different and special privileges, and even rights, clearly seemed to apply to us. We were in effect an avant-guard, exploring and staking out new territories where the usual norms did not necessarily apply, and new ones were being constantly designed and tested by ourselves. At any rate, I have nothing but the fondest memory of that trip, only made possible by my bicycle, one of the most outstanding material acquisitions of my life.

The Institute of Physiology

At the end of that summer, however, the fun was over and I had to confront very seriously the first realities of my budding professional responsibilities. Probably the last thing in my mind the day that I crossed the austere front door of the Instituto de Fisiología for the first time, was my future as a research scientist. I was simply there to meet with Dr. Middleton and get briefed on my new obligations as a demonstrator, an assistant in the Physiology course. That was all I could think about, and it was more than enough. For the reasons already stated I was quite scared, or at least very apprehensive, feeling incredibly ignorant in both the theory and the practice of physiology, which to me at least, was a brand new discipline, quite unrelated to my main background in chemistry. Besides, if I had had some practice at being found ignorant and wanting as a student, I had none in my capacity as a teacher, never mind how humble the position. Far worse, I had no idea about how to correct my deficiencies in this respect, a fact that would cost me a lot of grief and embarrassment for quite some time to come.

Preposterous as this may sound, I was then struggling with the fact that teaching at the university level was vastly inferior to the teaching we had been exposed to at the secondary level. High school teachers were trained for five years or so, not only in their chosen specialties, but in the art and science of teaching, or pedagogy. Further, the most distinguished among them had written and published small but most adequate text-books to fit the national curriculum. This had enabled us in high school to catch up from respectable sources whenever we missed a class or when our own notes were incomplete or inadequate.

In contrast, our university professors had direct knowledge and experience of only their own narrow specialties and, worse still, no training whatsoever in pedagogy. At the time of which I write, only two of them, out of some eighteen or so of our professors, had written textbooks that more or less corresponded to what they were teaching us. This problem was not, alas, peculiar only to the University of Chile, because I later met with essentially the same thing abroad. As for the rest, we had to make do with our own notes, frantically scribbled in class in a desperate attempt to catch it all, including the mistakes, the unfinished sentences, the non sequiturs, and even the coughs and sneezes, if we were really good at it. However, if our own notes weren't enough, there always were the more professional "notes" prepared by senior students for a price.

In the case at hand, the physiology course for the Chemistry and Pharmacy students, there weren't even those typed and mimeographed notes to consult because there were no senior students, since we were the first class to take the course. On that first meeting with Dr. Middleton, to be briefed on my duties, he did not in any way instruct me about this obvious and crucial problem, and I was too shy and too embarrassed to ask. I seemed to have gone on the assumption — as I would wrongly but consistently do for years to come — that I ought to have known how to learn all by myself, that this was somehow my own problem to solve, that needing help was a clear sign of my own incompetence, and therefore no one else's responsibility.

Gradually and painfully, by observing how the rest of the staff went about their business, I began to learn the ropes for acquiring knowledge. I soon found out that there wasn't just a neat small text-book of Physiology in Spanish that perfectly matched the course, but a whole library of severe tomes on the second floor of the premises. And then, eager to select from among them the one volume that would be the answer to my prayers, I was confronted with the shocking fact that just about everything on the shelves was either in English or in German. This was indeed my moment of linguistic truth. It was then that I realized for the first time, but with appalling clarity, that my majoring in French in high school had been a strategic mistake. Because, when I picked up one of these books and tried to understand even one full sentence, I couldn't.

Even though by that time I had already read a few novels in English with a reasonable level of understanding, this was scientific English, a lingo all its own, and I was not even all that familiar with its equivalent in Spanish. So, with the help of an English-Spanish dictionary, I began to write down my translations of English technical texts word for word, slowly and laboriously.

Although naturally I made very little progress on substance at first, my technical English improved considerably in a relatively short time.

But in the meantime the classes for the third year students had begun and I, probably excessively conscious of my inward sense of insecurity, tried as hard as I could to at least look professorial. While the students, wearing street clothes, sat in the lecture room furiously taking notes, Dr. Middleton and I, wearing neatly tailored white lab coats, took care of our business on the other side of the bench, in front of the blackboard. Except for listening while Dr. Middleton gave the formal part of his lectures, there wasn't much for me to do. But this gave me an invaluable opportunity to go over the whole course for a second time. The result was that I gradually became more and more familiar with the subject matter of the course and consequently more confident and assertive.

For reasons still not fully clear in my mind, the course included a considerable amount of muscle physiology, with its attendant practical demonstrations. These consisted of showing to the students that muscles, taken from just-decapitated little frogs and attached to instruments that could record their tricks on the surface of smoked drums, could contract when stimulated and be predictably affected by a variety of chemical and physical factors. While Dr. Middleton went on explaining what was about to happen, it fell to me to pick up a small frog, decapitate it with a pair of scissors, peel his snug skin down to his last little toes as if removing a body stocking and then, very carefully, remove from one of his legs a whole and still viable little muscle. Gruesome and even revolting as this operation appeared to me at the beginning, I became quite expert at it in due time, and almost inured to its implicit cruelty. But even to this day I feel responsible for the premature death of so many little frogs whose souls, I hope, are in frog's heaven, if there is such a place. They and I, their executioner, can take comfort in the fact that we were there in the service of science, for the laudable purpose of illuminating the minds of young university students.

This was the narrow context of my first year as a demonstrator in Physiology. As the months passed, however, and I was approaching the end of my four-year course and the beginning of the research for my thesis, I became increasingly acquainted with the Institute, its principles and its purposes. The Institute was located on the grounds of the old neoclassical Medical School building and, although grafted onto one of its corners, it was an autonomous and separate structure. At the initiative of Professor Francisco Hoffmann, it had been created by government law in 1936 and built in 1937, according to all the spartan, economical, but efficient specifications of Professor Hoffmann. Its two and a half stories, with space for eventual enlargement, housed four or five large research laboratories, a couple of teaching labs — later considerably expanded — a library and a seminar room, as well as a surgical room, animal quarters and a kitchen and dining room on the third floor. There was, in addition, a machine shop where a good many of the teaching and research instruments were built, as well as an electronics shop to serve the equivalent purposes. The difference between these facilities and those of any one department in the School of Chemistry and Pharmacy, consisting of only one teaching lab with its attached office, was truly awesome. Naturally, I was greatly impressed, but not nearly as much as I was when, during the course of that year, I got acquainted with the academic and support staff.

At the core of the senior staff, and its main source of direction and inspiration, there was Dr. Hoffmann, Chairman of the Department and Director of the Institute. Second in command, and Dr. Hoffmann's dynamic lieutenant, was Dr. Samuel Middleton, now also Professor of Physiology in the School of Chemistry and Pharmacy. And next to him in seniority, although considerably younger but equally able, there was Dr. Jaime Talesnik. And then there was the unclassifiable but equally influential presence of Dr. Helena Jacobi Hoffmann, Dr. Hoffmann's wife, who held no official position, but worked without remuneration, although with equal dedication, next to her husband. These people were assisted in their research work by three or four senior technicians, as well as, indirectly, by the machinist, the electronics man and a chemist. And, as far as teaching was concerned, there was a fluid group of half a dozen or so medical students who worked part-time as demonstrators in the laboratory courses. Once they had finished their regular medical course, some of them would help with the research work in the process of doing their undergraduate theses. Initially, I belonged to this group, except for the fact that I was the only one who was not a medical student.

The Institute had the primary responsibility of teaching the Physiology courses for the Faculties of Medicine and of Dentistry, and for the School of Chemistry and Pharmacy, a task which was equitably distributed among the senior staff. Otherwise, the place differed radically from most if not all other departments in that its members were exclusively dedicated to scientific research instead of practising medicine or holding other jobs on the side to make a living. All of this had been, almost singlehandedly, Dr. Hoffmann's achievement.

At the time I joined it, the Institute was just four years old, and Dr. Hoffmann himself only forty. He was a handsome and physically vigorous man, blond and blue-eyed, sporting a very impressive patriarchal reddish beard which was in perfect harmony with his role as head of this remarkable institution. In the late 1920s, while he was a part-time assistant in the then Department of Physiology, he had obtained a government fellowship to go to Germany to do post-graduate work in physiology. Well aware that the development of science in Chile lay far behind that of literature, the arts and other cultural elements, he took it as his mission to learn and absorb everything he could in the department of the renowned German physiologist Wilhelm Trendelenburg. He would then return to Chile to pioneer the development of scientific research.

While in Germany, he received a request from the Instituto Bacteriológico in Santiago to specialize and become proficient in the techniques available to measure hormones. For that purpose he went to the Department of Pharmacology at the University of Berlin, under the direction of Paul Trendelenburg, Wilhelm's brother, and an expert in the field. He worked there for many months under the guidance of Dr. Helena Jacobi, Dr.Trendelenburg's right-hand woman, until a new government in Chile cancelled all fellowships and he had to return home. In the meantime, the close professional relationship between the two young scientists had turned into a passionate romance culminating in their marriage just before he left for Chile, at the beginning of 1931. Helena Jacobi, however, had to stay behind in Berlin for many months because, as a result of Dr. Trendelenburg's unexpected and premature death, she felt obliged to complete the second volume of a treatise on hormones on which they had been working together. She, a native of Riga, the capital of Latvia, would join Hoffmann later in 1931 and become, together with other members of her immediate family, a most distinguished immigrant to Chile.

While she worked for some years at the Instituto Bacteriológico, he was developing and finally implementing his dreams of creating an Institute of Physiology, based at least partly on the German models he had become acquainted with, and directly supported with government funds. When this had been accomplished, in 1938, Helena Jacobi Hoffmann left her post at the Bacteriológico and joined her husband at the brand new Institute, where she worked full-time, but without remuneration, until the middle of 1951. To quote her own words: "It was unacceptable for a professor to hire a relative, even less a woman, and still less his own wife!" By the time I appeared on the scene "la Doctora Hoffmann", as we all called her, was an essential part of the team, so much so that it is hard for me to conceive of the Institute without her. She may or may not have held an official ad honorem position, but in practical terms I never knew her to take any part in our teaching obligations. She was the only member of the professional staff solely dedicated to research and, for my money, the most knowledgeable in the group.

And her knowledge extended well beyond physiology and the medical sciences to encompass everything from languages — she spoke six — to literature, and the arts in general. It was truly amazing, and for a very green young woman like me, thoroughly intimidating, even though she was, at least with us, very reserved and quiet and anything but ostentatious in her knowledge. On the other hand Hoffmann, or rather "el Prof" as we all called him, was, in her words again, "not particularly fond of reading". He was a doer, the most inventive, ingenious and enterprising doer I've ever known. This, coupled with his intellectual vision and understanding of the role of science in society at large and in teaching at the university level, as well as his ability to persuade officialdom of the merits of his ideas, were the main factors responsible for the success of his mission.

I had then, almost fortuitously, landed at the ideal place to try my wings at becoming a research scientist. My problems then and in subsequent years would therefore have more to do with my own inadequate background, as I perceived it, and my own abilities for scientific research, than with any real lack of facilities or opportunities as I had sometimes feared. It was all up to me now.

Exploring Politics and the Mountains

These were heady times indeed. At least two years before graduation I had a job that allowed me to help out at home. I was the proud and happy owner of a beautiful bicycle which had increased my mobility many fold. And, almost incredibly, I had found an entrance into nearly the ideal place in which to indulge my dreams of scientific research. But, as if all this weren't enough, I had also, and roughly at the same time, become involved in the University's political and sports activities.

Chilean university students, probably to a greater degree than students in other countries I have known, were intensely involved in the politics of the country. Each School or Faculty had a Students' Center made up of two or three delegates from each year, and a president selected from among them. I was one of the delegates from my class in second year. In turn, each Center contributed delegates to a central University body called FECH (Federación de Estudiantes de Chile, or Federation of Chilean Students). This body functioned in a couple of large rooms in an old downtown building and was therefore accessible to students from all the Schools scattered around Santiago. One would expect that, at least nominally, it should have dealt primarily with all matters related to students' concerns. In effect, however, it was almost a purely political forum at the time of which I write, in the early and mid 1940s. As such, it reflected in microcosm the politics of the country as a whole and, consequently, its participants represented all the major political parties then in place, rather than the more narrow interests of one faculty or another.

Raquel and I, being keenly interested in political matters, especially in those that related to the War, decided to have a look at the activities of the FECH by at least attending some of their meetings. Although I suspect that Raquel's sympathies already leaned towards marxism, I was, or at first saw myself as, only a naive and impartial observer. It didn't take me very long, however, to realize that the communist students formed the most coherent, well-organized and, most importantly, the most idealistic and well-informed group of the lot. My perception was that the rest, including from left to right the Socialists, the Radicals, the Liberals and the Conservatives, young as their members were, already represented mainly the vested interests of the well-established and generally accepted political parties. The undeniable idealism and commitment of the communists, in contrast, were instead directed to the eventual well-being of all the people, especially the powerless and unrepresented poor, and not just of those who were already well-off. To achieve this end they believed in the public as opposed to the private ownership of all the means of production and in the equitable redistribution of the profits to everybody, instead of only or mainly to the owners of capital.

Another powerful factor contributing to my interest in the communists was their position towards the war. The Battle of Britain was over, and on the Continent itself there was only the Soviet Union battling and desperately trying first to keep Hitler's armies in check and then to wipe them off the earth. Stalin's clamoring for the opening of a Second Front had echoed throughout the Communist parties around the globe, and been adopted as a battle cry. As I saw it, the Chilean Communist party, including its youth branch at the FECH, were the most committed and passionate anti-Nazis around, and this cause was, as I've already explained, very dear to my heart.

My interest had therefore been thoroughly aroused, together with my interest in the theories behind the beliefs of the communist students, and in some of those students in particular. Judging from my records I don't seem to have read very broadly on communism as a political doctrine, except, of course, for The Communist Manifesto which, nostalgically, I still own in a tattered Spanish version. Instead, I read a few tomes on dialectical materialism, the philosophical basis of the political doctrine, but mainly political propaganda straight from the source. The Soviet Union used to publish this sort of material in respectable editions in numerous languages for distribution around the world. These were accessible to us in Spanish at ridiculously low prices. After reading a few of them, especially a uniquely slanted and biased History of the Soviet Union, I had had enough of uncritical propaganda, and turned my attention to my friends at the FECH instead.

It should come as no surprise that the most numerous and the most active of the students at the FECH came from the Faculty of Law. Among them there was Ignacio Aliaga. By the time I appeared on the scene Ignacio was the charismatic leader of the communist group. Paradoxically, he didn't come from the ranks of the working class, or even from the low middle class, as one might have expected, but from a well-to-do and distinguished, if not aristocratic, family. He was tall enough and of fair complexion, but with no other distinctive physical features to explain his considerable attractiveness, especially to women. His undeniable appeal lay instead in his agile and cultivated mind, in his enormous and contagious enthusiasm for his cause and, most importantly, in his eloquence, his impressive ability with words. All these abilities combined to make of him a formidable and most successful speaker, a trait that he used to great advantage as a political leader. But he used the same combination of traits, although of course at a very different pitch, to seduce, to unashamedly attract women, but mainly for the sole sake of attracting rather than to enjoy the logical results of seduction. And, despite what I believed to be my comparatively wide experience of men and my worldly-wise ways, I fell for him.

I fell for him with reckless intensity, hoping against hope that if I made the right moves and honestly gave him a chance to see all the beauty and depth of my soul, he would reciprocate my amazing and earth-shaking feelings for him. And so I did, more awkwardly than convincingly, all the retrospectively embarrassing things that a young woman in love for the first time does. Or do they? I went assiduously to every meeting of the FECH where I knew I would find him. When the meetings were over I found ways to engage him in serious and what I believed to be profound discussions of marxist philosophy and even of tactical measures to defeat our reactionary opponents. And then, when I had succeeded in at least being recognized by him, I did all I could to be present at social gatherings more conducive to personal interactions than our action-oriented political meetings.

One of these occasions was a students' ball with a live orchestra and all the trimmings. That I agreed to go there with a group of friends (but with the only purpose of meeting him), is a true measure of the intensity of my passion, because this happened before I had joined Raquel's group of friends and therefore before I had learned to dance. Had it not been for my virtual certainty that I would meet Ignacio there, a ball would have been the very last place to find me. To my simultaneous delight and trepidation I suddenly saw him jauntily coming towards us with a big smile on his face. And then, what I most wanted in all the world but also what I most dreaded, happened. He asked me to dance. "Oh!" I said. "I would love to, but I'm afraid I don't know how to dance." "It doesn't matter", he said. "Let's go, and I'll teach you!" I refuse to describe what happened next. There has to be a limit to self-humiliating revelations! But, between the excitement of finally being in his arms, and the excruciating pain of stepping on his toes, and going right when I should have gone left, I found myself vehemently cursing the gods who had failed to make me know how to dance by divine grace. I am quite certain that this sweet and sour experience had as much to do with my subsequent willingness to learn to dance as Raquel's persuasiveness did.

At another time, on a beautiful late afternoon in the summer, a group of five or six of us, including Ignacio, decided to go for drinks to the Oriente, a then very fashionable cafe. This was truly the big time for me, since I had never been anywhere for drinks before, let alone with Ignacio, and to the Oriente to boot. I carefully listened to the waiter recite a long list of names and, since gin and ginger was the only one I even vaguely recognized, that was precisely what I ordered, with all the aplomb I could master. So there I was, pretending to be as cool and sophisticated as the surroundings required, when I heard Ignacio ask: "What do you think of Sibelius' ninth symphony?" To this day I curse the moment when I heard myself saying unashamedly: "Oh! I love it. I think it's great!" And I feel even worse when I recall Ignacio's roaring laughter and glee, saying quite loudly: "Good for you, Oriana, but Sibelius never got around to composing a ninth symphony, not even an eighth!" There are at most three moments in all of my life when I fervently wished that the earth would part under my feet and swallow me whole, drink and all. This was the first, and the most devastating of all, because it had a double edge. First, I, in my rather pathetic if not desperate attempt to please and impress Ignacio, had pretended to know and even to like a non-existent piece of music and, adding insult to injury, by a composer I didn't even like to begin with. And secondly, my hero, the object of all my love, was in fact a mean man, but clever enough to set such a trap for his friends, especially his unconditional admirer.

Were it not for the exasperating illogicality of love, my non-affair with Ignacio should have ended right there and then. That it didn't, is witnessed by the fact that when some time later Raquel and I organized a party of our friends at tía Olga's, he was invited and he came. Although comparatively small, this was a very animated affair that went on until the small hours of the night during which he played no tricks on anybody. To me he was not only gallant but positively amorous. So much so that when he left at about four or five in the morning of a Sunday, he told me he would call me at ten that morning at tia Olga's, where Raquel and I would stay for the remainder of the night. I was completely ecstatic in the knowledge that my feelings were fully reciprocated, and then some. But he didn't call at ten, or at eleven, or at twelve, or at one, when, discouraged and despondent, despite tía Olga's and Raquel's attempts at reassuring me, I left and went home to lick my wounds.

In the meantime, rumors were rampant in the communist youth group at the FECH that higher-ups in the party were very dissatisfied with Ignacio's behavior and personality, if not with his leadership itself. His case, it was said, was under disciplinary investigation. Presumably, the authenticity of his convictions and commitment to the cause were in question, as well as his personal behavior towards women. If the party condoned and even encouraged serious sexual relationships outside of marriage, it disapproved quite vigorously of promiscuity or any other flippant and careless casual behavior of the play-boy type. He was apparently under suspicion on both counts. Even so, I agreed to one more private date, in fact the first, more in an attempt to test my own feelings than his. Yet I was still hoping for the best, despite my already serious doubts about his character and integrity.

We had agreed to meet under a designated tree in a field adjacent to some of the fancy houses of the Barrio Alto where he presumably lived. When I arrived on time after the long bicycle ride from my home, he wasn't there. He arrived on his bike nearly an hour later, casually explaining that lunch at home had gone on far longer than he had expected. By then, I was no longer eagerly or anxiously awaiting the arrival of my dashing would-be lover, or of my knight in political shining armor. Instead, I was just waiting to tell off a miserable cad who seemed to think he could take any woman for granted, including me. When he tried to kiss me and set things right I momentarily nearly lost all my determination to put him in his place, but not quite. I am so angry in retrospect, that I can't even remember much else, except that, having learned my lesson the hard way, I gave up on him for good, right there under the designated tree, on a Sunday afternoon.

The end of my infatuation with Ignacio was not, however, the end of my involvement with communist ideas and ideals. If it is true that I gradually withdrew from the political activities at the FECH, I continued to interact with my other communist or fellow-traveller friends. I had, however, entered a new stage of my political development, the critical phase. If I still believed, at least to some degree, in the basic and fundamental tenets of marxism as a political doctrine, and agreed on quite a number of subsidiary issues or objectives, I was beginning to have some very serious doubts concerning its implementation in the Soviet Union, even if we hadn't yet heard of the atrocities committed by Stalin in the 1930s.

Eventually, even the claim that communism as a political philosophy was based on solid and unassailable scientific principles was beginning to crumble as I read, studied and discussed these things with better informed believers. My very choice of the term "believers" at this point reflects precisely my feelings and perceptions at that time. I could not escape the conclusion that many among my friends had turned their commitment to communism into a faith and themselves into worshippers. When, as a consequence, I realized that the dogma could not withstand critical scrutiny, but only be uncritically adopted and absorbed, I withdrew. I withdrew from the doctrine but not from my friends, some of the best people I've ever known, or from some of the more peripheral but no less important causes they then stood for.

First among them at the time was, of course, the anti-Nazi cause, winning the war against Hitler. In this, before the invasion of Normandy by the western allies, the Soviet Union, then the only communist country in Europe, had been heroically fighting the Nazis alone on the continent, and was in dire need of support. Of course, anti-Nazism never was the exclusive domain of the communists, but at the time of which I write they were most certainly as committed as anyone else, if not more. Secondly, I had also found some aspects of the communist ethic appealing, especially those that related to the sexual behavior of the human couple. Responsible sexual activity outside of marriage seemed to me a far saner and healthier approach than the rigid and hypocritical norms of the Catholic Church. Other cultures, especially in the west, have faced reality and adopted liberal sexual practices, but much later.

And lastly, I then came to espouse, I regret to say, the notion that the esthetics of art must be at the service of the message, that art without an inspirational social message is corrupt and valueless. Perhaps because I then knew so little about art and, probably more importantly, because all the artists I then knew personally were committed communists, I hadn't even heard the counter arguments which would allow me to draw my own conclusions. But don't despair. The time would come, much later in North America, when I would reassess this contentious issue and finally conclude that art stands or falls by itself, with or without a message.

This, in broad outline, was my involvement with university politics generally, and with communism in particular. Characteristically, it was more personal and intellectual than militant, and it shows very clearly an already well developed trait that would mark my future approach to other causes and organizations that would initially intrigue or attract me. I refer to a basically skeptical and critical approach to things which, despite initial interest, if not enthusiasm, would eventually preclude firm and unconditional commitments of any description. This critical ability would also serve me well in my subsequent scientific career. My initial interest in communism was partly circumstantial. I came across it in a university setting where it was not only acceptable but even fashionable to join, or at least sympathize with, leftist and quasi-revolutionary causes which, as in my case, appeared to be wholly consistent with my own beliefs and aspirations. Simply put, it was the thing to do for the young and the restless, especially in a country like Chile with its huge disproportion of wealth distribution. But my critical and analytical propensities eventually won out, thus preventing any further or firmer association with this, or for that matter any other, political party or movement.

Fortunately for me, none of these considerations applied to my whole-heartedly joining another student organization somewhat later, but with some degree of overlap. I refer to the Ski Branch of the Sports Club of the University of Chile. Whether playing hopscotch or climbing trees when I was little, or running up and down the hills of Valparaiso to bring warm bread to the breakfast table, or later playing basketball in high school or, still later, riding my bicycle virtually everywhere, there is no question that I had always tremendously enjoyed indulging and testing the physical attributes of my strong young body, especially in the outdoors.

Looking back, I can clearly see at least two salient features of all these activities. First, none of them required costly training by specialized instructors, or belonging to or attending equally costly but necessary facilities, such as swimming pools or tennis courts. The reason was quite simple. Neither my family nor our public schools could afford such luxuries. Secondly, for the most part, I consistently shunned team sports, much preferring activities that I could indulge in with one or two, or at most a few, of my friends in a freer and less structured setting than team sports require. The reason in this case is not quite so obvious, but I suspect that it relates to my rather ambivalent attitude towards rules, regulations and discipline. If I was obviously committed to all these things as a student, I clearly needed space in my spare time to let myself be and feel free to extend myself, without rigid restrictions, as near or as far as I wished to go. I wanted no rules, no time limits, no external authority present to dictate my norms.

By the time I had reached twenty-one, especially now that I had a bike, I had pretty well explored most of the possibilities in or near Santiago, and so my attention, as well as that of some of my friends, turned towards the inescapable in our setting. The mountains, the impressive Andes, the alluring Cordillera was right there, asking to be discovered and explored. And we, no longer dependent children, already had the means and maturity to embark first on a few tentative expeditions, and later in better organized ones.

During all of my school years I had been to the top of the San Cristobal many times. But it, a three hundred meter high hill encroaching on the city itself, was in effect a public park. It had a lift and a car road that reached the very top, crowned by a white statue of the Virgin Mary and also, to one side, it housed Santiago's zoological garden, a place better remembered for its foul smells than for the fascination of its animals. I had, of course, been to the San Cristobal many times with family members when I was small, and later with my classmates and teachers during our annual school picnics. Two memories remain. The full view of the city below and, if you turned around and looked east from the top, the close view and sense of the Andes themselves, of which the San Cristobal is but a small and insignificant toe.

Otherwise, the Cordillera itself was nothing but a gigantic and supposedly inaccessible monument, to my eyes and to those of all the people I knew, until I reached university. Except for two things. When I was in my early teens this apparently remote, enormous and inert wall to the east of us had come sufficiently alive to kill a number of young people, university students if I remember correctly, during a winter avalanche. It had been a skiing trip come to grief, a grief that spread through the whole city overnight because the accident was so completely alien to its culture and ethos, skiing being such a rare sport in Chile at that time. I still remember the horrifying pictures of the dead young people on the front pages of the papers, taken during the rescue efforts. Their bodies bloated in the surrounding snow, a painful and cruel warning of the indiscriminate power of the otherwise beautiful and majestic mountains. Although I must have been familiar with mountaineering and skiing through films, this was my first real if indirect experience and recollection of the sobering risks of such sports in my very own surroundings. From then on the Cordillera would never again look to me only as inoffensively beautiful and impressive, but also as awesome and mysterious, making it at some level of my mind even more seductive than before.

The second mountain experience of my school years, modest and quite commensurate with my own circumstances, happened when I was seventeen. Milena, still my mentor, and way ahead of me in virtually every respect, asked me one day whether I would like to go and climb the Manquehue with her the following Sunday. I was absolutely thrilled at the very idea of even trying to climb this one thousand meter high hill — or was it already a mountain? — adjacent to the San Cristobal but, to my eyes at least, towering over it. Since it exhibited no roads, no lifts and no statues of any description, I sensed that this was the real thing, true mountain climbing, as opposed to the Sunday morning strolls up the slopes of the San Cristobal. But, in addition, I was immensely flattered that my sophisticated cousin, already a medical student, would have thought of me of all people to be her companion in such a special and outstanding expedition.

I had no problems whatsoever deciding what the appropriate garb would be for our purposes because I simply didn't own sport clothes of any description. So, at the appointed time, I appeared wearing my brown school shoes, ankle socks, and a plain cotton summer dress. And off we took, each carrying a sandwich and some fruit, with Milena naturally leading the way. The beginning of the climb, through rather dense undergrowth and bushes, was hot and slow enough that I was convinced we would never reach what looked increasingly like an unreachable top. But we persevered, and things got somewhat easier and faster once we had left most of the vegetation behind, climbing up, step by step, with our noses virtually to the ground because of the rather steep slope, until we got to the top. I think that I persevered mainly because I felt I would rather die than quit in the presence of my superior cousin, whom I badly wanted to impress. And I apparently did because, once it was all over and we had returned to our respective homes, Milena told her older sister that she had been amazed at how strong a climber I was, especially since I had had no training or experience to speak of.

Now, if I were writing fiction rather than fact, I would undoubtedly describe in great detail and with all the skills at my command the glorious feeling of reaching the top of the Manquehue, of taking some time to contemplate the awesome beauty of the still taller peaks nearby from a completely new perspective, and whatever else people do and feel when they proudly stand on top of a peak and plant their flag. In my hapless actual case, the sad fact is that I don't remember the feat itself with any clarity, only that it happened. However, I do remember that the net result of climbing minor peaks or major hills, as in our case, is the full appreciation of how enormous the now much closer major peaks really are, thus turning what one imagined to be a major achievement into something quite modest, if not trivial. In other words, I now knew how puny the Manquehue felt next to the three or four thousand meter peaks nearby. And I also remember quite clearly how much faster and easier it was to come down than to go up the slope of the now cut-down-to-size Manquehue.

Further, the experience taught me with incontrovertible certainty the importance of one's previous experience, perspective or point of view, in the making of judgments. Because, when *tío* Antonio, Milena's father, learned of our rather innocent expedition, he was outraged. He raised hell with Milena about taking her younger cousin along on an expedition full of risks and totally unsuitable for two unaccompanied teenage girls. His indignation, however, had far more to do with potential sin than with the possible dangers of a bad fall, or of breaking a leg. I mean the sins and the crimes of men rather than our own, because his concern was all centered around potential kidnappers, rapists, and even murderers. I hate to admit, in retrospect, that he was probably right, but such is the nature of youth that not even the idea of such dangers crossed our minds, at least not mine. It seems that the challenge of a climb three times the size of any of my previous ones had engrossed me to the exclusion of everything else. But the idea of females as prey had been implanted, forever precluding the sense of unencumbered freedom to go wherever my individual desires and drives would take me. I would repeat a similar experience at least once more some time later, although the presence of fear of marauding men would corrupt its original sense of unadulterated adventure.

Oriana on a typical "excursion" in the cordillera.

During my first two years in university I never did anything as challenging as the climb of the Manquehue. My excursions, enjoyable as they were, consisted mainly of one day "paseos" or picnics to one spot or another in the foothills of the Cordillera with my classmates or, as I've already described, with Leonardo and Fusa. Until, in the summer of 1941, Fusa and I decided to go for a weekend to La Hermita. This was a spot with no more than two or three houses half way up the road to Farellones, a new and developing ski resort two thousand meters above Santiago. I think we had been there once before with Leonardo, but this time we would make it alone.

By now, three full years after the Manquehue expedition, we almost looked like true alpinists, fully equipped with proper walking boots, thick socks, shorts and knapsacks full of blankets and food. The one thousand meter climb to La Hermita, however, was a cinch compared to the Manquehue. It was just a hike, since we simply walked along the zigzagging dirt road that led to Farellones. But precisely because it zig-zags — thirty-five turns or so before it reaches La Hermita — it was a long walk in the hot sun, without a tree in sight to provide a rest in the shade. We must have been about three quarters of the way up, two or three hours later, when we heard the sound of horses behind us. It was two handsome huasos in full attire who promptly halted their horses when they reached us, and asked most politely where we were headed for. When they found out that it was La Hermita, they offered us a ride, because it was their home, they said, and we looked very tired. I presume Fusa had also already taken their measure because, as we looked at each other, we agreed simultaneously to accept the offer, and off we went, seated behind the riders.

Once we had reached La Hermita we thanked our huasos profusely for the welcome ride, while they tied their horses to a post in front of their adobe house. But, as we walked towards our previously chosen camp site we realized that the sun was gone and heavy dark clouds had appeared, presaging a rain storm. We didn't pay any attention, however, because, as everyone knew, it never rains there in the summer. Little did we know. We had barely begun to unpack and try to light a fire on the grounds of an abandoned farm house, not far away from the huasos' adobe house, when a heavy rain, which soon turned into hail, came pouring down. We were completely dumbfounded and totally unprepared for this tum of events because, as everybody knows, it just doesn't rain in those parts in the summer! We didn't have a tent or even a plain piece of canvas to take refuge under, and were pondering what to do next when somebody from the adobe house came to say we could come to their house while the rain lasted. We did, most gratefully, and that was the way that I found myself for the first time in my life inside a large adobe peasant hut.

A slightly built older woman, dressed in black, came to greet us at the door. Her sons, the huasos, had told her that two young girls from the city had come to camp in the surroundings, but in view of the heavy rain it would be best if we came in and had supper with them. In the circumstances, there was little choice but to accept this kind offer as graciously as we could, but I at least was beginning to feel very uneasy at the prospect of sharing a meal in such a setting. It was a comparatively large room with white-washed walls, a solidly packed and clean-swept dirt floor with a fire in one comer and a hole in the ceiling to allow the smoke out. Whatever light there was came from a small window high up on the front wall, and from one solitary candle sitting on a large long table to one side. The rest of the furniture consisted of two long benches, one along either side of the table, and half a dozen or so low stools with straw seats, scattered about.

I know that besides the woman and the huasos there were at least three other people present for supper. But, try as I may, I cannot recall them, or for that matter what we talked about before and during supper. I fear that all my emotional energy was concentrated first on trying to anticipate what kind of steaming concoction the woman was stirring in a large cauldron over the fire, and later on having to eat it without showing any sign of the suspicion and even dread that were increasingly seizing me. To this day I don't know for sure what we ate that night. All I do know is that, once we were all seated at the table, I was presented with a large soup bowl filled to the brim with something thick and smooth, and with a spoon. Since the gruel in question had no discernible smell and the lighting was so poor that I couldn't distinguish any color, it was left to my imagination to figure out the worst possible alternatives, including porridge, which I thoroughly hate. Having reflected upon this mysterious dish many times through my life, I've come to the conclusion that, in the absence of unfamiliar discreet chunks of any sort, such as rabbit or frog meat, and considering the abundance of corn in the region, it must have been corn meal, a perfectly acceptable dish, if only I had known that then. But I didn't, and so every spoonful became in fact a major effort to swallow.

This must have been a light evening meal for our hosts, as opposed to dinner at noon, because once the dish in question had been disposed of, we were all asked to leave the table and come and sit in a circle on the low stools for the nearly ritual drink of mate. Mate, much like tea, is a drink made with the dried leaves of a South American bush which contain caffeine. It is quite popular in the rural areas of Chile and neighboring countries, where it is invariably drunk in colorfully decorated gourds by pouring boiling water over the leaves and sucking the infusion through a straw or silver tube equipped with a fine sieve at the bottom. I hadn't even heard of mate since I had been a child in La Estrella, and had quite forgotten that among true Chileans, like our hosts, the gourd is passed around from person to person to sip, thus explaining the circle. When I saw our hostess, whose two front teeth were conspicuously missing, take the first sip and then pass the gourd to her immediate neighbor, I panicked. It was one thing to go through my mysterious gruel without much of a fuss. But to sip from a common straw was far too much. Since I was sitting exactly opposite the hostess I had enough time to whisper to Fusa, who was sitting next to me, that I was getting sick to my stomach, and to please explain that on strict doctor's orders I was never to even come near the stuff. To my profound relief Fusa did this so convincingly that our hostess nodded knowingly and smiled in such a way as to convey the notion that she was well aware of such conditions and, further, that she felt very sorry I couldn't partake of such a fine treat. As for me, all I can say is that this memorable dinner party is the closest I've ever come to total social disgrace and that, when it was all over, I felt as if I had been put through a grinder.

But we weren't through yet because our hospitable hosts were very concerned about where we would spend the night. At that point I prayed to God that they wouldn't invite us to share their beds in the dark. My prayers were answered immediately when the older woman suggested we might want to take refuge for the night in the abandoned farm house. It wasn't very clean, she explained, because it had gone unused for a long time, but at least it would be better than the wet outdoors, a shelter from the rain and the hail. When we agreed that was without question the perfect solution, our kind hostess sent one of the younger people with us to open the place. But not before we had warmly thanked her and her sons for all their kindness to us, poor stranded souls in the wild.

From the outside, earlier that day, the house had looked to us as a rather attractive, though clearly dilapidated place, with its white or light grey exterior and big paned windows. So it was with a light heart that we made the rather short trek from the adobe hut to our residence for the night. Once we were in, and only by the light of one miserable candle, we discovered to my horror that the floors were literally carpeted with rat droppings, and that the only piece of furniture in the whole place was a long narrow table equally carpeted. Since the rain had stopped we almost left in disgust but, on second thought, we decided that the rat infested indoors was preferable to a whole night on the very wet grounds. We cleaned the table and one side of the room as best we could, when Fusa decided that since I was more of a wimp than she was, she would sleep on the floor and I could have the table. Although I have slept on surfaces of every conceivable description, I have never slept on a table in the middle of a rat encampment before or since. That night I did, although probably not before counting rats instead of sheep, thousands of them.

The next day the sun was shining, and all was well with the world, when we realized we were alive and unbitten, and not the worse for wear. We washed in a nearby creek, changed into fresh clothes, and finally managed to light a fire to cook an oh! so welcome conventional and familiar breakfast. And, early in the afternoon, after saying good-bye to the good people next door, we set out on our long downhill walk back to Santiago. We wondered then, I still do, what these good people thought of two young women, one tall and fair, the other clearly oriental, wandering on foot and alone in the wilderness. Did they think, I wonder, that had it not been for their help we might have perished? It is more plausible, I suppose, that they thought, as I am doing now, that we were simply a little bit crazy, if not just plain dumb foreigners. And as for us, we had survived, hadn't we? And we had quite a story to tell in the bargain.

My acquaintance with the Cordillera and with myself, with my own drives, skills, limitations and stamina, changed radically when Raquel and I, as well as a few other friends, decided to join the Ski Branch of the Sports Club of the University of Chile. This happened in 1942, when we were taking the fourth and last year of our regular course. The Ski Branch, which, like the FECH, held regular evening meetings downtown, consisted of a very enthusiastic group of students from every faculty. And, unlike the FECH and its political strifes, it was solidly united for the main purpose of enabling its members to pursue serious mountaineering and skiing at a minimal cost. Although formally affiliated with the University, it functioned quite autonomously, its president, secretary, treasurer and other officials being students. For that very reason, it was also clearly democratic, in that every member had a voice and a right to vote on all major decisions.

At the time we joined, in the winter of 1942, the main activity was to organize weekend skiing excursions to Farellones, the nearest and most accessible resort. Since the Ski Branch was new, and its members not particularly affluent, we owned neither a hostel in Farellones nor our own means of transportation. For this reason, most of our expeditions were just for the day, on Sundays. We used to gather at a prearranged central location early in the morning and climb onto an open truck fitted with four parallel wooden benches the length of the truck's platform, capable of accomodating up to thirty or so of us, needless to say with the help of a great deal of good will. Our skis and our knapsacks, filled with food and water for the day, were placed wherever there was room left, mainly in the way of our feet, under the benches.

The trucks themselves were, of course, rented and often in pretty poor shape since it was the middle of the War and all imported vehicles were at a premium, or simply nonexistent. Under normal circumstances this would have been par for the course, but the road to Farellones was anything but normal. It was a one-lane affair with a steep wall to one side and a precipice to the other, that zig-zagged seventy-two times before reaching Farellones, two thousand meters above the outskirts of the city. Here and there, it widened just enough to allow vehicles coming in the opposite direction to pass, and here and there there were short stretches covered with gravel for better traction. I have nothing but the greatest admiration and boundless gratitude for the hired drivers of the trucks who maneuvered these jalopies with the precision and elegance of figure skaters. But still, if one was sitting near the tail end of the truck when it backed out over the precipice — often several times over — to negotiate any one of those seventy-two hairpin bends, one prayed, despite one's acknowledged atheism. Of course nobody, especially the boys, would ever admit to being afraid, but the disproportionately loud laughter at the mildest joke, or the enthusiasm with which we sang invigorating songs, especially those great songs of the Spanish Civil War, betray quite the contrary.

But we invariably made it quite safely to Farellones, except for once, two or three years after my first trip. On this occasion, we were only a few hundred yards from our destination when the truck, which had been moodily sputtering and spewing steam from its front end for some time, suddenly stopped altogether. Sergio Badilla, our leader on this particular trip, came to us after some serious consultations with the driver, to ask us to disembark and walk the rest of the way. The radiator had cracked and lost all its water, he said. And so we did, obediently, when, having reached the top, going cross-country, we saw the truck jerking and sputtering and finally coming to a halt at the top end of the road. I ran and hugged Sergio, the hero of the moment, and then stopped abruptly when I smelled what appeared to be huge amounts of alcohol in his breath. "You are soused!" I shouted. "You are completely drunk! Shame on you!" "I'm not drunk!" he shouted back, quite earnestly, "The truck is!" And the poor truck was, indeed. For lack of water, he and the driver had poured red wine into the radiator to allow it to cool down enough to complete the trip, but by now it was happily boiling and spewing its vapors in all directions. That is how, in order to save the truck, we sacrificed our precious cargo of red wine. And this is the worst that ever happened to us during all those years of countless trips up and down that incomparable road.

When occasionally we went for an overnight trip, we used a shack which had originally been built to store machinery for the ski lift. It was a wooden affair, no more than twenty by fifteen feet, with a tin roof and enough gaps between boards to allow for ventilation and for the snow to come in if there was a strong enough wind. It had a door but no windows, a counter, a sawdust stove and a dirt floor on which we all slept wrapped in our improvised blanket sacks, except for the rich among us, who had regular and utterly enviable sleeping bags. It was usually so crowded at night that when anyone turned in their sleep, everyone else had to follow suit, and turn in the same direction. How we washed, dressed and undressed, or how the boys shaved and so on, is quite beyond me now, because we had no toilet, running water or electricity. Just a paraffin lamp which was turned on for a while before we went to bed. Probably we sang our beloved Spanish Civil War songs again, just to give us courage.

The fact is, however, that despite these crowded and primitive conditions and all the young blood circulating about, everyone behaved with decorum and consideration, according to our own self-imposed rules. No practical jokes in bad taste, no fighting and, above all, no hanky-panky of any sort was allowed, let alone condoned. But there were arguments about everything, from politics to the best way of waxing skis and, naturally, about whose turn was next on the stove. Except for coffee, I never bothered cooking anything, since sandwiches, cheese, chicken legs and fruit were plenty for an overnight excursion. But some, especially among the boys, seemed to relish the idea of cooking the most improbable mixtures of things over the sawdust stove, the results being somewhat reminiscent of the gruel at La Hermita. I would then go out and glory in the crisp fresh air outside, never mind how cold it was.

Our shack was in a prime location, just at the top end of La Gran Bajada, the main downhill run of Farellones. Farellones itself, now a posh and flourishing winter resort, was then a comparatively small mountain village, a grouping of thirty or so privately owned and very smart Swiss chalets, one equally smart but small private club called, in English, the Ski Club and an inn, La Posada. None of this was, obviously, accessible to us, but the only two runs then in operation were. La Gran Bajada (The Big Downhill), for the more experienced skiers, was quite steep and reasonably long, while La Cancha de los Tontos (The Simpletons' Run), always crowded with novices like myself and most of my friends, was pathetically flat and short. Even so, it presented me with enough challenges to my nonexistent skills, and to my cheap and more or less improvised equipment, to keep me busy for more than one winter.

If it is true that my new status of "affluence" now permitted me the luxury of even thinking about skiing — still largely a sport of the rich at that time — it is equally true that, in keeping with our means of transportation and accommodation, I could only afford the cheapest possible equipment. I think it would be more accurate to say that I had to push my heavy wooden skis downhill, than that they carried me like wings over the ice and snow. And my equally heavy and coarse leather ski boots had been made to match. There was absolutely no danger that I would ever slide at great speed towards the edge of a precipice and beyond. I would have sunk in the snow like a stone long before. And I did, more times than I care to count. And when I did, my "ski" pants, made by myself, I'm proud to say, from a loosely woven wool fabric which I had got from The League of Poor Students, absorbed the snow and the moisture like a sponge, as did my equally self-made knitted sweater. In the end, it is no wonder that I never got very far, since I must have weighed a ton on each of these outings.

We learned the rudiments of skiing from whoever among us knew, or claimed to know, more than the others because, naturally, we couldn't afford formal instructors. By the end of that first season I had managed to learn to stop without necessarily falling on my bum, and to climb up to the starting line without, Sisyphus-like, sliding back further than I had climbed. I was rather surprised, if not shocked, when I eventually had to admit to myself that I was not a natural at this sport. If running and bicycling had seemed as easy as breathing from the beginning, skiing felt alien, and even contrived and cumbersome, by comparison. I could not reproduce on skis that delicious sensation of going downhill on a bicycle, this being one of my major motivations to try the sport to begin with. But I kept on trying for quite some time, hoping that practice would make the difference. It didn't. I suspect that the fear of falling and breaking every bone in my body was stronger than I would then have admitted. I may add, as a consolation to my somewhat bruised ego, that the skiing talents of many of my friends were not that much better either. But, all in all, my newly discovered snow activities were tremendous fun, especially since, in addition, they took place with a great group of people which included some of my old friends, as well as new ones acquired in the process.

Raquel, my best friend, was the first among them, and I shared with her the planning, the decisions, the shopping, the food, and everything else related to these excursions, as well as the never-ending exchange of ideas and impressions, and even gossip, once they were over. This was enormously important to both of us because the men outnumbered the women by a ratio of probably seven to three, at least at the beginning. Since we were clearly at the stage of actively looking for mates, whether consciously or unconsciously, a close and trusting relationship with someone of the same gender was crucial to feel secure, comfortable and supported but, above all, to share the whole experience with an equal at the deepest, though not sexual, level. This, Raquel and I found in each other, much as we already had in our studies and in our social and cultural life down in the city. Several members of our group in Santiago, especially Myriam and Sergio, were also active members of the skiing group to which Adela Ohlbaum would soon be added.

Adela, who would become one of my best and longest lasting friends, was two years younger, and consequently two years behind us in university. She and Wanda, my old high school friend, had registered in a newly created chemistry course at the Instituto Pedagógico, and transferred to the School of Chemistry and Pharmacy two years later, when their course was cancelled. It was approximately at that time that she became a member of our circle and began to share with us in our professional, cultural, social, political and sports interests, and in my view at least, became the sort of glue that kept the group together for a long time. To complete the cosmopolitan nature of my circle of friends, she was a bona fide Hungarian, who had come to Chile with her Jewish family when she was a small girl. But by the time I met her she was a total Chilean, deeply interested in the fate of her adopted country, and genuinely committed to the left in politics. Broad-minded and tolerant enough of my skeptical and critical attitudes, however, to buy and give me a Bible once when, walking along Vicuña Mackenna, we had seen a display of Bibles in a shop window. She was smart, quick and intensely keen about whatever caught her interests, and much less tormented than I by intellectual questioning and doubts. Equally important to me, she was also warm, caring and immensely generous though, fortunately for me, I don't think she ever took me as seriously as I did myself.

Building the Refugio

Ｎone of the men in the ski group was a particularly close friend at this point. Our interactions occurred almost exclusively during the Sundays or weekends at Farellones, and once a week at our evening meetings in Santiago, to discuss the business of the Ski Branch and forthcoming expeditions. After the meetings we would often go to a rather cheap cafe nearby to talk and dance by the music of a juke-box, social activities which might have led to closer relationships, but hadn't yet. On the other hand, these meetings during the winter of 1942 were becoming increasingly exciting. Somehow the idea of building a big *refugio* (hostel) for the students of the University of Chile had been suggested and taken root, and the group was consequently a hive of activity, initiatives, projects and dreams.

Since I personally didn't take part in this phase of the proceedings, I don't know the details of exactly how our leaders persuaded so many outfits to contribute, but they did. First, and most importantly, the problem was to secure an appropriate site in the still uncrowded Farellones. We felt extremely fortunate when it was announced at one of our meetings that Don Benjamín Claro Velasco, then closely associated with the University's Sports Club and later to become the Minister of Education, had donated his own personal property for our use. It was a prime site, just a few yards from our shack, consisting of an almost semicircular lot following the contours of a slope right in the middle of Farellones and overlooking the Santiago valley.

There was only one condition imposed by this inspired and generous man.

He would give us the lot provided we, the students, committed ourselves to do all the work. I don't know the particulars, but I presume that a formal contract was signed to this effect. There was enormous rejoicing at this news, of course, probably at least in part because the enormity of our own commitment had not yet sunk in, or was not yet fully understood. Soon afterwards we heard that a major copper mine not far away from Farellones, our plutocratic neighbors, were to donate an expensive copper roof for our refugio. Now we could visualize, as in an ultrasound image, the feet and the hat, if not the head, of our dream refugio. Subsequently, many other materials and fixtures were given to us free of charge by other donors. Don Enrique Marshall, Minister of Education, and Don Juvenal Hernandez, the President of the University, gave invaluable encouragement and support.

Once the lot had been secured, a competition was held in the School of Architecture for the best plan for an appropriate hostel. But the winning plan was apparently so ambitious, at least in size, that it failed to fit into our comparatively small lot. And so it was that three of my architect friends designed a new and more realistic plan to house between 250 and 300 people, and this was the blueprint that was subsequently implemented.

By the summer of 1943 we were willing and ready to begin making our own contribution of brains and muscle power. The first ground-breaking expedition was organized in January of that year, once our final examinations were all over. It consisted of thirteen men and two women. Following the conventional distribution of labor by gender, the men were going to dig the holes for the foundations, and the women, Raquel and I, to do the cooking and general housekeeping for the whole group. We all stayed together in our already nearly legendary shack, which we used only to sleep and change, since all the cooking and eating was done outside, something made possible only by the glorious weather.

The trip up to Farellones should have been easier than in winter since there were no skis or heavy knapsacks to carry, and only fifteen of us. But it wasn't, because virtually all the extra space was now filled with building equipment and with countless sacks of rice, potatoes, beans, lentils, onions, sugar and so on, to feed all these hungry and hard-working men for at least a week, until new provisions would arrive. Raquel and I should have been intimidated by the sheer volume of all the food we would have to process somehow before it could be eaten, but we were far too innocent and ignorant of what was to come to pay much attention. On the contrary, I felt literally on top of the world, sitting on a sack of slightly shifting but smooth lentils.

Once we had arrived, unpacked and stored the loot wherever there was some space, we built a stone fire-pit outside, near the front door, because the old sawdust stove inside was totally inadequate for the coming onslaught. I can no longer recall what Raquel and I thought we were getting into. The fact is that the only qualifications either of us had to volunteer for this job was the simple fact that we were women, as if there were a female gene for peeling potatoes or for making a soup. Neither of us had had any serious experience of cooking, let alone cooking for more than a dozen men engaged in hard labor, and under the most primitive conditions.

My own experience was limited to the preparation of dainty hors d'oeuvres and desserts in our home economics classes in high school, and to the rare occasions when my mother would ask me to help in the kitchen. But I had never, ever, cooked a whole meal from scratch for anybody, let alone fifteen people. I'm quite sure that Raquel's experience was equally limited. However, neither of us had any doubts about our ability to live up to the task ahead, or was tormented by any feelings of inadequacy. After all, the boys had never built anything either, not even a doghouse, I'm sure.

And so the first week began and we produced three meals a day of which we were quite proud, because they were not only good and nutritious, but even sophisticated, considering the conditions. In addition, the boys had requested "ulpo" at midmorning, as a fortifying snack to supplement the comparatively light breakfast. Ulpo is a local Indian food made simply by mixing coarsely ground roasted wheat with water or milk, and sugar. We made it with water, and thin enough to drink, thus dispensing with plates and spoons. So, every morning at eleven, either Raquel or I would go down the hundred-yard stretch to the building site, and deliver a couple of pails full of ulpo to our hard-working male counterparts and, in the process, check on their progress.

I'm quite sure they were doing the job with just pickaxes and shovels, because I do not recall any mechanized equipment around. Consequently, the progress of which I speak seemed painfully slow, especially when compared to the swiftness with which we, with equally primitive tools, were producing all those splendid meals several times a day! When I consider that we had to prepare enormous amounts of soups, stews, salads, mashed potatoes and so on, bending over an open fire which coated everything, including ourselves, with soot; that we had no tables to work on, and no shelves to store the stuff; and that even the water had to be brought over from the nearest, but still far-off, tap in pails (only the fancy refugios had running water), I can't help but wonder at our resilience and stamina, especially in view of the results.

Raquel and I were quite pleased with our cooking when, three or four days into our period of service, the foreman of the crew requested a meeting with the two of us. We were sure he wanted to compliment us, or at least to express his and the crew's thanks for our efforts, but, in great embarrassment, he told us he had come on behalf of the crew to complain and request some radical changes in the menu. Swallowing nervously, blushing and stuttering, the poor man explained that although the boys had nothing but admiration for our culinary talents and for the imagination, sophistication and delicacy of our near-gourmet meals, they were, to put it mildly, just plain hungry. The last thing in the world they wanted to do was to offend us. But, could we please forget the mayonnaise, the clear soups, the light salads and so on, and give them beans, large amounts of beans, every day if possible. We should realize, shouldn't we, that they, the diggers, were spending huge amounts of energy, and that energy had to be replenished daily, or they would all either perish or at least be rendered totally unable to continue with their commitment to the cause.

I had always known, of course, that men eat enormous amounts of food compared to women, but had invariably concluded that it was simply gluttony on their part. Gluttony not confined only to food, but to many other bodily and mental functions. But as a physiologist in the making, I had also learned, though only recently, that the basal metabolism of men is higher than that of women, and that consequently they require a higher intake of energy-providing food, to say nothing of the extra energy needed when the expenditure, as in the case at hand, is substantially higher because of the extra physical exertion. But apparently this had just remained sheer theory, until we were confronted with the reality of his semi-starved crew. He was immensely relieved of his fears, both of offending us and of the fate of his crew, when we promptly reassured him that, having understood his predicament, we would immediately change the menu as he had requested.

And so we did, but not before we had tried to console each other about our bruised pride, or perhaps even vanity, concerning the implied lack of appreciation of our culinary talents, by thinking "Why can't a man be more like a woman!" But beans we cooked, day in, day out. All kinds of beans. And when we ran out of beans it was chick peas, and then lentils, and then back to beans, until we had emptied all the sacks we had brought with us. To add insult to injury, we had to clean these things, handful by handful, of small stones, twigs and other extraneous debris in their midst, before soaking them overnight to soften them, and then boiling them for hours because of the high altitude. My original dislike for beans was so markedly accentuated by this experience that I refused to eat beans for years afterwards.

But life went on, until one day Raquel and I looked at each other and agreed, almost simultaneously, that we were dirty, filthy dirty, and probably stinking. There is hardly any vegetation at those altitudes in the Andes and, "as everybody knows, it never rains in the summer in those parts". The dryness of the place, the relentless sun, working all day around that hot fire, and the lack of facilities to wash, had all combined to make us as dirty as we had ever been. After a few inquiries, we were told that a sort of general caretaker of the fancy refugios might let us into one of them to have a shower. We found the man, and after we had explained who we were - it seems that the label of "university student" was a passport to everywhere - he let us into Dr. Orrego Puelma's refugio. He apparently didn't mind lending his place for respectable, even laudable, purposes. It was a lovely place, a dream place in that location, but we were in such urgent need of getting cleaned up that we hardly paid any attention, except for the bathroom and its shower.

Oh what a glorious feeling! To get rid of our sweaty filthy clothes, to soap all over from head to toes, to let the warm water run over our bodies for minutes on end, to dry slowly, conscientiously, and then to get into clean shorts and blouse, seemed and felt as the greatest treat ever. I've been dirty, badly in need of a shower many times before and after. But no other shower has ever come even close to that one, at the refugio of Dr. Orrego Puelma. We should have sent him the warmest of thank-you notes, but I don't think we even knew then whose shower it was that had provoked such inordinate pleasure. I found out only recently from his son Hector, who became a good friend many years later.

It was nearly supper time when we walked up to our shack, where someone else was stirring the beans over the fire. I don't know about Raquel, but I do know for sure that I've never ever made such a splendid entrance anywhere. The boys, back from their day's work, were milling about, waiting for supper. When they saw us they jumped to their feet, exclaiming such things as: "What has happened! What. . .is the Minister coming to inspect our work? Where have you been! You look wonderful! You are beautiful! What a change!", and so on. Compared to them, even filthier than we had been, and with a week-old growth of beard, we indeed looked gorgeous, and we knew it.

But after the clamor had subsided, and the appropriate explanations had been given, nothing else was said about our new looks. The next afternoon, however, the noise from the building site seemed to have stopped earlier than usual. Not long afterwards, Raquel and I, who were sitting outside minding the fire, saw one of the boys climbing up towards the shack. We did a double take when we realized that he too looked gorgeous. He had shaved, his slightly wavy brown hair was wet against his scalp, and he was wearing clearly clean and fresh shirt and slacks. "Guillermo", we cried, "You've had a shower!" "Yes" he said, "but not only me. Just wait!" We didn't have long to wait to see the other twelve of them come up, one by one, looking as fresh and beautiful as we ourselves had looked the day before. This was a triumphant case of persuasion by example only, because neither Raquel nor I had said a word to any of them the day before. But they now explained that the contrast between them and us had been enough to make them realize how offensively filthy they had been, and had made them decide to take the drastic measure of getting all cleaned up. After that, we all rejoiced together, and proceeded to eat our beans while smelling like roses.

At the end of two weeks Raquel left because she had other commitments in Santiago, but no one else came to replace her. Since I had volunteered for a month, I was now alone with my thirteen boys. We all agreed immediately that it would be impossible for me to do all the cooking alone, I clearly needed an assistant. Carnio, a dentistry student, volunteered to help me for the first week.

Oriana and her new assistant cooking for the builders of the Refugio.

Raquel and I had obviously shared our jobs as equals, but now I found myself in the unusual and privileged position of being the boss, of having an assistant rather than a partner, a staff of one at my command. I enjoyed this unprecedented experience enormously, especially since Carnio, probably quite devoid of any cooking experience, had to follow my instructions rather than contribute his knowledge and expertise. But, being a very good-natured young man, he did this with great good humor until one day when, after the crew had swallowed the first few mouthfuls of our cabbage stew, it became quite evident that something had gone deadly wrong. I looked at them, looked at the slightly foamy surface of the stew in the cauldron, and quickly tasted a spoonful myself. Soap! That was it! The taste and smell of cheap coarse laundry soap had overwhelmed any other subtle flavors that our laboriously prepared cabbage stew may have had.

My consternation at this disastrous development was such that I cannot remember anything else about this episode. Was the offending bar of soap ever found? If so, how on earth did it ever get there? Was it sabotage on the part of someone else deviously aspiring to displace Carnio and become my assistant? Had I been so tired and exausted that I had tried to wash my hands in the stew? Short of making a pilgrimage to Chile to locate and interview the surviving members of that legendary crew, I shall never know what happened. Neither, most regrettably, shall I ever know what Carnio and I did that night to quench the hunger of our famished clients, as well as our own. Tomorrow, no doubt, would be another day, when the two of us would be allowed to resume our cooking duties if for no other reason than the total lack of alternative options. Till the end of that week, when another member of the group would be substituted for Carnio.

In retrospect I realize that I didn't know any of the members of the crew well at all, since none of my own friends was included. I knew them only superficially, as members of our club, and this applied equally to Guillermo, of whom I knew only that he was a law student, vaguely associated with the university communist group before my time, and a terrific dancer. I had seen him dance a few times with his very attractive steady girlfriend at balls in our school, which I occasionally attended as almost the official wallflower girl, because this was before I had been inducted into the dancing corps by my own friends. I had been most impressed by the grace, vigor and agility with which this glamorous couple manoeuvered through all kinds of exotic rhythms, especially American swing, then very much in vogue. Our own version of Fred Astaire and Ginger Rogers.

They were so good together that the rest of the crowd would occasionally stop and let them put on a show to the delight, and no doubt a touch of admiration and envy, of everyone else. To me, their skills, glamor and even more, their clear ease and absence of inhibitions to put on these shows were as mysterious and seemingly unattainable as beauty, or wealth, or brilliance. In these realms I knew I would always be the eager but ambivalent spectator, never the participant. But, in the summer of 1943, here he was, the Fred Astaire of my jurisdiction, quite willing to peel potatoes, chop onions, clean the beans of their debris, tend the fire and haul the water, in his capacity as my very own assistant.

I've just realized that the simile with Fred Astaire is not as far-fetched as it sounds in that it applied not only to the dancing but also to the looks. Like Astaire, Guillermo was strong, lean, wiry and graceful as a cat, although perhaps not as tall, certainly not as tall as me, just tall enough. His features, except for the light brown wavy hair, were also reminiscent of Astaire's, but a little less angular, like a handsomer younger brother. To complete the picture, his seemingly innate sense of taste, rather than his clothes, made him appear elegant, a sort of casual outdoorish elegance accentuated by his nearly permanent tan.

This much I knew of the man with whom I would spend all my working hours during that last week of my tenure as a cook in Farellones. Guillermo was no sweet Carnio, I soon discovered. He had very definite and strong ideas about cooking and about everything else, and not the slightest reticence to express them. He had in fact been the perpetrator of those weird concoctions over the sawdust stove earlier in the winter, during our skiing excursions. As a result, our verbal interactions were as quick and forceful as table tennis matches, but in the end, perhaps because of my greater depth of experience in the cooking arts, I generally prevailed. At least there was no obvious change in our fare, and no complaints from our clients.

What was changing, however, was my sense of being a woman. For the first time during that month, and for that matter for the first time during all of those previous trips to the mountains, I began to feel, subtly and nearly imperceptibly at first, and then quite clearly, that I was being perceived as a woman instead of as just one more neuter member of a group dedicated primarily to the enjoyment of the mountains. The reverse was equally true. I was perceiving Guillermo along another dimension from the rest of the crew. Somehow he made sure that I knew I was in the company of a man, although nothing overt or explicit was ever said or done. But, since I understood he was involved in a serious relationship, I didn't dwell any further on his or my own feelings.

When the week was up, I left with my filthy and skimpy belongings in yet another of those notorious trucks, and with a keen sense of the need for one of my mother's good meals, a hot bath and a clean bed. Whatever feelings of accomplishment might have been associated with this rather unusual sojourn of mine, I feel them much more clearly now than then, when all there was to show for my efforts was the fact that the crew had survived instead of dying of inanition. And, indirectly, a very unimpressive hole in the ground, a mere dent on a tiny slope of the Cordillera. I would return many times to the site of my travails in Farellones, but never to work there again.

This, as well as the construction proper, was left to newer generations of students. The whole project was now organized ambitiously if not "pretentiously", as one of my oldest friends has recently qualified it. There was a General Directorate, as well as Departments of Engineering, Administration and Budget. The former was in turn divided into Works, Materials, Personnel and Finances. Several of my friends, including Myriam, Sergio and Chito - the architects - Raquel in Administration, and Julio Magri as Director General from March of 1944 onwards, would play key roles in the enterprise. By the winter of 1946, when I last saw it, the heavy construction was completed, and today this large and impressive building stands in the middle of a vastly enlarged winter resort in what is referred to as Old Farellones. A big sign in front proudly announces: REFUGIO DE LA FEDERACION DE ESTUDIANTES DE CHILE. But I wonder whether any of its present guests has the slightest idea of how and when it all began.

Oriana surveying the progress of the Refugio
in a later stage of its construction.

Farellones, where at night one can see the lights of Santiago two thousand meters below, is the crossroads to paths leading to a number of higher peaks above, ranging from the comparatively modest Colorado at three thousand meters, to the impressive Plomo at more than five thousand. As such, Farellones becomes the base camp for many climbing expeditions in the summer. Needless to say, we were so busy digging during that summer of 1943 that not even the thought of climbing anything ever even crossed our minds. Some of my friends would do this later on, but not me. Mountain hiking, as opposed to climbing, could be done in various directions, both from Santiago itself or from Farellones, to relatively modest altitudes. This, of course, I did many times and continued to find the experience most enjoyable, but also sobering.

I eventually found out, however, that I didn't have the soul of a climber, a real mountaineer. If I had ever entertained any dreams of reaching the top of important peaks, I had given them up by the time of which I write. Anything beyond two thousand meters became so laborious and painful that, at least for me, the payoff was not worth the effort. If only I could have accumulated climbing credits - as one can accumulate credits in other kinds of activities such as writing - I'm quite sure I would have reached the top of the Aconcagua before I got too old to climb anything. At the rate of a thousand meters per weekend, but provided I could start the next time from where I left off the week before, I could have done the Aconcagua in seven weeks, and proudly become the Queen of the Andes! But, alas, there are no such credits, and so it was that the highest point I ever reached - on skiis in another winter excursion a couple of years later - was four thousand meters, beginning from the three thousand level.

I don't think I realized then, as I do now with outstanding clarity, that my relative lack of stamina, shown through my mountain experiences, applies equally to many other totally sedentary activities, and that therefore I can't even invoke physiological deficits in self-defence. I work or exert myself in spurts, intermittent bursts of effort, rather than on a continuous and sustained smooth line. No marathon runner I, just a sprinter.

My mother, who never seems to have asked many questions about my rather unorthodox behavior and activities, thought that I looked very healthy, if rather unkempt. My acquaintance with a mirror, on the other hand, was somewhat shocking at first. I looked like a red Indian with a straw hat. My skin was not just coppery-brown, but tanned like leather, and my hair was bleached to a very light blonde, so dry that it had lost all its silkiness and stood on end wherever I placed it. But now it was time for this wild-looking creature from the mountains to put that challenging summer behind, try to look normal, and face the very serious business of her studies and, she hoped, of the beginning of her budding career as a scientist.

The First Research Steps

I had finished the regular undergraduate course very much as I had begun. High marks in those disciplines that interested me, and passing marks in the others. There were two further requirements before graduation. A thesis based on an original experimental research project, and six months of practice in a Pharmacy. Only when these requirements were fulfilled could we face a comprehensive final oral examination and graduate. I naturally looked forward very much to the thesis work, but not at all to the practice. During the four-year course I had definitely decided not only that pharmacy, either as a profession or as a business, was not for me, but also that it was clearly becoming an obsolete discipline. In my view, drugs and their formulations would soon be manufactured in large pharmaceutical firms instead of in small quaint corners of drugstores, thus rendering the "pharmacists", as we knew them, rather redundant.

Needless to say, such views did not make me particularly popular with some of my professors. Once, when I expressed them within hearing distance of one of our Organic Chemistry professors, a proud pharmacist, he came towards our bench during a lab course in pharmacy and, quite indignantly said: "Miss Josseau, you will be a disgrace to our noble profession!" I decided on the spot that he was a lost cause, unworthy of my lucid arguments, and so I was content with mumbling to myself, like Galileo, "However, that is the way things are."

None of the courses in fourth year turned out to be as interesting or inspiring as organic chemistry and later physiology had been. The closest might have been clinical chemistry but, as taught, it was solely a collection of analytical techniques applied to body fluids and tissues. As I recall, it lacked the necessary theoretical biochemistry context to turn it into a dynamic exciting discipline. In the circumstances, my decision to do my thesis at the Institute of Physiology, where I already had a foothold, was easy. Even though I was fully and painfully aware that I lacked the proper background to feel comfortable, the subject matter, living mechanisms, was fascinating, and the place, for the reasons I've already described, the best if not the only one where I could try my hand at research.

When I made my views known to Dr. Middleton, he immediately agreed with my intended plans but, as he explained, he would be away for a year in the United States, sponsored by the Rockefeller Foundation. Therefore, in the interim I would assist Dr.Talesnik, who would be left in charge of the physiology course, and otherwise respond directly to Dr.Hoffmann. And so it was that Dr. Hoffmann became my thesis director, and that my first in-depth academic relationship was established. This was both a privilege and a source of many tribulations on my part. A privilege because of the prized opportunity of making my first steps in research under the guidance of one of the best research scientists in the country. A source of much anxiety because I didn't think or feel that my training so far would be up to his expectations. I was quite right on the first count, especially when considering the fact that to his knowledge and experience were added those of Dra. Hoffmann, since they worked closely together in all their research projects. This circumstance added even further to my sense of being in a privileged position since I gradually realized that her theoretical depth in scientific matters was even greater than his. But at the same time, and for that very reason, it also aggravated my disturbing sense of insecurity to new and very troublesome levels.

In hindsight I realize that most of my anxiety on those counts was quite unnecessary. The Hoffmanns at that point did not expect me to have any profound knowledge of physiology or biochemistry which would allow me to ask profound and relevant scientific questions. That was their job. Of me, as it turned out, they only expected sufficient familiarity with chemical methods to tackle experimentally the questions they had raised. My scientific life would have been a great deal easier if, having understood this important point, I had been content with acting as their right chemi-arm, and not much more. From a practical point of view that is exactly what happened. Once my research project had been defined by them, I went to work as an analytical chemist of body tissues with relative ease. And yet, throughout the year and a half that the project lasted, I could not shake off the uncomfortable feeling that I was not on top of the problem, that I didn't comprehend, in depth, the context of the question, and that, therefore, I could not have asked the question myself, to begin with.

Oriana, with the determined look of a
would-be scientist while working on her thesis

What I didn't know then, and nobody bothered to tell me, was that that is the norm, that beginning graduate students rarely arrive with grand questions ready at hand with which to shake the scientific community. They arrive empty handed instead, are presented with usually a small, limited number of questions formulated by their supervisors, from which they select what they like best, and then set out to work. It is during the course of that work that, if they are any good, they will become gradually and increasingly familiar with the field, to eventually reach the point of maturity necessary to formulate new and exciting questions themselves. This, of course, applies to Ph.D. students but, not even knowing anything about graduate work abroad, I was applying these standards to my own piddling and utterly modest undergraduate thesis.

These feverish and unnecessarily ambitious and unrealistic expectations of myself were in fact aided and abetted by the presence at the Institute of at least two medical students who were doing their undergraduate theses more or less at the same time, Osvaldo Cori and Teresa Pinto. By definition, both of them were already far more familiar with the biological sciences than I was, a fact that greatly facilitated their understanding of physiology as a whole, and of the particular areas of research being carried out at the Institute. And, as their subsequent careers would prove, they were brilliant to boot.

With Osvaldo Cori, giving a "thumbs up".

To complicate matters even further, Osvaldo, the son of a very affluent Valparaíso family, had had his own chemistry lab at home since he was a boy. This luxury toy had of course provided him with unequalled opportunities to become familiar with both the theory and the practice of chemistry. Furthermore, he could read the scientific literature with far greater ease than I since, by the time he joined the Institute, he could speak English, German, French and Italian, in addition to his native Spanish. Teresa Pinto, the charming child of a distinguished family who counted one or two Presidents of Chile among her ancestors, was no budding chemist or linguist but, having chosen neurophysiology as her field of interest, was right in her element at the Institute, and later in important centers abroad.

And that was my problem. If I had soon realized that measuring my worth against the Hoffmanns was foolish, I couldn't help but compare my skills and achievements with those of my own peers as, alas, we are all so prone to doing. However, and even though the comparison, especially with Osvaldo, frequently left me at a disadvantage, I decided to do the best I could in my narrow little corner, and learn and study as much as possible to enlarge my theoretical comprehension of the field in which I found myself working.

It was a slow task. The Hoffmanns had decided early on to have all the staff work in the same field, to wit, the function and effects of the thyroid gland on the body. This was very wise on at least two counts. First, it allowed for a pooling of knowledge and expertise, facilitating cross-pollination among the various project staff and, secondly, it made the best use of resources and other practical matters in an otherwise small and not particularly well endowed group of laboratories. But, perhaps most importantly, this choice was almost an excuse to study virtually every function of the body, since the hormone produced by the thyroid gland seems to affect them all. The Hoffmanns themselves seemed to be most interested in the effects of either a deficiency or an excess of thyroxine, the thyroid hormone, on the functions of the nervous system.

It was well known at that time that nerve stimulation in animals that had been made hyperthyroid, by giving them an excess amount of thyroxine, releases toxic substances into the body with effects similar to those of cobra venom. It was also known that cholesterol, a rather obscure substance at the time, can bind chemically to the toxins of cobra venom, thus neutralizing it and rendering it non-toxic. So, the Hoffmanns postulated that the cholesterol already present in the body, especially in the central nervous system of hyperthyroid animals, might do the same thing. If that were so, they suggested to me, the amounts of cholesterol chemically bound or "esterified" to these toxins might be much higher in the nervous system of hyperthyroid than of normal animals. Consequently, the "free" or non-bound cholesterol would be simultaneously present in much smaller amounts. All that was needed, they thought, was simply to measure the concentrations of free and esterified cholesterol in the nervous tissues of normal, hypothyroid and hyperthyroid animals, to either prove or disprove this working hypothesis.

My task, said the Hoffmanns, was to develop reliable methods to extract and then measure accurately the amounts of these two types of cholesterol contained in the brain and nerves of rats. Easier said than done. I was confronted with at least two problems from the start. First, understanding the hypothesis, the theoretical background behind it. And, secondly, transfering the chemical techniques described in English in esoteric journals to the practice and reality of our very modestly equipped laboratory.

Since my training in endocrinology, of which the functions of the thyroid gland are only a part, amounted at the time to no more than a couple of formal lectures, I was in no position to understand this fancy hypothesis with any degree of clarity or depth. This inevitably meant that I was deprived of the intellectual excitement generated by seeking an answer to a novel question firmly based on previously accumulated knowledge. Such excitement is, of course, all-important in scientific research. It is the propeller, the source of impulse that motivates the researcher. In such a situation I had little option but to take the Hoffmans at their word, while, as the work proceeded, I tried to find my way through the all-necessary background literature.

But we, as undergraduates, were ill-equipped to do this because, remarkably, we had not been taught how to use the published literature for research purposes. Except for three or four textbooks, which dealt only with generalities, we knew nothing about scientific journals, or about how to search for specific topics in the myriad of publications available. Since neither of the Hoffmanns made any particular effort to enlighten me along these lines, I had to find my own way by observing what they and the other staff did, by asking questions, and basically by tedious and inefficient trial and error. But somehow, by the time I had completed the experimental part of my thesis, I was conversant enough with the theory to write my own introduction more or less convincingly.

The experimental part was another matter since it was in effect straight chemistry, though a branch, organic analytical chemistry, on which we had not had any specific training. But, since I was reasonably familiar with the general principles involved, as well as with the equipment, I was able to start my experiments with much more confidence than I could have in my ability to handle the physiological and biochemical concepts on which the working hypothesis was based. If Dra. Hoffmann was my unofficial coach with the latter, it was Francisco Hoffmann who helped me with the experimental part. Although he was not a chemist, I was amazed at the resourcefulness and ingenuity with which he helped me solve the numerous problems that arose along the way.

I labored for more than a year on this problem, at first all alone in a small improvised laboratory on the third floor — therefore well away from the rest of the staff — and later, back to civilization, in the main chemical lab on the second floor. The results were good and very consistent, but we couldn't get one hundred per cent of the cholesterol we knew to be present in the samples, only about ninety-five per cent. So I kept on trying all kinds of modifications to the methods described in the literature in order to make my results one hundred per cent right, but nothing worked. Therefore I felt compelled to report in my thesis — a detailed and critical account of all the tests I had carried out — that, in the last analysis, the results "were not satisfactory". But my thesis, published in September of 1944, and evaluated by three distinguished professors in the Faculty of Medicine, obtained the highest possible mark, twenty-one out of twenty-one points.

For the purposes of this writing I have re-read the thesis, my first published work, for the first time in fifty-two years. I feel compelled to say, with a mixture of regret and satisfaction, that, in the light of all my subsequent experience, I cannot agree with my own original conclusions. The results were actually highly satisfactory and remarkably consistent, but I'm afraid that neither the Hoffmanns nor I had enough experience in the field of organic analytical chemistry at the time to make a proper and justified judgment. Too bad, because in view of the conclusions we reached then, we never got to measure free and esterified cholesterol in animals with either a deficiency or an excess of thyroid hormone. For reasons that I do not need to explain here, my guess is that we would not have found what the Hoffmanns had conjectured. But that, besides being a moot point, is the way of research. I was beginning to find out that negative or unpredictable results are as common as results right on the dot. What we had in effect proved is that two physiologists, never mind how accomplished, plus a novice chemist, do not a biochemist make.

I had learned a good deal during the course of this exercise, including the tremendous importance of methods, of discovering or mastering techniques that allow one to either observe or measure whatever objects or phenomena one wishes to study. Many important and certainly great discoveries in science have come from the designing or invention of new techniques or gadgets. The invention of the microscope in the seventeenth century, opening up a whole new universe for study, comes to mind. I think I am being fair to myself if I say that during those many months of hard work I showed no signs of this particular type of talent. I was not inventive. On the other hand, my work showed thoroughness, perhaps excessive thoroughness, a quality that precludes the not infrequent phenomenon of making unwarranted claims.

As importantly, if not more, it showed a considerable amount of critical ability, of clear reasoning, especially when the time came to gather my daily results and put them together in the form of a coherent thesis. I also learned, however, that the progress of scientific research is amazingly slow and even tedious. That, regardless of how exciting or challenging the original problem or question may be, one can spend days, weeks, months and even years getting nowhere, or making very small progress. That the moments of great excitement are few and far between, and are often caused by minor achievements which can drive into ecstasy only the researcher involved, but most certainly no one else.

It is clear, therefore, that not everyone has the appropriate temperament to make a go of a career in science, regardless of whatever talents the aspirant may have. I suppose that by the time I had completed my thesis I should have asked myself that very question. If I had, I should have concluded that, as with my mountain climbing experiences, I did not have a suitable temperament to withstand protracted periods of time and effort for the sake of an elusive pay-off in the not-so-near future. I had shown to myself that I could do it, but that I was not particularly happy doing it. Other factors, however, played a significant role in my ultimate decision to stay with an academic career, of which research is a major component.

The first and foremost was that, on the basis of my performance as a student, I was given the opportunity. There was only one staff position for a chemist at the Institute. At the time I began to work there for my thesis it was occupied by a young woman who had graduated from the Instituto Pedagógico. That is, she had been trained as a high school chemistry teacher. The position itself was not academic but technical, in the same category as those of the machinist and electronics man, and as such it carried no teaching or research responsibilities of any sort. Because the occupant was much of a loner who hardly ever mingled with the rest of the academic staff, I never even found out what her work consisted of. But I presume she had been hired to assist with chemistry problems as they arose. Even though towards the end of my thesis work Osvaldo and I shared the main chemistry lab with her, she kept very much to herself, never befriending either of us.

In those circumstances, I was rather surprised and uncomfortable when one day Dr. Hoffmann came to ask me whether it was true that she had placed some glass dishes containing organic solvent solutions of fat to evaporate in an open-fire gas stove. With some embarrassment I said yes, she had, but that nothing had happened because Osvaldo and I had warned her of the danger of a big explosion and fire. Hoffmann was clearly furious at this near misadventure, but I heard nothing further about the episode. Not long afterwards, however, he fired the chemist and offered me the position, even though I hadn't graduated yet.

Secondly, after more than two years of assisting Dr. Middleton and then Dr. Talesnik with the teaching, it was quite clear that I enjoyed the experience of being on the "professor's" side of the bench very much indeed. I was learning very quickly that one of the best ways to master new knowledge is having to teach, to communicate lucidly and convincingly facts and concepts to minds even more naive and barren than one's own. Even when the experience was fraught with the danger of being found wanting, there was the thrill of success, of being able to establish objectively the fact that with each new assignment my understanding of the field and my confidence were increasingly more firm, more secure. And, as the self-conciousness decreased, the satisfaction of having taught something new to the students correspondingly increased. This was enormously gratifying, and gradually began to contribute significantly not only to my sense of self-worth, but to my enjoyment of the job as well.

Another factor contributing to my decision was the general atmosphere at the Institute. Even though at first I had found it intimidating, mainly because of my lack of familiarity with the discipline involved, a year and a half later I knew I was in the midst of a culturally and intellectually very stimulating group of people. We were the only department that worked from nine to five, with a short interruption for lunch. Everywhere else people quit at noon, and didn't come back until mid-afternoon. To facilitate our unusual schedule, a one-plate hot lunch was prepared on the premises and served in a spartan dining room which consisted of just one big rectangular table and its corresponding chairs. The seating arrangements were hierarchical. The Hoffmanns sat, naturally, at the head of the table, then the teaching staff on either side, followed in order of decreasing importance by the students and the senior technicians. At the time of which I write, I sat near the middle along one side.

The conversation around this table, for the most part initiated from the top, was often shop-talk, as might have been expected. Whoever had exciting results to report, or urgent practical or logistic problems to discuss, would do so. But, just as often, every conceivable topic of human concern would be brought up for discussion: politics or gardening, religion or nutrition, literature or cars, nature or fashion, music or bicycling, history or money, science or carpentry, Freud or gossip, business or some more politics. All of this was liberally sprinkled with typical Chilean humor and a good deal of bantering, so that the atmosphere was never pompous, and one never knew when one would be the target of one joke or another.

One day, for example, Hoffmann, who seemed quite intrigued by my proneness to blush, decided to test me scientifically. He wanted to know the time it would take me to reach a full blush, and so, as in a race, he warned me he was about to start, and then said: "Go!", in a loud voice, while looking at the second hand of his watch. I don't think I've ever blushed more quickly or more intensely, but my embarrassment and anger were such that I do not remember my timing, only the loud laughter all around me. Rather heavy-handed, I should think, but still I remember our lunch times at the Institute as very stimulating occasions, even if at times rather intimidating.

The leaders, the main participants, were Drs. Hoffmann and Middleton, as very well informed men of action, doers, and Jaime Talesnik and later also

Osvaldo Cori, as well-read and questioning intellectuals. But the soul of the group belonged to Dra. Hoffmann who, although deceptively quiet and soft-voiced, had the most penetrating, inquisitive and intellectually sophisticated mind of the group. She would discuss with equal ease the nutritional and economic potential of "cochayuyo", a seaweed commonly and abundantly found on the coasts of Chile — with which she could make a delicious souffle, she claimed — and the challenge of reading James Joyce's Ulysses in English, German and Spanish at the same time. Needless to say, my participation in these daily rituals was quite limited at the beginning, while I was still an undergraduate student. The combination of my low status in the hierarchy and the intimidation provoked by the high level of these interactions seemed to have inhibited my natural tendency for opinionated loquacity. Even so, lunch time at the Institute was yet another stimulating reason to make me wish to join in.

Finally, this was a full-time position with a corresponding salary and all the perquisites of a public servant. Considering the alternatives, there wasn't the slightest question that this was for me a golden opportunity to at least begin a scientific career. As things actually happened, I don't think I spent even one day pondering whether or not to accept Hoffmann's offer. What is rather remarkable in retrospect is that neither Hoffmann nor I paid the slightest attention to the fact that the official position was technical rather than academic, and as such not at all attractive to me. I simply took for granted that I would continue to do research rather than solve ad hoc chemical problems, and that in one capacity or another I would be involved in teaching. This tacit agreement between Hoffmann and me should have been very flattering to me, but at the time I wasn't at all aware that anything out of the ordinary was happening, and nobody else bothered to tell me. I was there, I had certain skills, and they should be put to good use. It was as simple as that.

Middleton's return from a year of research work in the United States made for exciting news to many of us. His vivid, colorful and lucid descriptions of life in general and of academic life in particular in the big, rich and powerful country to the north opened the door to brand new dreams of studies abroad, where the opportunities and the resources to do research seemed limitless. When it soon became apparent that Jaime Talesnik would go next, I allowed myself the luxury of dreaming that maybe one day, with any luck, my turn would come.

A New Job, a New House,
a New Language

It was crystal clear, however, that well before my travelling dreams got the best of me, there were at least two major hurdles to overcome. I had to graduate and, just as importantly, I had to learn English. But, to make matters even more complex, if not exciting, all of these academic achievements and dreams were obviously superimposed on my very busy private life. Despite the hard work and long hours at the Institute after that unusual summer of 1943, I had continued with my very busy social and cultural life in the city, as well as with my very frequent excursions to the mountains, and with the attendant activities at the Ski and Mountaineering Club. Because of the big building project at Farellones, our weekly meetings were now far more focused and business-like than ever before, and the social bonds among us much stronger.

It was in these circumstances that Guillermo and I met again. As usual, we went for refreshments and dancing after our meetings. Very quickly, Guillermo and I became regular dancing partners. I could now confirm first hand that he was indeed a superb dancer and, even more exciting, that I, not quite as superb, was nevertheless sufficiently skillful to follow him with some degree of grace. This was great fun because I really loved dancing but, not surprisingly, the fun soon developed into a more complex relationship which I am still at a loss to understand, at least as it concerned me.

As he began to walk me home after these dances, and to ask for dates, he explained that his affair with his former girl friend was over. If that impediment for a relationship between us was now out of the way, I had my own to contribute. I thought, quite honestly, that I couldn't possibly be interested in him because, simultaneously, I had an intense crush on someone else, one of those impossible infatuations with a very sophisticated married man, who, despite my best efforts, showed only the mildest of interest in me. This I kept to myself but, on the other hand, I didn't mislead Guillermo into believing that I was at all romantically interested in him. Further, I wasn't very clear about his studies or about his future plans. Although he claimed to be finishing his law studies, I never saw any concrete signs that that was in fact the case and, to this day, I have no idea what his means of support really were.

This was unsettling to someone like me, who liked to plan and know what lay ahead. However, the physical attraction, his persistence, and perhaps the frustration of my own unfulfilled emotional state were such that we soon became lovers. This affair, which lasted for the best part of a year, was obviously satisfying in some respects, but not at all in others, because, besides sex, the dancing and the mountains, there was not much else to share, at least not from my point of view. Sometimes one gets to love a lover, but that didn't happen. So, when his demands and expectations became more serious, and my realization of what was happening more clear, I left him.

It was a sort of deliverance because I couldn't possibly conceive of marriage, parenthood or anything else of lasting value with a man, never mind how attractive, with whom I shared so little. The contrast between my almost opportunistic behavior towards Guillermo and my highly principled and idealistic attitude to Claudio five or six years earlier, is striking and puzzling. I suppose that in the interim I had shed some of my excessive and unrealistic idealism concerning human relationships, and also that, considering the environment in which I found myself, a certain degree of experimenting was understandable and justifiable. But experiments have a tendency to become habits, and I was not about to let that happen.

As I've already said, the time had come for me to face my obligatory practice in a drugstore. Purely for convenience I chose a pharmacy that was virtually next door to the School of Chemistry and Pharmacy, and consequently very near my home. The owners, a young couple, both pharmacists, readily accepted me as a volunteer worker, and so it was that the least interesting, if not a dreaded, part of my undergraduate training began.

I was immediately assigned to assist the pharmacist in charge of prescriptions. He was a slight, pale, grey man, probably in his mid-fifties, who looked to me like an antique, as obsolete as the formulations over which he labored so conscientiously. But he was knowledgeable, kind and patient, and put up with me as best he could. By far the biggest challenge I confronted during my tenure in that comer of the drugstore was deciphering the doctors' prescriptions. I was in awe of the pharmacist's confidence in his own interpretation of the mysterious and to me illegible squiggles that passed for writing. The mere thought of filling the prescriptions with the wrong drugs, powders or liquids, and thus causing the intended patients to get sicker or even die, was horrifying. When nothing of the sort ever happened, my respect for the quiet gentle pharmacist increased by several notches.

We got along just fine, but the work, carried out in that claustrophobic, isolated comer of the otherwise open, bright and busy place, was as unchallenging, tedious and boring as I had imagined it to be. The tedium got so bad that at the end of three months I requested and was granted permission to work behind the counter, in the store proper. Of course, this had nothing at all to do with my technical or academic training, but it would do as a credit and, most importantly, it turned out to be a lot of fun, because of the direct contact with the public. Although most of the transactions were straightforward requests for over-the-counter medications, every once in a while something out of the ordinary happened which added spice to the routine.

Two examples come to mind. On one occasion, when I was alone in the store, a police officer in full regalia came in and, instead of addressing me directly, began to pace the floor looking perhaps embarrassed, perhaps just hesitant. "Can I help you?" I said after a prudent lapse of time. "Well", he said, while swallowing nervously, "I wonder if you have any athletic supports". I looked rather blank, since I had never heard of "athletic supports", and then said "I'm not sure, let me go and check." Suspecting the worst, I went to the pharmacist who was as usual deeply immersed in his wondrous powders, and explained. "Oh!" he said, "I guess I'd better look after this myself." Then, while I watched the two of them look at various packages and discuss sizes, the true meaning of the phrase hit me, and I blushed with appropriate decorum while otherwise pretending to be as nonchalant as the occasion required. Up to that point I hadn't known that men needed supports of any kind while engaged in athletic activities. But it made sense, considering their weird anatomy.

On another occasion, a tall, fair, slim woman, unmistakably a "gringa", came into the store and clearly waited until I was available to ask me for some AWL-co-hawl. I looked at her in some bewilderment while I said: "I beg your pardon, señora?" She carefully repeated: "AWL-co-hawl, please", but the sounds she had emitted added up to zero in my uncouth ears. She tried again in that nasal tone of some English-speaking people, and then, suddenly, as in a portentous revelation, I beamed and said: "Oh! you mean al-KOL!." She beamed back, more with a sense of relief than of amusement, as if to say: "But that's what I've been asking for from the beginning! ", and we completed the transaction without much further difficulty.

She probably thought that I, whom I'm sure she had chosen to speak to because of my own "gringa" looks, was a complete moron. Otherwise, why on earth did I not understand her "alcohol" when in Spanish the word is written identically: "alcohol"? Why indeed! Because, speech being what it is, it often bears very little resemblance to those symbols we read on the printed page, and because the ear is attuned to the familiar rather than to the unexpected. Sobering! So sobering indeed that this experience, plus similar ones accumulated in the course of my work, in addition to my ambitious plans for the future, led me to seriously consider the idea of learning English in earnest. Little did I know what that would lead to!

Since completing the last year of our regular course, Raquel had also been busy with the research work for her thesis. She had been so fascinated by viruses, covered in our Bacteriology course, that she had decided to choose that field for her initiation into research. Consequently, she was doing her work in the Department of Viruses at the Instituto Bacteriológico, under the direction of Dr. Raúl Palacios. Because this Institute occupied a building situated roughly half way between the Medical School and downtown Santiago, I often stopped there to pick Raquel up on our way to whatever concert, film, theater, meeting or social gathering we were planning to attend after work. As a result, I got to know quite well her bosses, the Drs. Palacios and Avendaño. These people did not do pure research as the staff at the Institute of Physiology did. Rather, they applied and developed the main advances in the field from abroad to the specific needs for sera, vaccines and so on, in Chile. But the undergraduate students, who came to do their theses there, were assigned genuine research projects which were carried out under their supervision.

That, of course, was Raquel's situation. And she, too, was beginning to make plans to go abroad, namely to the United States, to advance her training in viruses. Since her English was as meager as mine, we made inquiries jointly, and eventually joined a social and cultural organization called The Chilean-North American Institute of Culture, whose main activity was the teaching of English, American style.

For practically two years, from the middle of 1944 to the middle of 1946, we regularly attended two-hour classes twice a week during the winter semester. The courses were divided into three levels of complexity: beginners, middle and advanced. New students were assigned to each level according to their degree of mastery of the language, assessed by means of an initial interview, conducted exclusively in English. On the basis of our high school

English, and whatever else we had learned in the interim, we were enrolled in the middle course. The teaching was done exclusively by Americans of various ages, genders, levels of education, points of origin and accents.

The main thing in common among them was their amazing ignorance of the Spanish language, nicely covered up by the one overriding rule at the Institute, to wit, that all, absolutely *all*, verbal interactions within its walls had to be carried out in English. This meant that not even the simplest questions to clarify some obscure or unintelligible point could be asked in Spanish. Stressful as this was, it had its pay-off, because it forced us to think in English almost from the start, instead of thinking in Spanish and then translating. It was thus that we began to acquire some semblance of the rhythm, the inflexions, the sound of the language, even though our vocabulary was often anything but adequate.

But there were times, many times, when I fervently wished that the Spaniards had settled all, and not just parts, of North America. Compared to Spanish, a clearly and methodically organized language, English seemed chaotic, arbitrary in its rules, hybrid in its pedigree, and totally hopeless as far as pronunciation was concerned. Why fourteen or more vowel sounds when five could do so well? why so many silent consonants? why so many words with totally different spellings, but the same sound? Why? Why, indeed! The task was arduous, but, little by little, as I was increasingly able to understand our teachers, and respond more or less fluently and coherently, I began to feel less self-conscious, to enjoy the experience, and even to appreciate the unique beauty of the language.

In other words, while with French it had been a question of beauty at first sight, in the case of English it had to grow on me. I supplemented our lessons by trying to listen to the dialogue of the American and British films I went to see, instead of relying exclusively on the Spanish subtitles, and by reading as much as I could. By the time I had finished the advanced course, when I won the second prize for written English and the first in the oral examination, I felt quite confident that I could hold my own with the best of them. I had forgotten, however, that I was testing my command of the language almost exclusively against teachers attuned to our slow and laborious speech, and to our Spanish and even idiosyncratic accents. The definitive proof would come later, in the real English-speaking world.

In these circumstances, I felt extremely fortunate and flattered to be invited by the Talesniks to small dinner parties at their home, where the conversation would be carried out exclusively in English. The purpose was, of course, to practice their English in preparation for their projected one-year stay in Toronto, that was to begin in a few months time. These dinners, which usually included half a dozen or so of us, took place more or less regularly during the winter and spring of 1945. Although the food, as well as the hospitality of our hosts, were invariably great, the conversation, which in Spanish would have been a breeze, also invariably resembled much more the overcoming of an obstacle course than a breeze. To make sure that we kept on track, that there was someone around to get us out of trouble, and that our most grievous mistakes were corrected on the spot, the Talesniks always included someone who spoke fluent English in the group.

Even though we often serially murdered this beautiful language, and our halting and pathetic efforts would have been hilarious to an English-speaking witness, these reunions did indeed serve their purpose rather well. I, for one, began gradually and painfully to shed the accustomed crutches of teachers and books, and to rely on my own resources to retrieve and actually use the considerable knowledge of English that I had accumulated. However, this was just one of the very first steps in the laborious and open-ended process of trying to master a foreign language. It's tough. I've been at it for another fifty years, and I'm not there yet.

These developments in my personal and professional lives were running more or less in parallel with family and domestic events of considerable importance to me. Perhaps the most immediately and obviously significant among them was our moving to a new house. Shortly after I had got a full-time job at the Institute and I had, therefore, automatically become a contributing member of the Caja de Empleados Publicos — in effect a Credit Union of public servants — a house in the immediate neighborhood became available for rent. This was 154 Vicuña Mackenna, exactly between the impressive British Embassy and the del Campo mansion, two houses over from where I had grown up and the family had lived for about fourteen years. The Caja subsidized both the rental and purchase of houses for its members, so I was now in a position to rent this place for a sum that we could afford, since it was well below its market value.

The place, also owned by the del Campos, was truly amazing, especially when compared to any of the other dwellings we had lived in before. The handsome wrought iron gate led directly to a wide, block-long path framed by a tall, curved wrought iron arbor covered with grape vines and with a profusion of flowering and other bushes on either side. The arbor connected directly to a garden of bushes and tall trees immediately to the right, and therefore behind the del Campo house. And then, semi-hidden by the trees, there was the two-storey high, stained-glass front wall of the house.

The front door opened into a huge hall or atrium with a terrazo floor in earth tones from which a curved staircase led to the second floor. There were two rooms to the left of the staircase and two more large rooms and the kitchen to the right, in addition to servants' rooms separated from the house proper by the end of the arbor. The stairs led to a balcony that ran all the width of the house and looked out into the atrium. Opening onto the balcony were six rooms, a bathroom and a steep and closed staircase to the one room that constituted the third floor. Each of these rooms had, opposite to the door to the balcony, a window that looked out over the Parque Bustamante, a new and beautifully green open space, where the Symphony or the Ballet would give open-air performances on warm summer nights. Although in need of some cosmetic repairs, this was a grand house by any standards, and so different architecturally that I've never seen anything like it anywhere else, not even in films.

We moved at the beginning of 1945 and realized almost immediately that our meager belongings would barely furnish half of its fourteen rooms, to say nothing of the enormous two-storey atrium. While I had spent the previous fourteen years ferociously defending every inch of space and privacy I could muster, now at last, and for the first time ever, I had a room of my own, as did each of my three brothers. And my parents, in full possession of the master bedroom, next to the bathroom, no longer had to share it with what passed for a living-room. The latter was installed at one end of the largest room in the house on the ground floor, while the dining room occupied the other half.

This room had two large low windows opening to the park and thus providing both light and a view. They were promptly all dressed up in lace curtains made by my mother from old materials she had kept and nursed for years in that unforgettable chest where she kept all her assorted treasures to be used on a better day. Next to this room, and near the kitchen, was her workroom, where we also had our every-day meals, but which no longer served every other imaginable family purpose as the big room in the small old house had. My brothers and I were now far more independent of each other than we had ever been, but by the same token far more disconnected, since the physical opportunities for proximity had diminished substantially. This purely physical or geographical fact, combined with our getting older and perhaps more mature, no doubt accounted for a much more civilized behavior among the four of us than had previously been the case.

Once we had settled in and had distributed whatever furniture we had as equitably as possible, it became painfully apparent that the place, except for the living and dining rooms, looked nearly as stark and empty as a monastery. For my bedroom I had chosen an ample room at the end of the balcony. Its walls were covered with a clearly faded light green paper, and it had a good sized window overlooking the park. New wall-covering or even just a coat of paint would have instantly given it a badly needed lift, but such an enterprise, of nearly engineering proportions there at that time, was not yet in my repertoire of skills. Except for the outside walls of houses, which by law had to be repainted every two years, I had never seen a room repainted or recovered with wallpaper anywhere. It seemed as if the original finishing had been meant to last forever, with not a chance of an uplift, ever. Once I had installed my share of our furniture in this first room of my own, I realized with considerable dismay that it looked utterly empty.

I had a single bed, a night table with my legendary faded pink lamp and my precious new modern radio on it, and some small book shelves, also inherited from my affluent aunt. The radio, incidentally, had been my second big and important purchase after my bicycle, these two terrific new possessions that opened up my range of experiences so substantially. The radio, like the lamp many years earlier, had become all-important because there was one station in Santiago which played exclusively classical music, uninterrupted by commercials, every night of the week from 10 p.m. to midnight. But I had nothing else, not even a wardrobe to hang my clothes in.

Naturally, I had taken a day off from work to help with the move. But then, without letting anyone know at the Institute, I stayed home for another day and then another, without any apparent reason. By the fourth day Hoffmann himself appeared in person, late one afternoon, to find out if anything serious was keeping me away from my job. I was quite at a loss to explain my uncharacteristic behavior to him, but promised I would be at work the next day, and I was. Since I cannot quite remember my actual mood at the time, I can only conjecture that my immediate response to this major and positive change in my life was more akin to a minor depressive episode than to a more logical state of excitement. After all, if there was a lot to be very happy about, there was also a great loss, the loss of my home for the previous fourteen or so years, when I had evolved from childhood into full adulthood.

But, coming back to my obvious preoccupations at the time, namely what to do with my nearly empty bedroom, I improvised with some boxes and a rack while I investigated the available furniture styles and compared prices against my financial means. I quickly came to the conclusion that the pine furniture introduced by some very enterprising Catalonian immigrants was the thing for me. This stuff was as fashionable then among my young and iconoclastic friends as Scandinavian furniture would be one or two decades later among young North Americans.

I ordered a wardrobe, one half of which was for hanging clothes and the other half equipped with shelves above and drawers below, as well as an arm chair and a coffee table. I cannot describe the thrill I experienced when these pieces, with their happy and light natural finish, were delivered to the house. Utter luxury. It was not only the first new and extremely well made furniture ever acquired by any member of my immediate family since we had moved to Santiago, but beautiful and functional. Now I had an arm chair of my own to read in, in the privacy of my room, and proper well-designed places to keep all my stuff, duly sorted out according to their multiple functions.

The best measure of the importance I attached to this purchase is that I've kept the corresponding invoice from Tanago Labayen and Co. for all these years, and I'm now looking at it: 2810 pesos for the lot, with 500 pesos down and seven monthly instalments of 330 pesos each. Even though I cannot tell the relative magnitude of this transaction because I don't remember what my salary actually was, I know that I felt well satisfied and even proud of being able to make my payments without any difficulty while giving my mother her customary allowance and having enough money left for all my personal expenses, including clothes about which I was becoming much more discriminating and interested.

Our increasingly comfortable but still modest economic situation depended almost exclusively on my mother and me. The two of us were the major bread-winners for the family because my father continued to contribute unreliably, since his jobs and deals were as erratic and unproductive as ever. This proud and irascible man, by then in his mid-fifties, and with whom I had not been on speaking terms since the Claudio affair, seemed to spend a good deal of his time minding the chickens in our new large grounds, while still nursing his dreams. I am not conscious of ever having wondered then what he thought or felt about me or about the course that my life and career were taking. But I do now, with deep regret. Being so much like him, I know that his mute and apparent indifference was no more than a veneer covering a multitude of feelings, either repressed or at least unexpressed. Only I am the loser.

I can easily guess at all the things I did or stood for that he would have strenuously disapproved of, being the conservative old-fashioned dogmatist that he was. But I have not the slightest idea about what, if anything, about me he approved of, or was pleased by. There was never a greeting or even a simple acknowledgement of my birthdays. Never a word of congratulation for my academic successes. Never an indication of satisfaction for my being a responsible daughter. Never even a hint of approval or satisfaction for who I was becoming. Never a question about what was next. Nothing. So much of nothing that I never even raised this issue in my own mind until now, when I can no longer ask.

We couldn't count on Orlando either — the twins were now twenty-two — because in his last year of his law course he was completely immersed in his studies. Although Raúl's condition was more or less stable, he was too frail and thin to even entertain any idea of a meaningful career or job. And if he had, my mother, who watched over him with total dedication, would not have permitted it. And Fernando, now a very handsome twenty-year-old, had taken to the theater with a passion, but was still in training, with his sights set on becoming a director. Clearly, none of them earned or contributed anything to the household.

It is easy for me at this distance and in my present situation to be, or at least to sound, reasonably objective about my brothers' apparent lack of commitment to the economic plight of the family. It was another matter then. I was resentful and even bitter that the four men in the family appeared to take for granted that it was all right to let the two women carry most if not all of the load. I didn't mind so much for myself because I didn't perceive my work as any sacrifice. All the contrary, it was precisely what I wanted to do and be involved with. But not so my mother, who worked primarily for the money, and never ceased to remind us of the sacrifices she was making for us. It was their indifference to her plight that I resented, especially since every one of them enjoyed and expected the good things in life. I clearly remember thinking then that my mother and I could have lived like princesses by ourselves, if we hadn't had to support the rest of them. But we had to, because they were "us".

Looking at this family constellation from the present North American perspective it may sound odd that all four of us, already in our twenties, were living at home. But in fact there was nothing at all odd about it because in Chile it was, and I gather it still is, the rule rather than the exception for children to stay at home with their parents until well into adulthood. One left home after marriage, when going to school or university out of town — something that rarely applied if you lived in Santiago — or when you died. This practice was so prevalent and deeply ingrained in Chilean, and probably in most other Latin societies, that it was considered a bit of a disgrace, if not a scandal, to leave home for any other reason. It meant that there was something terribly wrong with the family, or at least that the young quitter was up to no good.

This custom, probably based at least in part on economic reasons, is of course in sharp contrast to what prevails in English-speaking countries, where the reverse is true: there is something wrong or odd if the children do *not* leave home by eighteen. I haven't the slightest doubt that each of these practices must have considerable social implications and affect the dynamics of family interactions profoundly, but that is the subject for another book. It is enough for me to say here that in my early twenties, and already financially self-sufficient, I didn't leave home because that would have been a serious break with the norms of my society. Further, and even more importantly, because it would have been a devastating blow to my mother, who could now count on me economically and in a variety of other ways. But I must admit that the thought of being on my own often crossed my mind.

Men as Friends, and a Lover

My life, however, was as independent of the rest of my family as it could be in the circumstances. I was away most weekends, and during the week I left home after breakfast and didn't come back until late in the evening, having often had dinner out with friends or other members of my extended family. And when I was at home it was usually because I had to work or wash my hair and do all those time-consuming things one must do to look good. With some minor additions and deletions, my social group of friends remained pretty well the same as I've already described, with Raquel, Fusa and Adela continuing to be my closest girl-friends. And, to make matters richer and even more interesting and complex, I had now found at least two close friends among the men of my acquaintance.

The ftrst was Gregorio ("Goyo") Gasman. Raquel and I had met him for the ftrst time at a concert of the Chilean Symphony Orchestra which turned out to be memorable on at least two counts, probably three. First, this was the occasion of the first performance in Chile, probably in 1943, of Shostakovich's seventh symphony, the *Leningrad Symphony*. Monumental and deeply stirring, this work had been inspired by the protracted siege of Leningrad in 1941. Considering the significance of this siege in the context of the Second World War, our political beliefs at the time, and the sheer power and beauty of this symphony, all three of us were so overwhelmed by it that we decided to go out and celebrate, instead of going straight home after the concert. Since, typically, none of us had much money to go anywhere, Goyo suggested we buy a bottle of whatever, and go to his place.

"His place" — which I immediately assumed to be where he lived with his parents, two blocks away from my home — turned out to be his studio downtown, right off the Parque Forestal. It was one of those places dreams are made of, at least my modest dreams of long ago. It was a very large one-room self-contained apartment with two wide windows overlooking my favorite park, on the ground floor of an old building. The very first impression was of books, hundreds of books lining all the walls as silent witnesses to his interests and tastes. But the books left enough of an inner chamber to accomodate a divan full of cushions, a large coffee table and two gorgeous dark green leather arm chairs, as well as a desk under one of the windows. I don't know whether it was the exultant mood, the literal euphoria provoked by the *Leningrad Symphony,* the company, or the place itself, but I thought I had landed in heaven, somewhere in the outskirts of Leningrad.

We toasted the victory at Leningrad, and everybody and everything else that had anything to do with an early victory in the war against Hitler's armies, with as much fervor and commitment as if our own country had been at the forefront of the struggle. But there was a catch. Goyo had bought a bottle of cherry brandy, of all things, and was serving it to us in highball glasses. Sweet and innocent looking, it went down very easily, almost like a dessert, to my unknowing and unsuspecting palate. A few hours later, after much animated talk and many toasts, as we got up to leave, it was quite obvious that all three of us were anything but sober, and rather unsteady on our feet.

Since a taxi in the wee hours of the morning was out of the question, the three of us walked to Raquel's place, which was more or less on the way to ours, and then Goyo and I walked some ten more blocks to mine. I remember being quite embarrassed at my slurred speech and other signs of intoxication, trying to explain to Goyo, on our first encounter, that I couldn't nderstand why I was so high since we hadn't drunk that much after all, and that I wasn't in the habit of getting drunk, ever. He was very gallant, apologizing and assuming all the responsibility for having served us this deceptively sweet and apparently mellow drink which in fact was as strong as a whisky while pretending or appearing to be a sweet wine. And then he left me at the door, wishing me a good night and a hangoverless tomorrow.

As I've said, Goyo lived a couple of blocks away, in that street where my brothers, and probably he, had played so much soccer when they were boys. But I had never met him until that night. I only knew him by sight, always a very good dresser, who frequently passed by our house, invariably carrying a book under his arm. I thought he was rather interesting — who wouldn't be, with a studio like his! — but, after the events of the previous night, I was absolutely sure he would now avoid me like the plague. It is funny that I thought so, since I most certainly wouldn't avoid him just because on such a special night he had had one too many. But girls ... that's different, or so I felt.

At any rate, the next day at about noon, there he was, fresh and well groomed, ringing the bell at our door. He was feeling guilty, he said, about pouring the cherry brandy as if it was water, and wanted to know if I was O.K. I reassured him that I was O.K., with only a slight headache, nothing to worry about if contrasted with the splendor of the night before, referring principally to the *Leningrad Symphony*. He agreed, and then we agreed about many more things such as music and literature and politics, as we walked along Vicuña Mackenna, chatting exactly as people do when they have just discovered a soulmate.

Since we were both free of other possessive relationships at the time, we became fast friends and went out together a lot, even though there never was any sexual or romantic attachment between us. We, Goyo and I, became just very good friends. For reasons that I do not remember, he had not gone to university, but at the time I met him he was the music critic of *El Siglo,* the official daily newspaper of the Communist Party, under the byline of Juan Sebastian! He was in effect a self-educated man, with a vast understanding of music and literature and with serious aspirations as a poet. At the time, he was working very hard on his translation into Spanish of Walt Whitman's *Leaves of Grass.* In this context he became my valuable and stimulating mentor and companion since, as I've already said, my liberal education had virtually ended with high school. Now, after several years of mostly science, I could enjoy becoming re-acquainted with all those other aspects of culture that still held great fascination for me.

Once, for example, he invited me to a Sunday morning recital of Neruda's poetry read by the great poet himself. He had recently returned from one of his many sojourns abroad and was to present some readings under the title of *Viaje Alrededor de mi Poesía* (A Voyage Around my Poetry), if I remember correctly. The stage of the Teatro Municipal contained nothing but a small kitchen table with a candle on top, and a chair, placed in such a way that, when Neruda sat down to read, he was seen in profile rather than facing us. The big balding man, one of my enduring heroes, read his own fabulously rich poetry in a strange singsong voice, more a lament than a song, for something like two hours, and left us stunned and amazed by the genius with which he took our own old familiar Spanish words and aligned and wove them together to produce such extraordinary effects. (This was 1943, before his partisan political poetry, about which I have serious reservations.)   It was magic.

Much of the audience, which must have included a Who's Who of the

Santiago literary world, and us, Goyo and myself, then celebrated and toasted the poet at a lunch held afterwards in one of those outdoor restaurants in the outskirts of Santiago called "quintas", and notable for their pure Chilean cuisine. Had it not been for Goyo and his connections I would never even have known that such an inspiring event took place. On another occasion, a Sunday afternoon this time, he invited me to go and visit Neruda's home in Los Guindos, an old-fashioned section of the Barrio Alto. Responding to the surprised look on my face, he explained that we had not been invited by Neruda to visit him but, rather, that on Sunday afternoons, when he and his wife retired to their bedroom for a siesta, the house was open to selected visitors who were given a tour by an elderly woman, his aunt, I think.

I didn't know what to expect, and when we reached the place, after a very long trip on street cars, I was beginning to wonder, why all the fuss? It was a wide adobe one-storey house, with a red-tiled roof, probably of nineteenth century vintage, the kind one found everywhere outside of the modern and prosperous areas of Santiago. But, from the moment the elderly woman had opened the heavy front door, I knew this was no ordinary old house. The living room, immediately to the left of the entrance, was a huge room with wide picture windows to the inner courtyard, and a massive stone fire-place on the opposite wall. The furniture, sofas and arm chairs, were all covered in coppery-brown and white calf skins, and the tables and other occasional furniture, in natural finished woods, appeared to have been custom-made for the place. And they probably were because, as Goyo explained, the gutted and re-done old house, as well as all its furnishings, had been done according to Neruda's own designs. I was beginning to discover that Neruda was not only immensely inventive and imaginative with words, but also with objects of every description, and that he had, to boot, the soul of a collector.

Since I had heard that he was a keen shell collector and had imagined that he probably had three or four small glass-covered cases of shells, I asked if we could see it. "Oh! Come this way", said Neruda's aunt, as we were shown into a large room whose walls were lined from top to bottom with showcases containing a truly amazing display of shells behind glass doors. And the center of the room was occupied by table-high display cases showing, I suppose, the prize items in the collection. As I began to look more closely I realized that every shell, or group of shells, on display was neatly labelled with its common name as well as its proper scientific name in Latin. Lo and behold! Neruda was not only a great poet, but also an original and gifted designer, a serious collector, and even a scientist! I was enthralled!

The shells varied in size from tiny ones which had to be looked at under a microscope, to massive huge ones which I never knew existed, but their subtly varied mother-of-pearl linings were all equally beautiful. When I asked the obvious, how had this very prolific and busy man collected so many shells, Goyo explained that when word spread that Neruda was an avid collector of shells, people, literally from around the world, had begun to send him prize examples from their own shores. This process apparently continued at such a pace that eventually, long after our visit, Neruda donated the bulk of the collection to the Museum of Natural History.

Once we were through becoming acquainted with the vastness and richness of the shell world we crossed the courtyard full of fruit trees and other old trees, and opened the door to what, for lack of a better name, I shall call the party room. This was a large rectangular space with windows all around its two exposed walls - something like a large sun-room - at one end of which there was a big round table and numerous dining chairs with straw seats -the kind one could buy at the market for a few pesos each, and immortalized by Van Gogh. At the opposite end there was a bar, a real old-fashioned bar that Neruda had found somewhere in the real world. At one end of it sat an antique phonograph, the kind with a big trumpet and a wind-up handle on one side. And on the shelves behind the bar there was a colorful collection of old wine and liquor bottles of every size and description. (Neruda later became quite famous for his collection of old bottles which he displayed with great panache in the several houses he would create in Santiago and elsewhere.)

The space between these two ends of the room had clearly been kept empty to serve as a dance floor, and was broken up only by the inside of the entrance door, which was fully covered, from top to bottom, with old campy post-cards from the 1920s, featuring the likenesses of Rudolph Valentino and Clara Bow types. After seeing the terrific tango danced by Neruda (Philippe Noiret) and his wife in that marvellous film, *Il Postino,* a few years ago, how I wish Neruda had stirred up from his nap that Sunday afternoon and tangoed with me in that unforgettable room, so full of nostalgia! But alas, he didn't, and Goyo and I left without being able to see the spectacular photo-mural at the head of his bed which, I had been told, was of one of the beautiful avenues of tall old trees in the Parque Forestal.

Neruda would go on to design several other houses in his extraordinarily creative and inimitable style, the most famous of which, *Isla Negra* on the Pacific coast, is now a national museum. And I could go on indefinitely wondering about what determines the creative imagination. I think it is freedom. Freedom from the shackles of the conventional. And the courage to make do without it.

My second man-friend was Osvaldo Cori, whom I've already introduced. My friendship with Osvaldo was of a very different nature since it grew among the test tubes of our shared lab at the Institute. Although at the time we met he was a medical student, the initial and primary bond between us was our common interest in, and commitment to, biochemistry. But he had been seduced into joining the Institute of Physiology by the very same reasons I had: it was the only department in the Faculty exclusively dedicated to research and teaching. It would take some time, however, before he could try his hand at biochemistry because, for reasons unknown to me, his undergraduate thesis dealt, as opposed to mine, with a problem in classical physiology. But, brilliant and persistent as he was, he created his own opportunities to become a biochemist. And he did it with a vengeance since eventually, in the late 1950s, he created the brand new chair of biochemistry in my own Alma Mater, the Faculty of Chemistry and Pharmacy.

At the time of which I write, however, we were two young undergraduate students, the only two at the Institute with dreams about biochemistry. In that sense I was no longer alone, I had found an ally. By the same token, however, I had also found a rival because we were both intensely competitive and treading on the same, as yet unexplored, grounds at the Institute. But, overall, we managed to keep our competitiveness nicely in check, and became firm friends instead.

Even though we had many interests in common, such as music, literature and especially the mountains, our interactions during this period were primarily confined to our working hours. This was so mainly because he spent most weekends and holidays at home in Valparaíso, where his fiancee Aida Traverso also lived. If Goyo's tastes and inclinations were those of a left-wing avant-garde poet, Osvaldo was a politically conservative classicist. I used to tease him that for him music had ended with Bach, and literature would end with Thomas Mann. And yet I enjoyed and found stimulation and comfort in both of my friends, an eclectic trait of mine that my brother Orlando often used as proof of his view that I had no personality to speak of. At any rate, Osvaldo's presence in the lab made my life among all the physiologists a great deal more comfortable than it had been at the beginning.

Through this period of a couple of years towards the end of my studies, and through all these new relationships, connections, moves, plans and preparations for the big things to come, Raquel continued to be my closest friend, in a way a sort of stabilizer that helped me to keep on track and to smooth over the rough terrains into which I occasionally ventured or at least felt drawn to. I continued to drop in at the Bacteriológico to meet with her after hours, and this, quite naturally, provided the opportunity to meet and chat with Dr. Raúl Palacios and her other colleagues. Palacios, one of Raquel's thesis supervisors, was an attractive, quiet, tall man in his early forties who differed from most of my friends not only in age, but also in that he seemed aloof or above our intense passionate commitments to political ideologies, modern trends in the arts, or even scientific research as a noble cause.

Raúl Palacios

This sort of serene detachment, I gradually learned, was not based on indifference, laziness or ignorance but, rather, on the conclusions he had arrived at after much observation and thinking. He was at heart much more of a philosopher than a scientist, in that he spent most of his efforts as a student of philosophy, keeping his work on viruses strictly within the confines of an ordinary working day. I found his intelligent and critical mind not only appealing but enormously challenging. I was already in the throes of my own critical examination and rejection of the dialectical materialism of the marxists, and so began to test my own mixture of beliefs and doubts against his sharp intellect, something that I think he found, somewhat patronizingly, both amusing and challenging. Be that as it may, our discusssions, casual at first, became engaging enough that we were soon spending hours together, often over dinner.

I would have strenuously denied at first that this was, on both our parts, purely and simply an intellectual seduction of the first order. But the fact became undeniable, at both the emotional and sexual levels, since we became lovers despite the best efforts of Kant, Hegel and Marx, and Kierkegaard and Sartre - for whom, incidentally, he had nothing but scornful contempt - to keep us at a loftier, higher level of philosophical discourse and interaction. Our relationship was fraught with problems and obstacles from the very beginning. I knew through Raquel that he had been a married man and the father of several children — six, I think — but that he was either divorced or separated, and now lived with his sisters. Otherwise, I wouldn't have allowed myself the liberty of getting involved to the degree that I did. Remarkably, the two of us never discussed this all important issue openly, not only because I never asked, but because he was the most reticent person — man or woman — I've ever known. The most he ever allowed himself to say was that he had "family obligations" which impinged both on his freedom and his purse. The question of our age difference was equally touched upon only obliquely, if at all.

I am at a loss to understand what made our affair work, because outside of the bounds I've already described, probably because of age differences and temperament, we had very little else in common. He was not interested in going to the theatre, to concerts, or even to the movies, while dancing, parties and most certainly the mountains, were as much out of the question as speaking Chinese. While on weekends and holidays he presumably spent time with his children, of whom he never spoke to me, I went my way with my friends, pretty well as usual. And yet there was much mutual love and fulfilment, feelings which grew deeper with time.

But, at another and more thoughtful level, I knew all along that our relationship could not be lasting. I think he knew this even better than I did. If it satisfied his needs at that stage of his life, it did not satisfy mine, because I was too young to forfeit so many of my desires — including marriage and family — and of my interests. Perhaps he expressed the essence of the whole situation most aptly when he said to me once, a little later: "You know, I would give everything to be able to spend a year with you abroad." In other words, he knew, and I knew just as well, that this was an interlude, a romantic period of his life, in brackets for him, and an exciting experience into mature love for me but which was, nevertheless, well ahead of my years.

Graduation, and the First
Taste of Discrimination

Despite my romantic May-September affair, I still had to face the other more pedestrian but pressing realities of my busy life. The first among these, towards the beginning of 1945 was, of course, to graduate. Since my thesis and my obligatory practice were already out of the way, the only obstacle left was my final comprehensive oral examination. This was a daunting task indeed because just to pass, let alone do brilliantly, one had to have a commanding knowledge of every one of the subjects covered in the four-year course.

The topics or questions would depend on which three professors eventually made up the particular committee one had to face, but this was confidential until the very moment of the ordeal. There was no choice but to review the whole field, including all those courses to which I had paid only minimal attention. It was an arduous task, and also boring instead of challenging, because being happily focused on my research and teaching at the Institute, I found myself having to go over material that I was not at all interested in, and would never use again. Since Raquel was pretty well in the same boat, we set out a program of joint studies, in part to relieve the tedium, and also to reinforce each other's flagging determination.

We crammed in as much stuff as our beleaguered brains could contain and naturally ended up with a rather lopsided body of knowledge: a good deal about organic chemistry, physiology, pharmacology and bacteriology, subjects we had been clearly interested in, and with a thin veneer of facts about pharmacy, pharmaceutical botany, food chemistry and such. When the dreaded day came, the only thing left to do was to hope fervently that my good luck with oral exams would hold once more, and that I would confront a committee made up of my favorite professors. Shrewdly, and as if to compensate for my scholastic deficiencies, I also decided to look my best, for which purpose I squandered my money at the beauty salon, and wore my new and elegant black suit, proudly made by my mother for this and other similar occasions.

When we arrived at the main administration building of the University, in one of whose wood-panelled and very formal rooms the exam was to take place, and were presented to the committee, it was obviously and pathetically clear to me that I had struck lead instead of gold. The professors of pharmacy and pharmaceutical botany, as well as the bad half of the duo who had taught us organic chemistry, the one who had told me I would be a disgrace to the profession, constituted the committee. I thought that, in the circumstances, no amount of good luck, not even my fancy hairdo, would make any difference. Yet when all was said and done, including my reciting, as a robot, the formulation for tincture of iodine and for something then called Fowler's solution, I had passed with some dignity, though not much else.

The young professional at last.

But passed we had, Raquel and I. And to observe such a landmark in our lives, our friends decided to celebrate with a big party in, of all places, my very own house. The choice of locale was obvious because that large stained-glass enclosed atrium just cried for a big party. Would my mother agree to such a disruption? Would my father tolerate such an intrusion into his well-guarded seclusion? There had never been a real party at home. Only occasionally my mother had had tea parties for three or four of my friends for my birthdays and, once a year, now that we were in the big house, my father would invite the one sister and two brothers of his that lived in Santiago, with their spouses and children, for one of his renowned baby lamb barbecues. This was totally in keeping with his complete refusal to socialize with anybody — not even my mother's family — except for his siblings, my Josseau aunts and uncles. Siblings who, in a way, were like his own children to him, since he had looked after all of them after his parents' tragic deaths. Although he never said a word to me about the party, or for that matter about my graduation either, he must have agreed to it, because the party took place in my home, in the spring of 1945, at the end of October.

By my standards it was a huge and unprecedented affair, in the planning of which neither Raquel nor I had any input whatsoever. We were the guests of honor, who should mind our own business until the day of the party itself. We did so gladly, but I couldn't help witnessing and occasionally overhearing Violeta Bedrak, the commander-in-chief of the organizing committee, discuss details of the preparations. The only one I remember was a sharp difference of opinion between Violeta and my mother about the first course, or antipasto. My mother, unaccustomed to Central European foods, thought that only a delicate chicken salad with home-made mayonnaise would be the appropriate first course, chicken being considered a luxury meat in Chile, while Violeta, of Hungarian extraction, wanted pickled herring, the height of ordinariness in my mother's opinion. In the end Violeta won, and herring we had, but my mother never forgave her.

By the time Raquel arrived, and the two of us had made our triumphant appearance downstairs, we realized this was going to be no small cozy affair for eight or ten of us, but a sit-down dinner for something like twenty-five or thirty people. Somebody had improvised a long rectangular table, covered with an equally improvised white table cloth, which ran virtually the whole length of the large living-dining room. I cannot recall the menu, except for the pickled herring, but it had all been brought in by my friends, as were most of the dishes, the glasses and the cutlery, as well as the wine and the flowers. In fact, everything had been arranged, contributed and prepared by our friends, so that my mother didn't have much to do but supervise the goings on in the kitchen, and generally conduct the traffic.

Violeta and company had invited all of our friends but no family, except when they were bona fide members of our now rather large group. This, of course, excluded my brothers who that night must have joined my father to sleep outdoors with the chickens because of the unbearable noise in the house. The multiple-course dinner, followed by the desserts, fruits, coffee and liqueurs, was a long and animated affair that continued until near midnight, when the dancing began. The organizers had brought records and a record player and so, when dinner was all over, we moved to the atrium, where we danced in every possible combination and permutation until the wee hours of the morning. People had begun drifting away gradually after a couple of hours or so, but I clearly remember that at five or six in the morning, a group of us was still sitting in the living-room telling stories and jokes, and sipping coffee. The party, to commemorate what Raquel and I very likely thought was the end of our studies, was a great success thanks to our wonderful friends. And I can report with some pride that at least one good and long marriage, between two people who met there for the first time, resulted from it.

Formally, I was no longer a student. My diploma, that neat piece of paper duly signed by university officials, testified to the fact that I was now a professional woman, legally entitled to perform a variety of functions which I couldn't have done just the day before, such as the running of a pharmacy. In my circumstances, however, it didn't mean anything of the sort because in my chosen field of chemistry applied to physiology, I now felt exactly as knowledgeable or as ignorant as I had the day before. Clearly, studying and learning had begun to look increasingly as a continuous open-ended process, with no discreet stages or endings. And yet, much as a marriage certificate does, the degree and its diploma had a subtle effect, in the sense of an improved and far better defined self-image and a feeling of entitlement to a much higher degree of assertiveness. Materially, on the other hand, my degree made no difference, since I had jumped the gun and gotten my job before the event.

But in terms of my responsibilities at the Institute, there was a big change. A few months after my graduation, at the beginning of the 1946 academic year, Dr. Hoffmann had asked me to act as a regular demonstrator for the laboratory course given to the second year medical students. I felt honored and terrified, both at the same time. Honored, because I would be the only demonstrator without a medical background to teach the course. And terrified at the very idea of having to confront a horde of students far better trained in the biological sciences than I was. This implied no mere standing pretty and looking professorial next to Dr. Middleton as I had done in the classes for the pharmacy students, a couple of years back. This was for real, since it meant being alone in charge of a group of approximately twenty-five students for a whole day, once a week.

A specific topic was covered every week and, to illustrate it, experiments were carried out either on animals or on the students themselves. It was, therefore, not only a matter of knowing the theory in order to answer all the questions that would inevitably arise, but also the practical and often vexing question of being familiar with all the instruments, equipment and gadgets that could, and often did, go wrong, to say nothing of the frequently unpredictable responses of live animals and humans. This time, however, I did my very best by mastering the theory as well as possible, and by rehearsing and testing the gadgets before each class. It appears that my very best was good enough, because my students, who were remarkably cooperative — probably because they sensed I needed as much leniency as they did — did as well as those taught by the senior and medical staff. It was a great experience overall, not only because I learned a great deal, but also because the initial terror gradually subsided, to be replaced by a modest but much healthier degree of confidence.

However, my new status as a member of the teaching staff was by no means my only, or even main, professional preoccupation. A few months earlier, in 1945, the Drs. Francisco and Helena Hoffmann had taken a study trip through several important research centers in the U.S.A. and Canada, including visits to Harvard and the University of Toronto. While in New York, Hoffmann had discussed with a Dr. Oliver the possibility of obtaining a fellowship for me from the Rockefeller Foundation, the very institution which was sponsoring the Hoffmanns' own trip. I can only surmise that Dr. Hoffmann's recommendation of me was very positive because Dr. Oliver had agreed at once to give me a fellowship, subject to approval by his representative in Santiago, a Dr. Janney. Consequently, Dr. Hoffmann wrote to suggest that I contact Dr. Janney in order to apply through the regular channels, a simple formality.

This was the most exciting news I had ever received. Not even the thrill of getting my precious bicycle, or of having just graduated, could begin to compare with the certainty that I was now in a position to spend a year of research and studies in an American university of my choice. Would it be in New York, in Chicago, perhaps in Los Angeles? Can you imagine me, poor me, who had never been abroad, who had never been to a foreign country, not even to Argentina next door, whose longest trip from Santiago had been to Concepción, a university town only a few hundred kilometers away, now going thousands of kilometers to the north, to the United States, the richest and most scientifically advanced country in the world? And with all expenses paid, and a handsome salary to boot? Surely, I was dreaming. But when I pinched myself .....

Once the worst of the euphoric hurricane had subsided some, but still simmering with excitement, I made the necessary arrangements to see Dr. Janney. He received me in his ample and very well appointed office, with large windows overlooking the Parque Forestal, and asked me to sit down. Although the proximity of the park was a good omen, his looks weren't. A tall, skinny man, probably in his mid-fifties, dressed in a three-piece business suit and wearing glasses as if they were his worst enemy, he didn't look at all like the Santa Claus I had expected, about to present me with a gorgeous gift. He, like his suit, was pure business. Methodically and martinet-like, he asked me a series of questions about my academic record, about my personal life, about my present work and, most of all, about my reasons for wanting to go to his country to do post-graduate work. I answered as methodically as he deserved but, when it came to my present work and to the urgent need for the Institute to have a really well trained biochemist, namely me, I tried my damnedest to be as eloquent and persuasive as I knew how.

He nodded, he asked yet some more questions, he commented about the difficulties we all had faced at the Institute to work effectively — the War, you know — and finally, when I was expecting that he, duly impressed by my skillful presentation of my case, would gladly rubber-stamp Dr. Oliver's decision, he got up and, practically showing me to the door, said something like this: "Miss Josseau, you have been highly recommended to us. Your record is clearly excellent, and your projects and plans quite estimable, but" — and at this point I thought he was going to say, "you don't have a medical degree, you are just a chemist", when he actually said instead — "you are a woman and, in our experience, women are a bad investment. You are young, you are going to get married, and when you do and have children, you are going to forget all about your present aspirations as a scientist. I am sorry, but I cannot approve this fellowship". My sense of unbounded optimism, and the exuberant euphoria which had just preceded it, were instantly replaced by a wave of surprise, rage, indignation and contempt so intense that I feared I would lose control and insult this powerful man right on the spot. But I managed to keep my cool as I heard myself uttering: "Surely, you don't expect me to promise I will never get married or have children. And if I did, you wouldn't believe me anyhow. Thank you very much. Goodbye!" and I walked out in a royal huff.

As soon as my intense emotions had subsided a bit, I realized that I had said something rather lame and stupid. That, if I had not been so taken by surprise and shocked, I should have demolished the man's theory in an instant by bringing to bear powerful sociological arguments. No doubt his conclusion that women were a bad investment was based on, and therefore applied to, only American women who generally did not have access to domestic help. That, whether rightly or wrongly, middle-class professional Chilean women like myself did, and were therefore quite able to carrry on with their careers after marriage and children. That, in case he hadn't noticed, Dra. Helena Hoffmann, the mother of two small children, and currently in the U.S., sponsored by his own Foundation, was a prime example. That he was committing the unforgivable mistake of talking statistically instead of recognizing the wide individual variations in drive, motivation, commitment, energy and ingenuity. And, finally, that in the circumstances, I would appeal to his superiors in New York, whom he was in effect overruling. But, alas, I had not brought these arguments to bear at the right moment and I thought it was now too late to do anything about it. Instead, I wrote to Hoffmann, who was then visiting Dr. Charles Best's Department of Medical Research at the Banting Institute in Toronto, and reported on the outcome of my interview with Dr. Janney.

I don't think that the feminist argument, invoking the right to equal opportunity, regardless of gender, even entered my mind at the time. Not so much because my consciousness had not yet been raised, a concept which would take another two or three decades to be developed, but because up to this point in my life, I had never confronted blatant sexual discrimination in my academic and professional experience. Obviously, this had been totally irrelevant in school, where everyone from the principal to the smallest first grader had been females. Since the curricula of the schools for boys and for girls were identical, except for those courses that dealt with manual skills, carpentry for the boys and sewing and embroidery for the girls, the educational standards at the end of high school were identical for the two genders.

Further, there were no formal restrictions or impediments of any sort for either gender to be admitted to any faculty or course at the university level, even though males and females characteristically tended to gravitate to "men's" or "women's" professions respectively. I had personally chosen a co-educational course which I had rightly assumed would offer me the same opportunities that my male classmates would have. This had been amply confirmed when, in my third year, I was offered a junior teaching job exclusively on merit, and not because I was a woman. Later, when Dr. Hoffmann first offered me the job of chemist at the Institute and trusted me with teaching responsibilities beyond what corresponded to my own job definition, he also did it on my record alone, because he could have chosen from any number of males in my course or others. The conclusion is therefore inescapable that my very first encounter with sexual discrimination at the academic or professional level came from that advanced and powerful country to the north, exemplified by the Rockefeller Foundation policy, rather than from my own "backward" and "underdeveloped" country. The euphemistic and all-encompassing phrase "developing country" had not yet entered the lexicon.

This is not to say that Chile was uniquely enlightened in this respect, or that I had never been discriminated against because I was a woman. Of course I had, at every turn, but not professionally. Even though my mother had made every effort to allow me the best and most complete education possible, these pages are a witness to the differential treatment that my brothers and I were subjected to. I don't need to repeat myself. In the church in which I had been brought up, the highest position I could have aspired to would have been that of Mother Superior of one convent or another, but never the priesthood or the papacy. Can one just imagine, Pope Oriana I? The fact that we laugh says it all. And in the society at large, any of the conventional rules that distinguished between men and women could only be broken at the risk of being labelled at best as mannish or unfeminine, and at worst as an immoral outcast, a fate to be dreaded more than hell if one aspired to be socially accepted and attractive to the opposite sex.

If I had broken some of these rules by, for example, smoking, or wearing pants on my mountain excursions, it was a calculated risk that I was not taking alone in the first place, and which did not seem to have any negative impact on the men of my social and university circles. On the contrary, doing away with some of these gender-associated conventions was seen as an attractive sign of an independent or emancipated personality by many of them. Just think of that poor English woman who had to climb Mont Blanc in the Alps — the first female ever to do so — wearing her rather dainty buttoned-up shoes and layer upon layer of crinolines! But going to university, and having serious plans to pursue a career in the professions, was not in this category, and it was seen by my contemporaries at large as a perfectly acceptable aim for a woman. Hence my shock and astonishment at the response of the representative of the Rockefeller Foundation in Santiago. In the years to come, I would learn a great deal more about the fact that not all countries are created equal.

It is difficult to remember my thinking on feminist issues at this distance because the topic was not a well-defined set of beliefs at the time. We were to a large degree in a sort of dormant state between the suffragette movement of the turn of the century, and the women's movement that would explode a couple of decades later. As far as I was concerned, the second World War itself had amply demonstrated that women, when allowed the chance, could do anything. Further, I still half-believed that, at least theoretically, the marxist doctrine on which the Soviet Union was presumably based, allowed for total equality between women and men. In my own society, I honestly believed that any woman, including myself, could achieve anything if she was willing to make the effort. Hadn't Gabriela Mistral just received the 1945 Nobel Prize for literature, the only Chilean to have been so honored up to that point?

More important to me then was the not unrelated issue of the fulfilment of the human couple, a man and a woman, through a union of mutually supporting and inspiring equals, something like the Curies in my own imagination. In such a case, no potential would be thwarted or denied to either individual, the total would be more than the sum of its parts, and the fulfilment of each individual all the greater. This thinking of mine had at least two direct consequences. First, and despite my trying ever since Claudio, I had not yet found my match, the man to whom I would be a source of inspiration and who would in turn allow for the full blossoming of my own potentials. But I would continue the search. And secondly, the theory tacitly implied my belief in profound but matching, complementary differences between men and women, males and females.

By differences I do not mean the silly and superficial differences codified in societal conventions, such as the length of the hair, but genuine biological and biologically based differences having a direct impact on various fundamental aspects of the male and female personalities. This, more than the laudable but more limited achievement of social equality of the sexes, is what interested me most then, and has ever since. I shall come back to this later, even though, as I've already said in another context, this is indeed the subject for another book.

I did not have much time to stew over what at that point appeared to be my dismal fate, because I received Dr. Hoffmann's answer to my letter almost by return mail. Instead of renegotiating or even pleading with the Rockefeller Foundation, as I had half expected, he had talked to Dr. Charles Best in Toronto. Dr. Best, he explained, could not match a Rockefeller fellowship, but he would be happy to have me work in one of his departments for a year as a research assistant. This meant $1080 (Canadian) for the year, and no travelling expenses, compared to the Rockefeller's $2500 (US) a year and all travelling expenses paid. When, in addition, I soon ascertained that the return fare between Santiago and New York alone then cost $2000 (US), I knew this was an impossible proposition.

My feelings of despondency and defeat were further aggravated by the realization that this would specifically prevent me from training with Dr. Best's group. The Department of Medical Research at the Banting Institute and the Department of Physiology at the University of Toronto were not only world renowned but, like ours, their main lines of research were in experimental endocrinology, although focused mainly on diabetes and insulin. Jaime Talesnik, one of my senior colleagues at the Institute, had already chosen Toronto as the site of his study leave for 1946 precisely for those reasons.

Even though at the time Raquel had got herself an American fellowship of another description to pursue her studies on viruses, but which included travelling expenses, I don't seem to have considered other openings or possibilities. I can't account for this apparent lack of initiative on my part, except to say that I was very ignorant of the North American fellowship system overall, and had never even heard of the British Council or other European sources of help for foreign students at all. One learned of these things almost exclusively by word of mouth, and I was therefore relying only on my own rather meager connections. I should have relied instead on my present considerable and impressive hindsight!

I was in the middle of these very depressing academic and financial deliberations when I found myself one afternoon having tea at the Cheethams, my very affluent cousins. Since both Nora and Eric had always followed the progress of my various doings with great interest, I told them about my fiasco with the Rockefeller Foundation and about Dr. Best's offer. Eric was most interested in the latter, and asked me all sorts of questions related to the implications of the offer. Once I had filled him in on all the relevant details, he concluded that all I needed to go to Canada was a loan to pay for my travels. To which I responded, laughing: "Sure. Everything is settled. All I need now is for someone to lend me some piddly couple of thousand American dollars, and I'm all set!" The sum sounded to me then as two million would now. But, instead of laughing with me, he said, quite seriously: "Can you come to my office tomorrow? I would like to discuss this with you some more." I was absolutely amazed at this turn of events because he seemed to be implying, or at least suggesting, the possibility of making the loan himself.

When I met him at his office the next day — he and his brother Alan were the exclusive representatives of General Motors in Santiago — I was very impressed with the size and trappings of his enterprise, as well as with the fact that he really appeared to be a big and important business man, surrounded by mechanics in their overalls, salesmen in business suits, solicitous secretaries and so on. He immediately wanted to know what my salary at the Institute actually was and, most importantly, whether or not I would continue to be paid during my leave. When I said yes, I would indeed be paid, and he had made some quick calculations, he suggested the following: he, Eric, would lend me the money for the return fares between Santiago and New York; during my absence he would collect all of my monthly salaries; he would then give my mother her usual allowance, and he would keep the rest as term payments on my debt, which would in effect be fully cancelled by the time

I would be back. This way I would be able to accept Dr. Best's offer and be fully in the black on my return a year later.

Incidentally, Eric didn't say a word about interest on the loan, and I was so naive about financial matters that I have only now, as I write, realized that he was offering me not only the possibility of going to the University of Toronto, but the gift of an interest-free loan as well! He repeatedly asked me instead whether or not it was possible to live in Toronto on an income of ninety dollars a month. I said that I wasn't sure, but that I would try to find out. But we closed the deal in principle anyway, and after thanking him as eloquently as I could for his generous and totally unexpected offer of help, I walked out of his office in a sort of trance, just beginning to ponder the multiple implications of this rather short, superficially business-like, but to me enormously significant agreement.

Dr. Hoffmann, who had already returned from his North American tour, was very pleased with this news. He felt, however, that I should wait a while, partly because Jaime Talesnik would be spending the whole of 1946 in Toronto, so that I was needed for the teaching in Santiago, and partly to allow for enough time for me to make my arrangements both there and in Toronto. He further suggested that I write to Jaime asking him to be our representative at the Banting Institute. Jaime responded most gallantly, and from then on both he and his wife, Rebeca Elvira, answered all my questions about both the academic and domestic aspects of life in Toronto. He explained that Dr. Best and Dr. Hoffmann had already agreed that, considering my background and the interests of both departments, it would be best for me to work with Dr. Colin Lucas, one of Dr. Best's senior associates. Dr. Lucas, Jaime wrote, was a kind and charming man with a vast knowledge of the chemistry and biochemistry of fats. Since this was precisely the field Hoffmann and I had decided I should try to master, this was very good news indeed.

On the domestic front the Talesniks advised me that ninety dollars a month was just enough for a single person to get by on, but not much else. It would largely depend on the kind of lodgings I would be able to find because, as a result of the lack of new construction during the war, accommodation was scarce and expensive. They themselves had had to be content with only one room and a kitchenette in a boarding house where they shared the bathroom with other tenants. This, I must admit, was surprisingly bad news. Probably because my notions of life in North America were based almost exclusively on Hollywood films, I had pictured myself, from the very beginning of my dreams of going north, living in some gorgeous modern apartment, of the type inhabited on the screen by the likes of Katharine Hepburn, the delightful Jean Arthur, or Claudette Colbert. I began to wonder what other sobering surprises were still in store for me.

But with my characteristic stoicism I resigned myself to the idea of one room which would, of course, be sumptuously large and have huge windows overlooking those fabulous pine forests of Canada. I must have gotten this idea from the films of Nelson Eddy and Jeannette Macdonald, because the truth is that I knew precious little about Canada as a whole, except for the climate, and even less about Toronto's layout, architecture, and accommodations for students of modest means. In the meanwhile, Hoffmann and I had decided that September was a reasonable time of the year for my departure, a date which would, in addition, give me the benefit of the Talesniks' company in Toronto for two or three months before their return to Santiago. Consequently, I spent those last few months primarily focused on my eventual trip to Toronto, making all the necessary preparations. But otherwise I carried on my private, professional and social affairs pretty well as usual, without any new departures worthy of note.

North to the Future

In the summer of 1946, I went south with a small group of friends, including Goyo, on my longest camping trip yet, about four weeks. We travelled by train to Temuco, a few hundred kilometers south of Santiago, and then on foot, in whatever trucks would give us a lift, and even on ox-carts, to a region of beautiful lakes and forests near the Argentinian border, completely out of the way of the main touristic lake region. Despite the hardships of rickety tents, scarcity of provisions and battered and soot-covered utensils, I was enchanted because this part of the country was totally different from Santiago's surroundings.

Among other adventures, we forded a wide river on horseback, we met with the only native Mapuche Indians I would ever see, and we crossed the border into San Martín de los Andes in Argentina. The contrast between the sleepy little village on the Chilean side, with its neat adobe houses, and San Martín was staggering. This town had been planned and fully serviced well before it had been settled. So we found ourselves in the core of the town with smart shops, restaurants, cinemas and all the rest, surrounded by paved, well-designed streets, even with lamp posts, but no houses. Not yet, anyway. It had all been planned well in advance, presumably to attract new settlers. We were utterly amazed at this unpredicted discovery and I, for one, could now begin to understand why the Argentinians generally tended to look down on us as their poor cousins.

But we still inhabited a gorgeous contry and, turning around towards the west, we saw much more of it by travelling down-river to the port of Valdivia, near the Pacific. This time, instead of walking or swimming down-river, we made the whole and totally novel trip on timber rafts, courtesy of the local lumber yard officials. Valdivia itself was yet another revelation, because we suddenly felt transported to Germany, as if on a magic carpet. The preponderance of blond blue-eyed people, and of neatly painted frame houses, in contrast to the brick or adobe dwellings of Santiago, was such as to give one the feeling of being in a foreign country. This had been the result of substantial German immigration to the area a century earlier. After getting properly and thoroughly clean in Valdivia, and eating some hearty and well prepared meals, we took the train back to Santiago where, a few days later, we all met again to exchange photographs and drink strawberry milk shakes, the one thing we had most missed and longed for throughout our trek in the south.

Then, in the winter of that year, there was what I've come to remember as the most physically active day of all my life, before or since. Our Ski Club had been invited to visit La Disputada, a copper mine on the slopes of a four-thousand meter peak, just north of Farellones. We would be the guests of the miners themselves, who had offered to provide us with rooms and food for a whole week-end and, as it turned out, with entertainment as well. A truck-load of us arrived at the mine to make plans for the following day when we would all climb the peak on skis, or so we thought. Compared to our still primitive conditions in Farellones, the mine was luxury, because the rooms were warm, the meals modest but decent, and the miners most friendly and eager to make us comfortable.

The next morning, before we had even begun the one-thousand meter climb from the mine to the peak, we had to deal with our first casualties. Several members of the group had to drop out because a pocket of rarefied air, just a short way from the mine, had made them thoroughly mountain-sick. But the rest of us went on up the zigzagging route towards the top, huffing and puffing, but quite exhilarated by the experience. Eventually, some one hundred meters from the top, which was bare rock without snow cover, it became obvious that it could not be done on skis. I think that only two of the group took their skis off and climbed the rest of the way to the top. The rest, including me, turned around and began what, at least for me, was the most humiliating descent ever. Although I supposedly knew how to turn and put the brakes on, I didn't manage one single turn without falling on my behind. But, although bruised and exhausted, I managed to reach the mine more or less intact.

We had barely had enough time to wash and have a light lunch when the miners announced that the scheduled visit to the mine was about to begin. It was probably four o'clock in the afternoon when, guided by the miners, the trek through the most gorgeous green-blue tunnels began. We were walking along a very narrow path carved from the copper rocks, and all around us, hanging from the ceiling, were spectacular stalactites of copper salts, shining like so many jewels. I felt like Alice in Wonderland but, after an hour or so of steady walking I was truly exhausted, and asked one of the miners how much was there left to walk. "Oh! another two hours", he said, quite nonchalantly. "In that case" I said, "I'm turning back. This, after all that skiing today, is far too much!" "I'm sorry Miss" he said with a smile, "but nobody turns back, nobody is allowed to walk alone along these corridors." Confronted with such a categorical statement, there was no choice but to go on. The miner had been right. It took at least another two hours to complete the circle and return to base camp. I was so exhausted that even the unique, unprecedented beauty of the mine was by now completely beyond my ability to grasp.

Once back in our quarters, we freshened up again, and then went for dinner in a big room with long tables and benches, kept nicely warm by means of a big iron wood-stove. Despite the exertions of the day, everybody was in a great mood, recapitulating the day's experiences and telling stories and jokes. After dinner and coffee, somebody produced a phonograph and some old scratched records, and the party began. Still wearing our ski pants and our heavy boots, we began to dance, and then we danced some more until — hard to believe — it was two in the morning and no one could move any more. No doubt, tomorrow would be another day, but neither it, nor any other one, would begin to compare with the day during which I had climbed to the highest altitude I ever would — nearly to four thousand meters, and on skis to boot.

Back in Santiago, things had gone from busy to hectic, especially because Raquel had set her departure for August, more than a month before mine. She was going to Washington University in Saint Louis, Missouri, to do postgraduate work on viruses. But before reaching Saint Louis she was to spend a month in Baton Rouge, Louisiana, presumably to polish up her English and generally learn and become accustomed to the North American ways. My modest arrangements with Toronto did not allow for such luxuries. It will be clear by now that most events in Chile, never mind how superficially minor, call for parties, and these occasions naturally include arrivals from and departures to foreign countries. As Raquel's fateful date became imminently close, it naturally fell upon me, her best friend, to organize a farewell party which would measure up to the importance of the event.

Since Raquel was the first member of our group to be going to the United States for a whole year, I took my responsibility with utmost seriousness and consequently organized a very dignified dinner party at the Restaurant Capri, an elegant downtown establishment, which took place on July 15, 1946. The guests, sixteen men and thirteen women, included her sister, a couple of her cousins and of course all her friends, among whom, for obvious reasons, there were several of my own old ones, such as Wanda and Fusa, and newer ones including Palacios, Goyo and Osvaldo Cori. This shows the degree to which her life and mine had come to intermesh and our friends to become something akin to an extended family. A family by now made up mostly of university graduates with responsible professional positions, groomed accordingly, and unable or unwilling to dance until all hours. As I recall it, this was a serious, dignified and measured affair, whose primary purpose was to let Raquel know of her friends' warmest wishes for her success abroad.

But for me none of this was quite as easy. For the first time in six years we would be a long distance away from each other, meeting and making friends with totally different people and, obviously, working and pursuing knowledge in quite unrelated fields. The sisterhood, the close daily exchange of impressions about almost everything, the constant sharing and the deep caring for each other, would at best be drastically interrupted for a whole year, and at worst for ever. We did, of course, agree to keep in touch and to meet whenever possible while in North America, but those intentions would, I knew, play second fiddle to our more pressing obligations and commitments. Even though I still had many wonderful friends, Raquel's friendship had been unique and consequently not replaceable, a sad fact that left me feeling very much alone, though in the midst of a very caring crowd. But when we finally parted, as she left for Saint Louis, we pretended it was just one more of so many other partings, and no doubt we would soon meet again, somewhere, sometime.

When I then turned my attention to my own affairs, I soon discovered somehow that there was an American freight line, the Grace Line, whose fleet of ships made frequent round trips between Valparaíso and New York. This line, I was told, had very good accommodations for about thirty passengers in each ship and, most important of all for me, it gave a twenty-five per cent discount to students! Since the full fare was the same as by air, this meant that I could make the whole return trip for fifteen hundred instead of two thousand dollars. In my circumstances this was like a gift from heaven because it would immediately reduce my debt to Eric by five hundred dollars! But there was a catch in that the trip took three weeks instead of one day, and I wasn't sure I could afford the time.

I immediately consulted with Hoffmann, and with the Talesniks in Toronto, and everybody agreed it would be crazy not to take advantage of such an opportunity. And so it was that I bought my ticket to sail from Valparaíso in the middle of September, and learned in the process that the ship would make stopovers in Peru, Ecuador, Colombia and Panama before reaching New York. All this meant that, in addition to a substantial discount on the actual fare, I would enjoy a three-week holiday in a very nicely appointed ship, and the opportunity not only of practicing my English, but of visits to four Latin American countries that I knew only in theory. How lucky could I get!

Since I had already got my passport, all I needed now was my Canadian student visa. It was only then that I discovered, I must admit with considerable surprise, that at that time there was no Canadian embassy in Chile, just a consulate. So to the consulate I went, there to realize that the consul himself would process my papers, and be a charming and most helpful man in several other respects. He turned out to be none other than a young Jules Leger, the very same man who many years later would become one of the most distinguished Governors General of Canada. During my several visits to the consulate it was invariably M. Leger who most gallantly looked after my affairs, and from whom I learned more about Canada than from any other single source.

I had the impression that he was both amused — probably at the earnest naiveté of my questions — and delighted at the chance to deal, very likely for the first time, with a graduate student. Be that as it may, he answered all of my questions in excellent Spanish, and spared no compliments on my laborious English. But when the time came for me to apologize for being unable to speak French — my automatic assumption being that every Canadian spoke both English and French fluently — he was wonderful. With a smile that I was unable to interpret at the time, he said to me "Miss Josseau, I don't think that your lack of French will be any serious inconvenience to you in Toronto." Even though somewhat surprised, I don't think I pursued the point any further, so relieved was I at this news. Eventually, I would discover, of course, that his had been the understatement of the century. And then later, on my last visit with M. Leger, after I had mentioned in passing that I was having trouble buying dollars at the official price, he most generously offered to sell them to me himself. I accepted the offer on the spot, and so it was that we sealed our flourishing relationship with a most advantageous transaction of a couple of hundred dollars, to my benefit and my everlasting gratitude. It is very likely that at that point I thought if all Canadians are like this, I'm staying there, country unseen. No question!

Meanwhile, on the home front, nobody, at least not outwardly, seemed very excited at my imminent departure, except for my mother, of course. She was very concerned on at least two counts. First, we had to make sure that I had plenty of warm clothes so that I wouldn't freeze permanently in Canada. And second, that I should look like the daughter of the good and expensive modiste that she was. Somehow, I managed to convince her that Toronto itself was not all that horrendously cold, that in fact it even had a summer of sorts, and that my winter clothes would probably do all right. And her second concern was taken care of by adding a few items to what already was the biggest and best wardrobe I had ever had. She made me a dressy in-between-seasons black coat, a light blue wool dress with a fringe on the collar and cuffs, and a perfectly tailored light brown suit in which I thought I looked like a million dollars. And on, and on. So much, in fact, that I had to buy myself a very large suit case, something that in the end I could hardly carry by myself. The rest, shoes, purses and so on, all went into a very ordinary canvas bag.

Ready for the North!

I felt truly all set to go and conquer the world, except for money, of which I had very little, even though I had been unforgivably reckless when I turned my beloved bicycle into cash. It had been one of those deals that made me feel at best unpardonably disloyal and at worst like a crass philistine, but about which I had had virtually no choice. It was at this point that my dear friend Adela came to the rescue with a brilliant and characteristically practical and generous idea. Instead of throwing a fancy dinner party at an expensive restaurant, as I had done for Raquel, she organized a buffet party at her own home, and at minimum cost. The guests, however, were asked to contribute as if she had resorted to caterers or to an expensive restaurant, and the difference between the sum she collected and the actual cost was given to me for travelling expenses. This amounted to the grand sum of two hundred dollars, far more than I had dared to dream I would have available for unpredictable expenses.

I have been given many thoughtful and even wonderful gifts throughout my long life, but this particular one stands out as exceptional in my mind because it expressed such a degree of understanding of my situation, and of collective caring on the part of my wonderful friends. The party itself, which I hardly need describe any more, was a particularly crowded and noisy affair at the Ohlbaums' large apartment where, it seemed to me, everybody I had ever known was present. ¡Salud!, my friends!

If my life during these last few months in Santiago is beginning to sound like an uninterrupted series of vacations to exotic lakes and snow-capped mountains, and of countless parties while in town, it was nothing of the sort. These distractions occurred only during legitimate holidays or free evenings, while I continued to work and to teach as conscientiously as ever, and to the very last day before my departure. But even there, in the austere setting of the Institute, the idea for yet another farewell party was germinating. Not among my colleagues or staff, as might have been expected, but among the students. I was absolutely amazed one day in early September when one of the students of my group came to ask me whether I would accept an invitation to attend a tea-dance in a downtown cafe in my honor. Naturally, I said I would be delighted, and a date for this most unexpected of events was immediately set.

As the day approached, I felt increasingly unsure of myself and as to what to wear because, although tea-dances were still popular in some circles, I had never attended one. But, even more importantly, there was no precedent whatsoever for a group of students throwing a party for one of the staff. Should I look severe and wear glasses, thereby putting them off? Should I look elegant and frivolous, and thereby undermine my authority over them? Or should I compromise and therefore walk that narrow line between the severe and the glamorous, and probably impress nobody, but still be safe? In the end, after much excruciating pondering, I compromised by having my hair done up in curls as they had never seen me before, but wearing my elegant black suit, totally appropriate for a tea-time party, but not dressy enough to startle them, who after all had never seen me wear anything but my white lab coat before.

When the day came, we all gathered at the Ramis Clar, an old genuine Edwardian cafe, with marble-topped tables, cane chairs and a suitable orchestra and, I've been told, the meeting place of the Santiago intelligentsia. If this sounds quaint and old-fashioned now, it felt the same even then, because as far as I was concerned the cafe had been at that central corner of the Alameda Bernardo O'Higgins forever, or at least from the early years of the century. Soon after the students, about twenty-five of them, and I had sat down at a big rectangular table, the orchestra began to play and the students to dance. After two or three dances I noticed, with my usual perspicacity, that nobody had asked me, the guest of honor, to dance. But I had barely had time to interpret this awkward situation when Mario Miranda, the tallest, most handsome and best student in the group, came over and rather timidly asked if I cared to dance. Of course I cared, and off we went to a tango — my favorite ballroom dance — and then another, and so on.

Mario, who went on to become the Dean of Medicine in Costa Rica, his native country, was most charming, but didn't make any specific comments. We had, apparently, put on quite a show because, when we were back at the table one of the students said: "Miss Josseau, you are a terrific dancer. We didn't know. We thought, probably, that you didn't care about these things." While the others nodded in approval, I reassured them that I loved dancing a lot, and from that moment on everybody relaxed and we had a grand time. All of which goes to show how the doors to fun and enjoyment can be closed by just a rather minor difference in age, but a major one in rank. As I've already said, this inspired event stands out in my memory with amazing clarity because, to the best of my knowledge, the students had never given a send-off to any of my colleagues before.

By the middle of September I was ready to go. I had cleared my desk at the Institute and said goodbye to everyone there. I had made the rounds of the homes of all my aunts, uncles and cousins who lived in Santiago, and most especially of my lovely and charming grandmother. I had gone to the dentist, gotten my shots and made sure that my clothes were all clean, neat and ready to pack. And, finally, the day came when I had to part from my family. This would have been difficult in the best of circumstances, but in this instance they were not the best. My parents, but especially my mother, knew that Raúl was very seriously ill, although still up and about. Not too long before, my mother had asked me to go and see Dr. Hector Orrego Puelma (he of the ski chalet in Farellones, where we had all showered during the building of the Refugio), one of his doctors, and probably the best chest specialist in the country. He had told me that it was only a matter of time, that there was nothing else that could be done for him.

Orlando, although in good physical health, was also a cause for concern. A year earlier, confronted with the final oral exams of his law studies, he had been taking amphetamines on the advice of a friend to keep awake for long hours of intensive studying. A day before the scheduled exam he had discontinued the drug and shortly afterwards he had collapsed, literally. I still remember him, lying flat on his back for at least twenty-four consecutive hours, barely responsive to any attempts to rouse him. I had called Lalo Markovich, one of my physician friends, to see him, and he had said that Orlando was not in danger, that in due time he would wake up and recover. He did wake up and recover physically but now, more than a year later, he had been unable to face his exams and appeared quite idle and aimless, although he was, presumably, still studying.

With the wisdom of hindsight I can state with utmost confidence that Orlando had "crashed" or, in more technical terms, that he had had a severe amphetamine withdrawal reaction, the main symptoms of which are prolonged deep sleep and subsequent depression. The only problem was that neither amphetamine addiction nor its corresponding withdrawal reaction were then known or recognized. It would take many more years of accumulated evidence and much medical argument before this syndrome was generally recognized and accepted. Ironically, even I would eventually be a participant in the resolution of this problem. In the circumstances, however, we were left quite bewildered by the causes and the outcome of Orlando's misadventure with these then very fashionable drugs. It was not at all easy to leave when two of my brothers, especially Raúl, were clearly not well. But leave I did, to pursue my own aims, though with the knowledge that I would be back in one short year, far better equipped than before to help and support as best I could.

I must have said goodbye to my father despite our long-standing quarrel, because my conscience would not have allowed otherwise, but I don't actually remember doing so. Then we all left for the train station where relatives and friends had gathered to see me off, except for Palacios, Goyo and Fernando, who were accompanying me to Valparaíso. I had already given a big hug to my mother, who had shown remarkable composure throughout, when Raúl, whom I had not been able to find anywhere, suddenly appeared, to hold me and wish me the very best. I was so moved by his unexpected presence there that I can remember nothing else of that scene at the station. Only his sad, drawn, handsome face, and his tall slim body in my arms. My brother, of whom I knew so very little.

Fernando, on the other hand, was thriving professionally, though not financially. At twenty-two he had already produced and directed two plays of his own, Caesar and They Waited for the Dawn, and had pretty well gone through all the formal theater training that was available in Santiago at the time. He was, unquestionably, the most sociable and well adjusted of my three brothers. In characteristic Josseau fashion, we both kept our personal things to ourselves, never asking probing questions, or in any way trespassing our tacitly agreed-upon boundaries. However, during the last few years he and

I had become good friends, to the point that he would occasionally come to our parties, and at least once had joined a little holiday trip to Constitución in the south, with three of my girl friends. Therefore, it was totally natural that he would come to see me off in Valparaíso.

Once my three male escorts and I arrived there, and I had gone through all the required formalities, we set out to discover and inspect the good ship Santa Barbara. Considering that it was primarily a freighter, I was absolutely delighted to discover that the limited passenger accommodations were ample and sparkling, if not elegant. Each cabin, for either two or four passengers, had a complete private bath, something I had never enjoyed in my very limited experience of hotels. I had been assigned to a four-bed cabin which so far I would share with just one other traveller. She was a Mrs. Ruby, the middle-aged wife of an American engineer who was still in Punta Arenas, of all places, exploring for oil. She was on her way back to the United States to prepare for their retirement. So, right off the bat, I would be sharing in the North American way of life, including the language. The dining room, with a bar to one side and a most comfortable lounge on the other, was positively elegant, with long white table cloths and flowers on each table. And, to complete the picture, there was a passenger deck with an outdoor lounge next to a small but sparkling and beautiful swimming pool. Everything, including the officers, looked white and spotless, and I genuinely got the feeling that I was in Hollywood after all. A great beginning indeed to my presumably modest adventure.

It had been a long, tortuous, sometimes stormy but never dull trek from Patagonia to this point in my life. On the way, I had run into many obstacles and difficulties: unfair treatment and criticism as a girl and as a young woman, from family, school, church, politics and most recently, sexual discrimination from unthinking bureaucracy. I had also had great pleasure, joy, inspiration, even moments of true exhilaration, from wonderful friends and colleagues, the discovery of the arts, the beautiful Chilean landscape, and the challenge of science. I was certainly no saint, and I was well aware of my failings and limitations, but I had held to my own judgments and values, and now I was about to test them in this great new exploration of the "True North" — and of myself.

Once the four of us had finished the tour of the ship, Goyo and Fernando discreetly found an excuse to leave Palacios and me alone. I dreaded the moment, but there was no way out, it had to be faced. I dreaded it because this particular goodbye differed from all the others in that it was not for just one year, but forever, for good. He knew it and I knew it, though not one explicit word was said to that effect. It was one of those exchanges between two people who have shared a good deal, made up of two tiers of feelings and thoughts. The overt and fully articulated one, and the parallel, silent, underground one, which cannot or must not be overtly acknowledged, but which is as clearly understood as the first. I was leaving him. I would be back in a year, but not to him. No promises, not even to write. He was sad, but gallant enough to at least pretend he was sharing in my excitement. I was very sad, but so genuinely excited at what was to come that I didn't have to pretend anything, when Goyo and Fernando re-appeared and it was time for the three of them to leave. A final goodbye to each of them, and then, when it was already dark, and the lights on the hills of Valparaíso shone like so many stars in the background, I turned around and figuratively dipped my toe in the American pool nearby, on the way to my first American meal. And that will be the beginning of another story.

Epilogue

Oriana spent two years rather than one in Toronto, and then returned to Chile with an M.Sc. in Biochemistry and a Canadian husband. After two years they returned to Canada permanently. She obtained a Ph.D. in Physiology and had a successful career as a scientist at the Addiction Research Foundation of Ontario. Raquel acquired a Ph.D. and an American husband, had three sons, and also had a long and successful career in cancer research. Both of them thus showed the emptiness of Dr. Janney's argument. Oriana did indeed begin to write that other story, but did not live to finish it. She died of recurrent cancer at the age of 81 years and 15 days, having outlived all her family except her youngest brother Fernando Josseau, who is now one of the "grand old men" of Chilean theatre and literature.

H.K.